KU-009-387

First Level Management

An Active-Learning Approach

Peter G. A. Lang

Edited by Jill Hussey

DP Publications Ltd
Aldine Place
LONDON W12 8AW
1992

Acknowledgements

My thanks go to Steve Hender, Sue Pierce and Margaret Lang for their help in bringing this book to publication.

A CIP catalogue record for this book is available from the
British Library

Illustrations
Pages 138-140 and 229-233 © Cath Chadwick
Page 240 permission kindly granted by Pitman Publishing

ISBN 1 873981 11 2
Copyright P. Lang © 1992

First edition 1992

All rights reserved
No part of this publication may be reproduced, stored in a
retrieval system, or transmitted in any form or by any means,
electronic, mechanical, photocopying, recording, or otherwise,
without the prior permission of the copyright owner.

Typeset by
    DP Publications Ltd
Printed in Great Britain by
    Ashford Colour Press, Gosport, Hants

Preface

Aim of the book

First Level Management is written for students on NVQ 3 and 4 management programmes (Management Charter Initiative Standards M1 and supervisory subset) and for courses such as NEBSM certificate and CMS. It will also be of considerable use to students following other courses which include management studies. Students on such courses, many of whom may already have some supervisory or managerial work experience, need material that is both practical and interactive.

The book also provides the support needed by lecturers implementing active-learning methods. This is not a conventional textbook but a combination of reference manual and workbook. It allows the student to follow a course of supported self-study. In this approach the student is an active participant in the learning process, rather than the passive recipient of theory. Guidance for implementation is given in the Lecturers' Supplement (free to lecturers adopting the book as a course text).

Structure of the book

First Level Management is divided into three sections.

❏ *Section 1*

This section directs the active-learning process. It is divided into seven units, each covering a separate management topic. Each unit commences with a list of objectives and is arranged in logical sequence, leading the student through a series of *quick answer questions*, *tasks* and *scenarios*.

The **quick answer questions** encourage students to use their own experiences and common sense to tackle problems. They can check their answers to these questions by looking at the comments given on the following left-hand page.

The **tasks** require a little more thought than the quick answer questions and students may need to research the answers. Their common sense and general knowledge will help them solve these problems, but they are also directed to appropriate data in the information bank which is contained in Section 2.

The **scenarios** illustrate typical managerial and supervisory problems which students may have come across already or are likely to encounter in the future. The **problem-solving activities** help to relate students' own experiences and general knowledge to the knowledge they have gained from studying each unit. In the same way as the tasks, students are directed to the relevant data in the information bank which is contained in Section 2.

On completing each unit, students can progress to the equivalent unit in Section 3 (for more demanding assignments on the same topic) or can move on to the next unit of section 1.

Any materials produced when answering the tasks and solving the problems in this section should be retained as they may give an indication of the student's level of competency and thus contribute to a vocational award (NVQ).

❏ *Section 2*

This contains the information bank which provides a summary of the theory, legal requirements, principles and practice of management. It also incorporates useful checklists. The information is arranged alphabetically, as in an index, and there are cross references to other items in the information bank, appropriate units in Section 1 and Section 3 and to wider reading in the form of recommended texts.

❐ *Section 3*

This contains a number of *activities* which are arranged under the same headings as the units in Section 1. These assignments are similar to the scenarios in Section 1, but require a greater depth of research and knowledge. Students are directed to the appropriate data in the information bank in Section 2 and to the recommended texts.

Students should not attempt the activities in Section 3 until they have worked through the appropriate unit in Section 1.

Using the book effectively

First Level Management can be used effectively in a number of ways:

❐ *As a workbook.*

The lecturer explains the theory summarised in Section 2 and the students attempt the quick answer questions, tasks and scenarios in Section 1 in class. The activities in Section 3 are carried out in class/workshops as appropriate. Approximate timings and outline answers are given in the Lecturers' Supplement.

❐ *For supported self-study.*

Students attempt the quick answer questions, tasks and scenarios in Section 1 using the directions in the text to the appropriate information sources. The lecturer conducts tutorials for those experiencing difficulties and brings the class together for discussion, role play and giving presentations.

❐ *As a combination of the above.*

The lecturer uses the book in combination with the Lecturer's Supplement for planning a tailor-made mix of the activities which are most appropriate to the students and the course.

Immediately following the *Contents* pages are two analyses:

❐ *Coverage of topics by scenario / activities*

This is intended for lecturers planning their courses as well as for students planning revision/wanting to deal with specific topics only.

❐ *Management Charter Initiative Standards – Index of scenarios / activities*

This is intended for both the lecturers planning their courses and for students needing to retain material as possible *evidence* towards competency-based awards.

Lecturers' Supplement

A separate Lecturers' Supplement is provided free of charge by the publisher to lecturers who are recommending the book as a course text. This gives guidance on how to incorporate the book into a course including role play suggestions and outline answers to all tasks and scenarios in Section 1 and to the activities in Section 3.

Peter Lang
May 1992

Contents

			Page
Preface			iii
Coverage of topics by scenarios/activities			vii
Management Charter Initiative Standards – Index			viii

Section 1   Scenarios, quick answer questions & tasks

Unit 1	Management and supervision		3
	1.1	Objectives	3
	1.2	Organisational structures	3
	1.3	Authority, responsibility and delegation	5
	1.4	The role of management	7
	1.5	The role of supervision	8
Unit 2	Managing work		10
	2.1	Objectives	10
	2.2	Organisational objectives, strategies and policies	10
	2.3	Methods of control	12
	2.4	Work study	17
	2.5	Decision-making and problem-solving	19
	2.6	Time management	21
Unit 3	Managing others		23
	3.1	Objectives	23
	3.2	Interpersonal skills	23
	3.3	Groups	25
	3.4	Leadership	26
	3.5	Workplace communications	28
Unit 4	Individuals at work		31
	4.1	Objectives	31
	4.2	Personality and motivation	31
	4.3	Attitude	33
	4.4	Change and stress management	35
	4.5	Job design	38
Unit 5	Employee relations		41
	5.1	Objectives	41
	5.2	Personnel management	41
	5.3	Employment legislation	43
	5.4	Health and safety legislation	45
	5.5	Trade union legislation	47
Unit 6	Recruitment and selection		49
	6.1	Objectives	49
	6.2	Manpower planning	49
	6.3	Job analysis	51
	6.4	Recruitment and advertising	52
	6.5	Selection and induction	54
Unit 7	Development and retention		57
	7.1	Objectives	57
	7.2	Job evaluation	57
	7.3	Pay structures	58
	7.4	Appraisal and promotion	60
	7.5	Training	62

		Page
Section 2	**Information bank**	
	Attitude	73
	Authority	75
	Budgetary control	77
	Change management	79
	Communications	81
	Control	86
	Counselling and listening	88
	Data protection legislation	89
	Decision making and problem solving	90
	Delegation	93
	Discipline	94
	Discrimination and equality	98
	Employment legislation	99
	Groups and teams	104
	Health and safety	109
	Job analysis	113
	Job design	115
	Job evaluation	117
	Leadership	119
	Learning	124
	Management by objectives	128
	Management qualities and activities	130
	Management theories	132
	Manpower analysis and planning	133
	Motivation	135
	Non verbal communication	137
	Organisational objectives, policies and strategies	142
	Organisational structures	144
	Performance appraisal	145
	Personnel management	154
	Production control	156
	Quality assurance	159
	Questionnaires and surveys	166
	Recruitment, selection and induction	167
	Redundancy action checklist	178
	Responsibility	179
	Salaries and wages	180
	Stress management	184
	Time management	190
	Trade unions and the law	192
	Training	199
	Work study	202
Section 3	**Practice and development of skills and knowledge**	
	Unit 1 Management and supervision	209
	Unit 2 Managing work	215
	Unit 3 Managing others	222
	Unit 4 Individuals at work	232
	Unit 5 Employee relations	237
	Unit 6 Recruitment and selection	241
	Unit 7 Development and retention	266
Index		271

Coverage of topics by scenarios/activities

Below is an analysis showing which *units* in Sections 1 and 3 refer *directly* to Section 2 (*Information Bank*) for help in solving problems.

Note: It will be useful for *lecturers* planning courses, as well as for students planning revision.

Section 2 Information Bank Topics	Coverage of Information Bank Topics													
	Section 1 units							Section 3 units						
	1	2	3	4	5	6	7	1	2	3	4	5	6	7
Attitude				•										
Authority	•		•					•						
Budgetary Control		•												
Change Management	•		•	•							•			•
Communications	•		•	•				•		•				
Control									•					
Counselling and listening			•					•	•	•			•	
Data protection legislation														•
Decision making and problem solving		•							•	•				
Delegation	•		•					•						
Discipline					•			•						
Discrimination and equality		•											•	
Employment legislation		•		•		•						•	•	
Groups and teams		•								•	•			
Health and safety				•								•		
Job analysis					•			•						
Job design			•	•							•			
Job evaluation						•					•			•
Leadership			•	•						•				
Learning						•								•
Management by objectives		•						•	•					
Management qualities and activities	•		•											
Management theories	•								•	•				
Manpower analysis and planning					•									
Motivation			•	•					•	•				•
Non verbal communication		•						•		•				
Organisational objectives, policies & strategies		•						•	•				•	
Organisational structures	•							•						
Performance appraisal						•		•					•	•
Personnel management					•								•	•
Production control		•							•					
Quality assurance		•							•		•			
Questionnaires and surveys								•		•				
Recruitment, selection and induction					•						•			
Redundancy action checklist											•			
Responsibility	•													
Salaries and wages		•				•				•				
Stress management				•							•			
Time management		•						•	•					
Trade unions and the law					•							•		
Training		•						•						•
Work study		•							•					

Management Charter Initiative Standard Index

The following table lists scenarios and activities which can be used *to contribute to* achieving the MCI level 1 standards.

It will be useful to lecturers planning courses, and students should retain material produced in doing these activities and scenarios as it may be of use as evidence towards a competency based award.

Units	*Elements*	*Scenario/Activity*	*Page*
1 Maintain and improve service and product operations	1.1 Maintain operations to meet quality standards	Starlight plc	17
		Bill's biscuits	218
		The quality issues group	217
		A question of control	219
	1.2 Create and maintain the necessary conditions for productive work	A hazardous occupation	239
		Better safe than sorry	237
		A question of rights	238
		TC Installations	11
		Accidents will happen	46
2 Contribute to the implementation of change in services, products and systems	2.1 Contribute to the evaluation of proposed changes to services, products and systems	All change at Brooks Ltd	233
		New ways of working	232
		High Speed Engineering	18
	2.2 Implement and evaluate changes to services, products and systems	Alan's girl	4
		Space Systems Ltd	36
		The Haywood effect	25
		The Amos project	34
		Restructuring at Hardings	266
3 Recommend, monitor and control the use of resources	3.1 Make recommendations for expenditure	Lectronics Ltd	216
		John Jones v the management information system	13
	3.2 Monitor and control the use of resources	Work study	220
		What does it mean?	50
4 Contribute to the recruitment and selection of personnel	4.1 Define future personnel requirements	The caretaker	243
		BCC Ltd	241
		What do your people do?	52
		What does it mean?	50
	4.2 Contribute to the assessment and selection of candidates against team and organisational requirements	The handyman	53
		John Goodland & Sons Ltd	55
		Velop Ltd	245
		Personnel policies	265
5 Develop teams, individuals and self to enhance performance	5.1 Develop and improve teams through planning and activities	The Haywood effect	25
		The transport office	222
	5.2 Identify, review and improve development activities for individuals	Midas Ltd	223
		A question of style	228
		Last minute training	63
		What should I do?	212
		Learning style inventory	267
		A quick appraisal	61
	5.3 Develop oneself within the job role	Are you likely to suffer from stress?	235
		Individual and organisational goals	212
		Are you a team builder?	228
		Discovering your own learning style	268

Units	Elements	Scenario/Activity	Page
	6.1 Set up and update work objectives for teams and individuals	Trialpack Ltd	15
		Nimbiville	223
		What should I do?	212
6 Plan, allocate and evaluate work carried out by teams, individuals and self	6.2 Plan activities and determine work methods to achieve objectives	Stanley Engineering Ltd	39
		Clockwise Ltd	215
		Norance Plastics	232
		Pete's problems	209
	6.3 Allocate work and evaluate teams, individuals and self against objectives	The finishing shop	9
		Do you to do too much?	212
		Smudger Smith	32
		Arctic survival	20
		Individual and organisational goals	212
	6.4 Provide feedback to teams and individuals on their performance	Technoplast Ltd	44
		Deliverance	26
		A quick appraisal	61
		No singing at work	226
	7.1 Establish and maintain the trust and support of one's subordinates	Deliverance	26
		The transport office	222
		The Haywood effect	25
		A question of style	228
		A message from the management	29
	7.2 Establish and maintain the trust and support of one's immediate manager	Deliverance	26
		Queuing at the checkout	210
		Vernal Ltd	6
		Induction procedures	265
	7.3 Establish and maintain relationships with colleagues	The finishing shop	9
		Smudger Smith	32
7 Create, maintain and enhance effective working relationships		Are you a team builder?	228
		Belloc	24
		Basis for authority	211
	7.4 Identify and minimise interpersonal conflict	Who's the boss?	211
		No singing at work	226
		Playing by the rules	8
		Smudger Smith	32
		Closed shop	48
	7.5 Implement disciplinary and grievance procedures	A question of rights	238
		An employer's dilemna	238
		Deliverance	26
		Back home	222
		Technoplast Ltd	44
	7.6 Counsel staff	A quick appraisal	61
		Midas Ltd	223
		Body language	229
		The chosen few	256
	8.1 Obtain and evaluate information to aid decision making	Take your time	219
		Nimbiville	223
8 Seek, evaluate and organise information for action		Bill's biscuits	217
		Johnsons' Valves	59
		Rights and wrongs	239
	8.2 Record and store information	Computers and appraisals	267
		High Speed Engineering	18
	9.1 Lead meetings and group discussions to solve problems and make decisions	High Speed Engineering	18
		Nimbiville	223
9 Exchange information to solve problems and make decisions	9.2 Contribute to discussions to solve problems and make decisions	The quality issues group	218
		Focus on the client	42
		Pay points	58
	9.3 Advise and inform others	Call the fire brigade	21
		The quality issues group	218
		Redesigning a job	236
		Why are some jobs boring?	236
		The new supervisors	209
		The Amos project	34

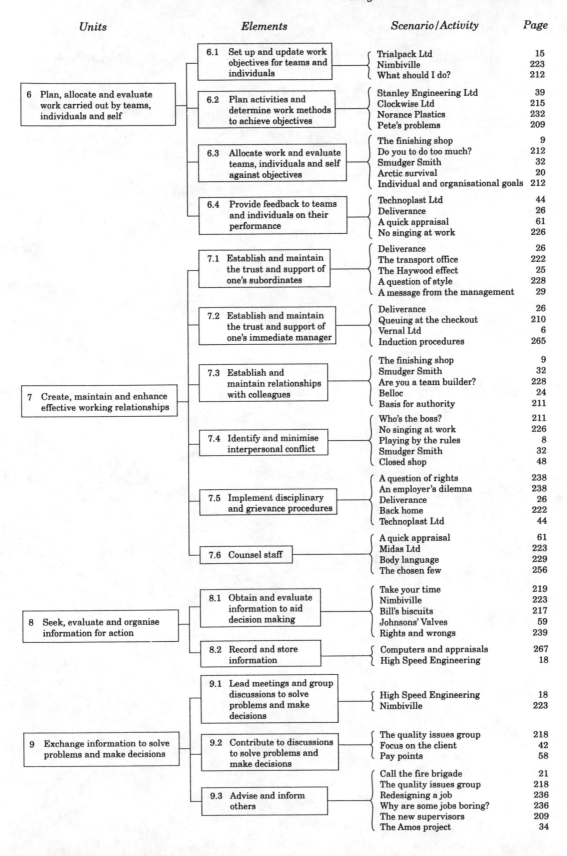

Section 1

Scenarios, quick answer questions and tasks

Introduction

This section directs the active-learning process. It is divided into seven units, each covering a separate management topic. Each unit commences with a list of objectives and is arranged in logical sequence, leading you through a series of *quick answer questions*, *tasks* and *scenarios*.

The *quick answer questions* enable you to use your own experiences and common sense to answer a problem. You can check your answers to these questions by looking at the comments given on the next left-hand page.

The *tasks* require a little more thought than the quick answer questions and you may need to research the answers. Your common sense and general knowledge will also help you solve these problems, but you will also find it useful to direct your research where directed to the appropriate data in the information bank in Section 2.

The *scenarios* illustrate typical managerial and supervisory problems which you may have come across already or are likely to encounter in the future. The *problem-solving activities* will help you to relate your own experiences and general knowledge to the knowledge you have gained from studying each unit. In the same way as the tasks, you will also find it helpful to follow the directions to the relevant data in the information bank in Section 2.

It is very important that you retain any materials you produce when answering the questions and tasks, and solving problems in this section, as they may contribute to a vocational award.

You are now ready to start the first unit.

Unit 1: Management and supervision

1.1 Objectives

At the end of this unit you should be able to:

- ☐ describe the formal and informal structures of an organisation;
- ☐ differentiate between line authority and functional authority;
- ☐ construct an organisation chart;
- ☐ classify managerial tasks according to the main functions of management;
- ☐ compare the role of a manager with that of a supervisor.

1.2 Organisational structures

All organisations, whether profit or non-profit making, need a structure. A formal structure ensures that all the workers, whether voluntary or paid, can identify their position in the organisation in relation to others. They need to know what their responsibilities are, to whom they are accountable and the nature of any managerial or supervisory responsibilities they hold.

In addition to the formal structure, there is likely to be an informal structure which arises from personal relationships, patterns of work etc.

Quick answer questions 1.2

i) *What position do you hold in relation to others in the organisation at work or, if you are a student, at college?*

ii) *To whom are you accountable?*

iii) *What are your responsibilities?*

iv) *Do you hold any managerial or supervisory responsibilities?*

v) *What informal structures can you identify in your organisation?*

Task

Collect any information that describes the structure of the organisation where you work or study.

| HELP | ? | See the information bank in ***Section 2: Organisational structures***, page 144. |

Comments on quick answer questions 1.2

i)   You may have decided to answer this question by indicating your position in your own particular department or section, or in your department or faculty at college if you are a student.

ii)   You should have given the position of your boss here if you are working or your course tutor if you are a student.

iii) You should have jotted down the main responsibilities of your job or what you perceive are the responsibilities of being a student.

iv)   You may have noted any number of responsibilities here. If you are working you may have listed such items as making decisions, solving problems, drawing up plans, monitoring progress, supervising work, liaising with other departments, record keeping, etc.

v)   Informal structures include such groups as social club members and sports teams, smokers, parents with children at the in-house creche (if there is one), shift workers, those who take their meal breaks together at work and those who go out together, etc.

Scenario: Alan's girl

Here is an extract from a conversation between a newly-appointed manager and one of his supervisors.

"The procedure is to give one week's notice to the Computer Department using a slip that must be signed by the Department Supervisor, who in this case is you. This is then returned to us with the information that we need and permission to go ahead.

Luckily Alan's girlfriend is a supervisor in the Computer Department, so he 'phones her and gets the figures, but we still fill out a slip and put it into the system. Because of Alan's contact, we get a turnaround of 2 days instead of 2 weeks.

It usually works well, though on a couple of occasions, when Alan and his girl weren't getting on too well, she refused to help, which meant we couldn't keep to our promised delivery time. I don't suppose the Computer Manager would be too pleased if he knew – he's a real stickler for procedures and always insists that every detail on the slips is filled in correctly. Worse still, he's so busy, he's hardly ever in the office which means that the job's long finished before he even signs the slips!

Still, we're like water in this department: we take the path of least resistance. I did try to get the system changed once, but the Computer Manager likes it as it is, so we've adapted..."

Problem-solving activity

1. *What do you think about the department's approach to the problems that they have?*

2. *Would you make any changes, and if so what would you do?*

HELP **?**

See the information bank in *Section 2: Organisational structures*, page 144; *Responsibility*, page 179.

1.3 Authority, responsibility and delegation

Most organisations adopt a pyramid structure in which authority and responsibility extend downwards in a hierarchical pattern. At the top of the pyramid senior managers make the executive and policy decisions. They have overall responsibility for the success or failure of the organisation's policies and the authority to carry them out. Status, responsibility and authority decrease as you move down the pyramid.

There are two forms of authority in an organisation. Line authority is the direct relationship between a superior and his or her subordinates. Functional authority refers to the responsibility for specialist functions in an organisation, such as finance, marketing, personnel, production etc.

Authority may be highly centralised, with only one or two people making the decisions, or it may be decentralised, allowing certain decisions to be made lower down the chain of command. In this way, authority can be delegated. Although delegation is a simple process, it is often a major managerial problem, mainly due to the human behavioural aspects involved.

Quick answer questions 1.3

i)   *What rights do the holders of authority have?*

ii) *What workplace symbols of authority can you think of?*

iii) *Is it true that authority can be delegated but responsibility cannot?*

iv) *Does a manager or supervisor normally have complete authority over his or her team?*

v)   *Why might a manager want to delegate?*

Task

From the information you collected in Task 1.2, construct an organisation chart showing the line authority. Indicate the position you hold on the chart.

HELP **?**

See the information bank in *Section 2: Authority*, page 75; *Delegation*, page 93; *Organisational structures*, page 144; *Responsibility*, page 179.

> ## Comments on quick answer questions 1.3
>
> i) Authority gives the holder the right to make decisions, issue instructions and insist that they are carried out.
>
> ii) You may have included in your list of symbols of authority such things as company cars, the position of the office in the building, its size (or the size of the desk), privileges, badges, uniform or colour of overalls.
>
> iii) Ultimate responsibility cannot be delegated, although by accepting authority some responsibility is also accepted.
>
> iv) Authority is only valid if it is accepted. The group or team may reject a manager's or supervisor's authority, by working to rule, striking or leaving the organisation. The authority of the management only extends to the workplace.
>
> v) Managers usually want to delegate in order to allocate work, relieve themselves of detail or make use of others' technical abilities.

Scenario: Vernal Ltd

Recent figures in the accounts of Vernal Ltd show a big drop in profits this year. One of the reasons for this was a large increase in labour costs. Consequently, every department has been told that it must economise. Roger Smith, the office manager, has been given strict instructions that permission for overtime must now be approved by his boss, the branch manager. This is a change in policy as Roger always used to deal with overtime allocations. He is feeling very worried about the change and discusses the matter with Pete Allen, one of his colleagues.

ROGER   I don't know what I've done wrong, we've always had a low overtime allocation compared with other departments and that's because I've kept a careful eye on it.

PETE   Yes, I know what you mean, but I hear the company is really struggling at the moment and there's talk of people being laid off, so if I were you, I'd keep a low profile on the issue.

ROGER   It's not that easy. We've got a big order that has to go out at the weekend and three of my staff are off sick. My boss is away on a course until the weekend and I've tried to get in touch with his deputy but he's never in his office.

PETE   Well, it's their problem. You've done what you can. If I were you I'd just let the customer wait; after all, orders are orders!

Problem-solving activity

i) *Why has this situation arisen?*

ii) *What should Roger Smith do now?*

iii) *What would you advise Roger to do in order to avoid this happening again?*

See the information bank in **Section 2: Authority**, page 75; **Change management**, page 79; **Delegation**, page 93; **Organisational structures**, page 144; **Responsibility**, page 179.

1.4 The role of management

Anyone who has had any kind of work experience knows something about management. You may be a manager or a supervisor yourself or you may have been on the receiving end of management instructions.

Some people believe that managerial skills are inherent. However, many large organisations set aside considerable sums of money for management training, since most of the skills required can be learned.

Managers carry out such duties as *forecasting, planning, organising, co-ordinating, commanding, controlling* and *motivating*, and possess *authority*. They aim to achieve the organisation's objectives through effective planning and use of resources. They may delegate certain tasks to their subordinates.

Sometimes a title other than that of manager is used, such as chairman, chief executive, chief cashier, director, headmaster, head of research, matron, partner in charge, president, principal, etc.

Quick answer questions 1.4

i)   *Do you carry out any managerial duties at work, at home or at college? List them.*

ii) *From whom do you receive authority for these activities?*

iii) *Which of the following duties do you consider are **not** normally part of a manager's job?*

controlling quality	*appraising staff performance*
dealing with staff grievances	*stocktaking*
setting production levels	*sending invoices*
designing products	*reducing waste*
decision-making	*motivating staff*
negotiating with trade unions	*setting budgets*
ordering stationery	*issuing press releases*
maintaining machinery	*drawing up advertisements*
dismissing staff	*recruiting staff*
problem-solving	*typing contracts*
training staff	*deciding work methods*
setting pay levels	*bookkeeping*

Task

Classify the managerial tasks in the above list according to the main functions of management. Exclude the non-managerial tasks.

HELP **?** See the information bank in *Section 2: Management qualities and activities*, page 130; *Management theories*, page 132.

Comments on quick answer questions 1.4

i)   You should have listed only those duties which in general terms involve planning, organising, motivating and controlling, and which you carry out with authority.

ii) You may have referred to the organisation chart you drew up in Task 1.3 if you are answering this question as a manager or a student. If the only managerial duties you carry out are at home, you do not require authority from anyone to manage your household, although you may share these duties with other members of your family.

iii) In some small organisations, managers may find themselves carrying out a mixture of managerial, executive and administrative tasks. This is particularly true in cases of staff absence, when managers must ensure that the day-to-day work is completed. However, for larger organisations you may have decided to exclude:

    bookkeeping   designing products

    sending invoices   ordering stationery

    typing contracts   maintaining machinery

Scenario: Playing by the rules

Geoff has been manager of his department for two years. He has a better knowledge of his firm's products than anyone else in the organisation and his expertise is widely respected. He manages his department strictly according to the rules.

One day Phil, one of the clerks in Geoff's department, had to take his wife to an out-patient's appointment at the hospital and was half an hour late returning from his lunch break. Geoff docked the half hour from Phil's pay.

On another occasion the new word processor operator, Sue, had an argument with Geoff's long-standing secretary, Muriel. Geoff told her, "Fit in or leave".

When Bill, Geoff's assistant came into work one morning and told him that his wife had left him, Geoff told him to make sure his personal problems didn't interfere with his work. Geoff's boss is aware that staff morale in Geoff's department has dropped considerably since Geoff's appointment.

Problem-solving activity

i)   *Think about Geoff's approach. Are there any alternatives?*

ii) *Do you think Geoff, who is an acknowledged expert in the firm, is the right person to manage the department?*

iii) *What action would you advise Geoff's boss to take?*

See the information bank in *Section 2: Management qualities and activities*, page 130 *Management theories*, page 132.

1.5 The role of supervision

All managerial positions contain an element of supervision which decreases as you proceed up the management ladder. The difference between management and supervision varies from one organisation to another, but essentially supervision contains a far greater element of close contact with the workforce than management.

Supervisors carry out supervisory duties such as overseeing and controlling, often dealing with situations on the spot as they arise; they also possess authority. They are concerned with the day-to-day supervision of a group of workers and may delegate minor tasks to their subordinates. In addition they may carry out a number of managerial duties (see Unit 1.4).

Task

List the qualities you would look for in a successful supervisor.

HELP **?** | See the information bank in *Section 2: Management qualities and activities*, page 130 *Management theories*, page 132.

Scenario: The finishing shop

Steve Cameron has worked in the finishing shop for nearly ten years and has recently been promoted to supervisor. He was a popular choice for the job.

Recently there have been an unusual number of operators absent, due to a particularly bad strain of 'flu which has been going round. As a result the finishing shop has fallen badly behind schedule.

Steve knows the work well and decides to help out by running one of the machines himself. Dennis Ludwig, the plant manager, on returning from a meeting at head office, finds Steve working at the machine. He is not impressed and calls Steve into his office and lectures him on his role as a supervisor. "It's time you realised that you're not one of them any more; you're part of the management team now and you can't go off doing their work for them every time we're short-handed."

Problem-solving activity

i) *Imagine you are Steve and write a brief report defending your actions.*

ii) *Using popular theories of management, explain Dennis' views.*

HELP **?** | See the information bank in *Section 2: Communications, report writing*, page 81; *Management qualities and activities*, page 130 *Management theories*, page 132.

 You should now be able to attempt the activities in Unit 1 of Section 3, page 209.

Unit 2: Managing work

2.1 Objectives

At the end of this unit you should be able to:

☐ differentiate between an organisation's objectives, strategies and policies;

☐ describe the main techniques of management control;

☐ describe the method of work study;

☐ understand the role of decision making in planning and control.

2.2 Organisational objectives, strategies and policies

It is the function of top management to determine the *objectives*, *strategies* and *policies* of the organisation. In Unit 1.4 you learned that one of the aims of management is to achieve the organisation's objectives. The prime objective or *mission* of any organisation is to meet the needs of its customers.

Long-term objectives or strategies set broad targets such as profit maximisation or growth maximisation. If objectives can be measured and relate to a specific period of time, they become *targets*. Strategies may usually take five or more years to achieve.

Medium-term objectives or policies are likely to be more specific. For example, a publishing company may have a policy of only using recycled materials or manufacture all its products in Britain. Middle management is responsible for drawing up programmes of work to achieve the objectives. Programmes of work usually take between one and five years to achieve.

Detailed short-term *plans* and *budgets* must be established to manage the operations of the organisation during the current and coming year. It is the job of the first line managers to ensure that these plans and targets are achieved by the workforce, thus producing the products and services to meet the customers' needs.

Q *Quick answer questions 2.2*

i) *Who are the customers in the organisation where you work or study and what products or services are supplied?*

ii) *When do objectives become targets?*

iii) *Should first line managers be given objectives to attain when the results depend on the people they have to manage?*

iv) *Who is responsible for deciding an organisation's objectives, strategies and policies?*

v) *What is middle management responsible for?*

Task

Find out what your organisation's or college's mission, general objectives and policies are.

HELP ?

See the information bank in *Section 2: Organisational objectives, policies and strategies*, page 142.

Scenario: TC Installations Ltd

TC Installations Ltd produces a wide range of air conditioning products and employs about 300 people. Terry Stone, the factory manager, is eating his lunch in the company canteen with Sue Smith, the stores manager, and Ray Brown from the sales office. They are discussing a common complaint, that the company has no written policies and that because of this they sometimes have problems when making decisions.

Terry deplores the fact that some of the employees eat their lunch at their work benches. He feels that there should be a policy to stop this. Sue and Ray both feel that there should be a clear statement about leave of absence. Ray is also concerned about some of the sales staff turning up at work wearing casual clothes. The three of them conclude that the best way to solve the problem is to confront the managing director with their concerns and ask him to define company policy in these and other areas.

While they are conversing, Alex Adams, the quality control manager, joins them. 'Are these really matters for the managing director to decide or should we all be making our own decisions on what is best for our own departments?'

Problem-solving activities

i)   Are company policies necessary to cover every possible contingency?

ii) What problems might arise if each department or section makes up separate policies?

iii) What problems might arise if policies are laid down by the managing director?

iv) What are the advantages and disadvantages of TC Installations having clearly defined mission and policy statements?

HELP ?

See the information bank in *Section 2: Organisational objectives, policies and strategies*, page 142; *Management by objectives*, page 128.

Comments quick answer questions 2.2

i)   In some organisations the customers are private individuals; in others they are other firms or whole industries. If you are at college, you and your fellow students are the customers. The products or services provided depend on the organisation, but can range from a silicone chip to a complete ship, a domestic appliance repair service to the National Health Service.

ii) Objectives become targets if they can be measured and relate to a specific period of time.

iii) A manager's job is to manage the resources, which include the workforce, to achieve the objectives of the organisation.

iv) An organisation's objectives, strategies and policies should be decided by top management.

v)   Middle management is responsible for drawing up programmes of work to achieve the objectives set by top management.

2.3 Methods of control

Control is closely linked to planning. After plans have been set and implemented it is an essential part of management to monitor performance against the plan, to identify any deviation from the plan and initiate corrective action. Careful preparation of plans minimises the need for corrective action. There are three main methods of control and we will look at them one at a time:

☐ budgetary control

☐ production control

☐ quality control and quality assurance

Top management is supplied with control information, usually financial, to keep a check on broad policy and programmes. *Budgetary control* is a widely used method. It involves setting plans (*budgets*) which lay down the policies for which individual managers are responsible. A continuous comparison is made of what is actually achieved against the plan, so that managers can remedy any divergence from the plan or revise the plan if necessary.

A budget is a quantitative and/or financial statement and normally gives the income and/or expenditure, including any capital expenditure, needed during a financial period to achieve a given objective. Individual budgets are incorporated into a *master budget* which include a budgeted profit and loss account and a budgeted balance sheet. The period of time for which the budget is intended is known as the *budget period*.

Quick answer questions 2.3a

i)   *Is it true that most employees dislike the constraints put on them by budgets?*

ii) *Do you agree that the manager who is responsible for a budget should be party to its calculation?*

iii) *Is it important to ensure that a budget for expenditure is always utilised?*

Task

What are the advantages and disadvantages of budgetary control?

HELP	?	See the information bank in *Section 2; Budgetary control*, page 77.

Scenario: John Jones versus the management information system

They called it a management information system when it was first installed nearly a year ago. Computers were put in all the offices and every section head had to give a detailed breakdown of how much was spent by their section last year and on what. A few weeks later all section heads received a budget. Actually there were three budgets: one for manpower, one for consumables and one for capital.

John Jones is an acting section head and hopes to take on the job permanently. His section deals with packing and dispatch. The goods are packed in cartons and each carton has a label bearing some printed information and a bar code. John punches the information on each carton into a computer and it prints the labels complete with bar code.

As usual a printout from the management information system had arrived at the beginning of the month and it showed that John had overspent on consumables, was on target on manpower levels and had underspent on capital.

The other day the laser printer that prints the labels for the cartons ran out of toner. John sent out an order for another toner cartridge, but it was returned with a note attached to it stating that as he is over budget on consumables the order cannot be authorised. Later in the day John was talking to Shirley Thomas, one of the accounts clerks. She said that it would be a waste of time arguing with the accounts people and that the simplest way round the problem would be to buy a new printer out of his capital allocation.

John went back to his office pondering on his options. He could:

❐ telephone the toner supplier himself and thus bypass the accounts department altogether;

❐ write a memo to the general manager explaining the problem;

❐ buy a new printer out of his capital budget as suggested by Shirley.

Problem-solving activities

Consider each of John Jones' options and make your recommendations, giving your reasons.

HELP	?	See the information bank in *Section 2; Budgetary control*, page 77.

Comments on quick answer questions 2.3a

i) In general people dislike being controlled and therefore dislike the constraints of budgets. However, most people recognise the need for some control.

ii) Usually, if you give people a say in the decisions that affect them they are much more likely to be committed to them. Therefore the same is also true of budgets.

iii) The idea that a budget is an indication or a guideline is often overlooked. As a result there is a temptation to spend to the limit in case the budget is cut in the following period. This can lead to wasteful or ill-considered purchases at the end of the budget period.

Production control and planning are closely allied and often the two functions are combined. A number of separate plans are combined to form an overall plan for production. Plans drawn up include labour, machines, tools and equipment, materials, batch quantities and safety measures among other resources. A time-scale and realistic targets must be set.

Production control can be broken down into:

☐ scheduling which results in a programme of production;

☐ stock control which can be divided into materials control covering the purchase and cost of materials, and stock control proper which controls the quantity and quality of materials according to the production plan;

☐ manufacturing order control which results in documents authorising production according to the schedule and the production plan;

☐ machine and labour usage which co-ordinates the two resources and reduces idle time to a minimum;

☐ progressing which co-ordinates the production programme by monitoring progress through the production department, comparing it with the schedule and taking the necessary action to correct any deviations.

☐ dispatching which results in work orders and production sheets authorising and allocating work in accordance with the standard method, using allocated tools, drawings and scheduled information;

Quick answer questions 2.3b

iv) *Managers have to make three production decisions:*

   ☐ *what needs to be done;*

   ☐ *who will do it;*

   ☐ *how it will be done.*

   What factors do you think influence a manager's production decisions?

v) *What aids or techniques are there which might help decide who will do what and how?*

Task

If you had to investigate a complaint about the level of productivity in your department, at work or at college, which items would you look at?

HELP ? | See the information bank in **Section 2; Production control**, page 156.

Scenario: Trialpack Ltd

Trialpack Ltd produces samples of consumer products in small bubble packs which are then sent by post to the consumer as a free sample. The process is a three-stage one. Each stage must be completed before the next can be started. The stages are moulding, filling and packing.

At each stage there is one machine with two operators. Each machine can handle 250,000 items per eight-hour day. The supervisor receives his or her instructions on what would usually be produced a week in advance, but this is not always so. On Monday the production needs for the week were 250,000 shampoos, 750,000 coffees and 500,000 jams.

Problem-solving activities

i)   *How should the operators be allocated for the week?*

ii) *How might the supervisor check on how the work is progressing?*

iii) *If a rush order for 750,000 tomato ketchups came in on Wednesday, could it be completed by the weekend?*

iv) *How much overtime would be need to complete all orders by Sunday evening?*

v)   *Trialpack Ltd intends to buy two new machines which will have much higher capabilities. Production levels will be more dependent on the speed and skills of the operators. This should significantly improve on present production levels. How could the pay for the operators of the new machines be determined?*

HELP ? | See the information bank in **Section 2; Production control**, page 156; **Salaries and wages**, page 180.

> ## Comments on quick answer questions 2,3b
>
> iv) What needs to be done depends on the orders received, the delivery times promised, how highly the customer is valued, the priorities of other members of the management team.
>
> Who will do it depends on capabilities, level of training and experience, which other jobs are in progress, who will be the most effective.
>
> How it will be done depends on the equipment available, safety considerations, operator skills, procedures devised by the use of method study.
>
> v) Aids and techniques used may include charts such as Gantt charts, critical path analysis and work study. Computers are often used in complex scheduling problems.

Quality control and *quality assurance* are concerned with *product quality* which can be broken down into quality of design, quality of conformance, quality of performance and reliability. Product quality is necessary and desirable for legal, competitive and economic reasons. The main methods of achieving product quality include:

- ☐ *quality control*, a traditional approach which involves establishing standards and specifications, and carrying out inspections to separate defective goods from those conforming to the standard of quality laid down by management;

- ☐ *statistical quality control*, a form of the above which uses the theory of probability to establish a set of control limits for each production process;

- ☐ *quality assurance*, a more modern approach than quality control whereby the supplying or manufacturing organisation is organised in such a way that quality products or services are assured;

- ☐ *total quality management*, a form of the above where the onus for achieving quality lies with all staff, not merely those concerned with quality;

- ☐ *quality circles*, an approach to quality based on motivation by participation whereby small groups of employees who are engaged in similar activities meet regularly to identify problems and present solutions.

Quick answer questions 2.3c

Are the following statements true or false?

	True	False
vi) *In some industries quality can never be too high.*	☐	☐
vii) *Quality problems are usually solved by employing more inspectors.*	☐	☐
viii) *Quality control principles only apply in manufacturing industries.*	☐	☐

Task

Find out what measures of control are taken at your place of work or study concerning the quality of products and services.

HELP ?	See the information bank in **Section 2; Quality assurance**, page 159.

Scenario: Starlight plc

The grinding wheel industry is intensely competitive and even Starlight plc, whose specialist grinding wheels have always sold well, have had to cut their profit margins. Last month Alan Marsden, the sales director, secured a large order to supply wheels to a giant Japanese car manufacturer. The contract was for 15,000 wheels over 18 months with delivery dates at three monthly intervals. Failure to meet the delivery dates would mean the loss of the order and a large penalty payment.

To cope with this large order, the production line has had to work at full capacity. However, the result of this has been a fall in quality, shown by an increase in rejects and a letter of complaint from another customer. Alan called a meeting of the senior management and the following solutions were suggested:

i) Buy higher quality materials.

ii) Reduce machine speeds.

iii) Employ two more inspectors.

iv) Form a committee to investigate the problem.

v) Inform the workforce that they are all responsible for quality and that the loss of any order will mean job losses in the company.

Problem-solving activities

Before any decisions are made, all first line managers are invited to make comments to senior management. Write a memo to Alan Marsden with your views on the five suggestions outlined above and your recommendations.

See the information bank in *Section 2: Quality assurance (British Standard 5750)*, page 159.

2.4 Work study

Work study is specific management technique which involves studying the ways of doing a particular job more efficiently and cheaply. It consists of a *method study* to compare existing methods with proposed methods and *work measurement* to establish the time required by a qualified worker to do the job to a specified standard.

Quick answer questions 2.4

i) *For what reasons might a work study be carried out?*

ii) *Who is the best person to carry out work study?*

iii) *Where should the work study be conducted?*

iv) *What techniques are used for communicating plans for improved work methods in your place of work or study?*

v) *Are there any channels for communicating ideas from the workforce about improved working methods in your place of work or college?*

Comments on quick answer questions 2.3c

iv) False. If quality is too high it is a waste; too low and customers complain. A standard must be agreed between the customers and the producer.

vii) False. Quality cannot be inspected into a product; it is concerned with the organisation's philosophy and policies.

viii) False. Quality principles are being used in service industries too, in education for example.

Comments on quick answer questions 2.4

i) Reasons include the following:

❑ to make the most effective use of economic resources available;

❑ to achieve more effective control;

❑ to improve planning;

❑ to increase productivity;

❑ to achieve a more even spread of work among the workforce;

❑ to establish fairer wage schemes through the assessment of job values;

ii) Work study is a highly specialist area and should only be carried out by those who are trained.

iii) Work study must be conducted in the workplace.

iv) Communication methods may include meetings and presentations, videos and/or written communications.

v) Channels for communicating ideas from the workforce about improved working methods might include suggestion boxes, quality circles, or financial incentives; documents such as employee reports, employee newspapers or news bulletins.

Task

What are the main advantages of work study and what major problems might arise?

HELP ?

See the information bank in *Section 2; Work study*, page 202.

Scenario: High Speed Engineering

High Speed Engineering is going to make 20 people redundant. Everyone knew it was coming and, though the public announcement has yet to be made, there is general acceptance of the fact. High Speed Engineering is a family firm and it has been a matter of some pride to the owners that they have never made anyone redundant before. As a result, they don't really know how to go about it. How will they choose who must go? Will it be last in first out? Should the least productive ones be the ones to go? What about loyalty – does it count for nothing?

The Managing Director has called a meeting of the department heads. At this meeting a policy is to be decided as to how the 20 will be selected. The MD has already stated that the decisions must be based on what is best for the company, though a secondary consideration will be the individuals themselves. Three months ago, the company did an in-house work study and looked at every job in the production area in an effort to find improvements. Most people were involved in this and even though it was stated at the time it was the jobs not the people who were being looked at, inevitably comments were made about the individuals concerned and the records were kept. The MD sees these records as being the basis for the decisions on redundancy.

Problem-solving activities

i)   *Should the work study records be used as suggested?*

ii) *How might the decision on who is to be made redundant be reached?*

See the information bank in *Section 2: Employment legislation*, page 99; *Redundancy action checklist*, page 178, *Work study*, page 202.

2.5 Decision making and problem solving

Managers constantly make decisions. Collectively an organisation's decisions determine its objectives, strategies and policies. They determine its size, its products and services, its profit levels, the size of its workforce, its life span; in fact, without decisions being taken, the organisation would not exist. It is therefore very important that management decisions, which are often made under adverse circumstances, are made as rationally and objectively as possible.

Decision-making is based on information. Information is necessary to define and structure problems, explore and select solutions and review the effects of the choice once it has been implemented.

Quick answer questions 2.5

i)   *What is a problem?*

ii)   *With sufficient planning and control, can all problems be foreseen?*

iii) *Should managers seek out problems?*

iv)   *Is there only one solution for most problems?*

v)   *Are problems merely deviations from standards?*

Task

List the advantages and disadvantages of brainstorming as a method of making decisions and solving problems.

See the information bank in *Section 2; Decision making and problem solving*, page 90.

Comments on quick answer questions 2.5

i)   A problem is a difficult matter requiring a solution.

ii) It is unlikely that all problems can be foreseen.

iii) Part of a manager's job is to foresee problems.

iv) Often there are as many solutions as there are people offering them.

v)   A deviation from a plan may be a problem, but not all problems concern matters which can be planned.

Scenario: Arctic survival

You are a member of a commercial expedition to the Arctic to test a new product. As a result of an accident you, your crew and your vehicle are stranded some 200 miles from the coast where you are to rendezvous with the expedition's mother ship. Most of your equipment has been lost in the accident and survival depends on reaching the ship.

Problem-solving activities

Rank the 15 items below, which are all that remain of your supplies, in terms of their importance to you and your crew in helping you reach the rendezvous.

(1 = most important, 15 = least important)

life raft

box of matches

magnetic compass

food concentrate

5 gallons of water

50 feet of nylon rope

parachute silk

first aid kit containing hypodermic needles

portable heat unit

2 × 0.45 calibre pistols

1 case dried milk

2 × 6 gallon fuel tanks

stellar map

signal flares

solar-powered transmitter / receiver

HELP ? See the information bank in *Section 2; Decision making and problem solving*, page 90.

2.6 Time management

One decision which has considerable bearing on the management activities of planning and control is that of how to use time effectively. *Time management*, which takes place at all levels in an organisation, is important whether the activity is carried out by an individual alone or by a group or a team.

Quick answer questions 2.6

i)   *What would you expect the symptoms of poor time management to be?*

ii) *What aids are commonly used for planning time?*

iii) *How might managers avoid wasting time?*

Task

Answer the following questions by ticking the appropriate column.

		Yes	No	Don't know
i)	Do I know what my main goals and priorities are?	☐	☐	☐
ii)	Do I know the best sequence in which to do what must be done?	☐	☐	☐
iii)	Have I checked in detail how I spend each working hour in an average week?	☐	☐	☐
iv)	Do I spend time operating when I should be managing?	☐	☐	☐
v)	Do I do work that I should be delegating?	☐	☐	☐
vi)	Do I spend long enough doing things that must be done and which only I can do?	☐	☐	☐
vii)	Do I do things that need not be done at all?	☐	☐	☐
viii)	Do I concentrate on my main goals and priorities?	☐	☐	☐

HELP ?	See the information bank in *Section 2; Decision making and problem solving*, page 90; *Time management*, page 190.

Scenario: Call the fire brigade

Last August, when most of the workforce were on holiday, you were left in sole charge of the site; only the maintenance personnel and a skeleton staff remained. A fire broke out in a store room next to the main office. It was quite serious and was discovered by one of the caretakers. Using a fire extinguisher, he managed to put it out, burning himself slightly in the process. He believed that the fire may have been caused by an electrical fault, because an electrician had been working on some equipment in the storeroom earlier that day.

The caretaker reported the incident to you and you went to inspect the damage. Then you returned to your desk to write a list of all the things you would have to do as a result of the fire.

Problem-solving activities

i) *Number the following items on the list in order of priority:*

(1 = most important, 12 = least important)

Get a message to senior management ☐

Fill in a hazard report form ☐

Make sketches and take photographs ☐

Arrange for the cleaners to come in ☐

Turn off the electricity supply to the building concerned ☐

Call the fire prevention officer to ask for advice ☐

Record the incident in the accident report book ☐

Close the area off to personnel ☐

Replace the used fire extinguisher ☐

Notify the office manager ☐

Reset the fire alarm system ☐

Write a report for the Safety Committee ☐

ii) *How did you decide on the order?*

iii) *Draw up a simple guide for making decisions of this nature.*

HELP **?**	See the information bank in **Section 2; Decision making and problem solving**, page 90.

Comments on quick answer questions 2.6

i) The symptoms of poor time management tend to be unfinished or late work, people in a rush, people under pressure.

ii) Commonly used aids include diaries, forward planning wall charts and lists.

iii) Time-wasting activities include holding meetings with unwanted visitors, dealing with other people's problems, gossiping, taking unwanted telephone calls, attending unproductive meetings, dealing with irrelevant papers, mislaying essential papers, correcting earlier mistakes.

You should now be able to attempt the activities in Unit 2 of Section 3, page 215.

Unit 3: Managing others

3.1 Objectives

At the end of this unit you should be able to:

☐ explain what is meant by interpersonal skills;

☐ understand the nature of groups;

☐ describe the characteristics of effective leadership and compare different leadership styles;

☐ give examples of workplace communications;

☐ list the common causes of distortion or breakdown in communication.

3.2 Interpersonal skills

In addition to learning the various methods for controlling work discussed in Unit 2, managers need to possess good *interpersonal skills*. The ability to deal confidently with interactions in the workplace, where there may be differences in power, status or role as well as cultural and social class backgrounds, is a key management skill. In order to control work effectively, managers must also communicate effectively.

An awareness of other people is an essential requirement. If managers and supervisors are sensitive to the different *attitudes* and *motivations* of others, the distorting effect of their different *perceptions* will be reduced. Managers should strive to be assertive rather than aggressive in their dealings. They may need to take into account their *leadership* role, and *non-verbal* methods of communication.

Quick answer questions 3.2

Give examples of the following:

i)   *an attitude you hold;*

ii)   *something that motivates you in your present course of study;*

iii) *your perception of the person sitting next to you, or who works with you;*

iv)   *the roles you play in different settings.*

Comments on quick answer questions 3.2

i)   An attitude is a belief or opinion you hold on a particular issue. Your behaviour usually reflects this.

ii) You may consider that improved career prospects is a motivating factor in your present course of study, for example.

iii) Your perception of the student sitting next to you may include the information you already know about him or her plus a number of assumptions you have made. These may include categorising him or her according to various stereotypes: appearance, gender, marital status, occupation and status.

iv) You may have thought of your role as a son or daughter, a sibling, a parent, a student, an employee, a member of a club, team, etc.

Task

An important part of communication is non-verbal communication. List some forms of non-verbal communication you have come across, and the messages that are being communicated.

HELP ? See the information bank in **Section 2: Non-verbal communication,** page 137.

Scenario: Belloc

The following story was told by Douglas McGregor (of Theory X and Theory Y fame).

A new manager was appointed in a mill. The manager came into a weave room the day he arrived. He walked directly over to the union official and said "Are you Belloc?". The union official acknowledged that he was. The manager said "I am the new manager here. When I manage a mill, I run it. Do you understand?" The official nodded and then waved his hand. The workers, intently watching this manoeuvre, shut down every loom in the room immediately. The union official turned to the manager and said "All right go ahead and run it".

Problem-solving activities

i)   *How should the manager have made his position clear?*

ii) *What should he do now?*

iii) *Comment on the attitude and perceptions of the union official and the manager.*

HELP ? See the information bank in **Section 2: Leadership**, page 119; **Motivation**, page 135.

3.3 Groups

Whenever people come together, whether at work or for social reasons, they form *groups*. *Informal* and *formal* groups in the workplace can greatly influence productivity.

Quick answer questions 3.3

i)   What is a group?

ii) What formal and informal groups do you belong to?

iii) Do the groups you belong to have a leader?

Task

Consider the people you know and try to identify small groups among them. Can you identify what draws them together? Now draw up a list of people you know who would make the worst possible group. List the problems that might arise in such a group.

| HELP | ? | See the information bank in *Section 2: Groups and teams*, page 104. |

Scenario: The Haywood effect

The machine room is set apart from the other offices. There have been virtually no staff changes over the last few years and the old supervisor, Ted, has recently retired. The operators in the machine room have been working together for a considerable length of time. They admit to being bored with their work, but get on well together and enjoy working as a team.

After taking some time to look at the way things are done in the machine room, Jason Haywood, the new supervisor, has introduced some big changes. No one is allowed to spend more than a month on any one job and machines have been moved and screened off so that the operators cannot talk to one another easily anymore.

To his surprise, Jason has found that the changes have not resulted in increased productivity. Instead, overtime has increased and absenteeism and sickness are becoming an increasing problem. Jason cannot understand it. He only made the changes to improve efficiency, give the operators more interesting work and to cut down on the amount of idle chatter.

Problem-solving activities

i)   What do you think has gone wrong?

ii) If you were Jason, what would you have done?

iii) If you were Jason, what would you do now?

| HELP | ? | See the information bank in *Section 2: Change management*, page 79; *Groups and teams*, page 104; *Job design*, page 115. |

Comments on quick answer questions 3.3

i)   A group is a number of people who are located close together, are classed together or who consider themselves to be a group. Members of a group must be able to interact and there should be some incentive for members to join or remain in the group.

ii) Formal groups you belong to may include clubs, societies, a church group, a work section or department, a course or study group or family groups; informal groups may include people you associate with who are fellow smokers or non-smokers, those who share a common interest in, say, health, diet, fitness, the arts, etc.

iii) The groups you belong to may have a formal leader or you may have noticed that the person leading the group varies according to the circumstances in which the group finds itself. Individuals may also take on other roles in the group.

3.4 Leadership

Effective *leadership* is an important management skill and is crucial to the management of others. It is concerned with being able to influence the *opinions*, *attitudes* and *performance* of others. This can have a powerful effect on the achievement of an organisation's objectives. A manager who wants to become a more effective leader must have a professional outlook and should recognise the need for continual personal development.

Quick answer questions 3.4

i)   *What is leadership?*

ii) *Are all managers leaders?*

iii) *Do men and women make equally good leaders?*

Task

*What **style** of leadership does your lecturer or manager adopt? List the characteristics and qualities of a successful leadership style.*

HELP	?	See the information bank in **Section 2: Leadership** page 119.

Scenario: Deliverance

The Red Van Delivery Company Ltd employs some 20 people, most of whom have worked for the company since it began trading 15 years ago. They are a closely knit group. Business has increased steadily over the years, but particularly in the last two years. So much so that Colin Sayers, the general manager, can no longer supervise all the staff personally and Maurice Twills has been appointed recently to assist him.

The newly created job was promotion for Maurice. He had previously been employed as a clerk in another company. After a week to find his feet in the new job, Maurice was put in charge of the drivers. Efficiency began to deteriorate almost immediately and it soon became apparent that the other employees did not accept his authority. Furthermore, the layout of the offices made it very easy for the office staff to continue to take problems to Colin Sayers thus bypassing the new deputy manager altogether.

Despite these problems, business continued to grow and the resulting increase in his workload forced Colin to delegate more and more of the decision-making to Maurice. Since he had been more or less ignored in the past, Maurice was reluctant to use much initiative in making decisions and whenever possible relied on the rule book. Often the van drivers used up so much time disputing the interpretation of the rule book that they were unable to make deliveries in time.

Maurice began holding a 30-40 minute meeting each morning to discuss operating procedures and problems. The van drivers soon regarded these meetings as an attempt by Maurice to emphasise his authority and gain prestige. Their response was to add the time taken for the meetings to their normal hours and claim overtime.

When Colin noticed the increase in overtime claims, he demanded to know what was going on. He soon learned about the resentment caused by the daily meetings and directed Maurice to discontinue the practice unless there was an urgent problem.

Maurice resented this, but even more he resented the fact that the drivers had ignored him by going directly to Colin with their complaints about the meetings. Soon Maurice became quite disagreeable with the drivers and began to rely entirely on an autocratic approach to carrying out his duties.

Meanwhile, the company continued to expand and a new supervisor was appointed. Maurice's job developed largely into an administrative post and his contacts with the drivers became minimal.

Problem-solving activities

i) *Why was Maurice not accepted by the drivers?*

ii) *Why did he initiate the daily meetings?*

iii) *If you were Colin, how would you have handled the situation?*

iv) *If you were Maurice, how would you have handled the situation?*

v) *Is there anything that might be done now to improve matters?*

HELP ?

See the information bank in *Section 2: Authority*, page 75; *Change management*, page 79; *Counselling and listening*, page 88; *Delegation*, page 93; *Groups and teams*, page 104; *Leadership*, page 119; *Management qualities and activities*, page 130; *Training*, page 199.

Comments on quick answer questions 3.4

i) A leader is a person who is followed by others. Leadership can be defined as influencing followers' behaviour to achieve results.

ii) Although some people seem to have inherent leadership skills, others acquire them with experience and training. Therefore not all managers are necessarily leaders.

iii) Gender is only a leadership issue if the group being led has preconceived expectations.

3.5 Workplace communications

Communication between people is common to all jobs and is one of the most important activities in any organisation. It is essential in the management of others. All forms of communication have four basic elements:

❐ the message

❐ the source (the transmitter)

❐ the medium

❐ the receiver

Good workplace communications require a *two-way flow* of information. The transmitter must try to ensure that the message is understood and should listen to and take account of any reaction to the communication. Workplace communications is a term used to cover:

❐ the information provided;

❐ the channels along which it passes;

❐ the means of passing it.

Messages are transmitted for a variety of reasons:

❐ to inform

❐ to command

❐ to negotiate

❐ to report

❐ to co-ordinate

❐ to co-operate

❐ to motivate

Employees need to be informed about their duties and rights; they need to be able to communicate with managers and supervisors about them. Many employees want more information than just basic instructions on how to do their jobs. They want the management to keep them informed on what is happening within the organisation and why. They may want to know how they can contribute to the organisation's objectives, policies and strategies, especially any that affect them directly. To do this, they need to be able to ask questions and receive answers.

Quick answer questions 3.5

i)   What are the advantages of good workplace communication?

ii) What are the common means of communication at work?

iii) What are the common causes of distortion or breakdown in communication?

iv) Why should communication always be a two-way process?

v)   Do actions speak louder than words?

Task

Select three examples of workplace communications from your answer to quick answer question (ii) above and identify the ways in which non-verbal communication can be used to reinforce the message.

| HELP | ? | See the information bank in ***Section 2: Communications***, page 81; ***Non-verbal communications***, page 137. |

Scenario: A message from the management

John Moss is the chairman of Moss & Son Ltd. It is a family business and John took over as chairman on the death of his father ten years ago. He likes to be called Mr John by his staff.

Every month the company newsletter, *From the Chairman's Desk*, is sent to all employees. John believes that this is an ideal means of communicating to staff. However, when there is a major crisis he summons all the managers and supervisors to a meeting in the oak-panelled board room. This is to show them that they are part of the management team and participate in making the important decisions. John always arrives last at these meetings and those present are expected to rise and remain standing until he has indicated that they may be seated.

Business has been difficult lately and John knows that in order to retain the company's market share he must lower their selling prices. He decides to call a meeting. When everyone is finally seated, he opens the meeting: 'I have called you together to explain the gravity of the situation we are in. We will have to cut our prices and, as a consequence, cut our costs. If we are to survive, we must all pitch in and pull together.' After he has finished speaking, he glares at everyone round the table. No one speaks. They all know that they are expected to remain silent.

'Firstly, we must have some positive thinking to implement a cost reduction programme, so I have gone outside the company and hired a top manager. Secondly, we have to improve our quality. Quality is everything in this business. From now on every machine will be inspected regularly by the supervisor; nothing is too small to overlook when we are considering quality. Thirdly, we need more team work. Unless we work together we won't survive. Leadership is what team work is all about and striving for the same goals. You are the leaders and you know what our goals are, so let's all put our shoulders to the wheel. And remember, we are all one big happy family in this firm!'

With this, John stood up and left the room. The meeting was over.

Problem-solving activities

i) *What was the purpose of the meeting?*

ii) *What was communicated at the meeting?*

iii) *How could Mr John improve his workplace communications?*

| HELP | ? | See the information bank in *Section 2:* *Communications*, page 81; *Leadership*, page 119. |

Comments on quick answer questions 3.5

i) Good workplace communication helps:

- ☐ to increase motivation;
- ☐ to improve productivity;
- ☐ to create trust between management, trade unions and employees;
- ☐ to reduce misunderstandings;
- ☐ to increase job satisfaction.

ii) Common means of communication at work are letters, memos, reports, newsletters, bulletins, telephone conversations, meetings and presentations.

iii) Common causes of distortion or breakdown in communication are:

- ☐ differences in perception
- ☐ language problems
- ☐ unclear purpose
- ☐ inappropriate medium
- ☐ inappropriate recipient
- ☐ problems of differences in status
- ☐ bureaucracy
- ☐ geographical distance
- ☐ distraction of the receiver
- ☐ hostility between the transmitter and receiver
- ☐ frustration or stress

iv) Communication is not just about passing a message, but making sure that it is understood. It should always be a two-way process to allow feedback.

v) Actions are important, especially where the issue involves some form of leadership.

 You should now be able to attempt the activities in Unit 3 of Section 3, page 222.

Unit 4: Individuals at work

4.1 Objectives

At the end of this unit you should be able to:

☐ explain what is meant by the term 'personality';

☐ give examples of motivating and demotivating factors in the workplace;

☐ explain what is meant by a person's 'attitude';

☐ give common reasons for resistance to change in organisations;

☐ describe the relationship between job design and job satisfaction.

4.2 Personality and motivation

The term *personality* is a term that refers to the whole person. It takes into account all the qualities that are revealed by an individual's general behaviour and attitude to life. Personality is not necessarily stable since some aspects are innate and others acquired. Consequently, personality may develop and change during a person's life. The interpersonal skills, leadership qualities and communication skills discussed in Unit 3 are all aspects of *personality development*.

Informal *personality* assessment takes place continually in both business and social situations as people interact and attempt to judge one another's personalities. More formal assessments may be made during the recruitment process in the form of personality tests.

Motivation is concerned with the goals a person seeks to achieve and the decision-making process that leads him or her to pursue particular goals. One way to define motivation might be to say that it is what causes people to act in a certain way. From a manager's point of view, the problem is motivating people to meet the organisation's objectives.

It is important to distinguish between motivation and movement. Motivation means more than just doing a job well; it also includes the spirit in which the job is done. Do the people you are supervising do as they are told (movement) or do they seek problems and solutions on their own (motivation)?

Q Quick answer questions 4.2

i) Is it true that people who do not work hard are not motivated?

ii) If people are doing as they are told, does it follow that they are motivated?

iii) How would you motivate machine operators to make up for lost production after a machine breakdown?

iv) Rank the following motivating factors in order of importance to you:

(1 = most important, 4 = least important)

pay

working conditions

job prospects

interesting work

v) What factors do you think might demotivate people at work?

Task

Carry out a survey among your friends and family to try and establish whether men and women are motivated by different factors.

HELP **?** See the information bank in *Section 2: Motivation*, page 135.

Scenario: Smudger Smith

Smudger Smith has been the assembly room supervisor for nearly twenty years. Recently many of the older members of his work team have left or retired and they have been replaced, mostly by married women. Smudger's team still meet its targets, but he senses a lack of interest and commitment to work, unlike in the days of the old team. During the tea-break one day he discusses this with a fellow supervisor, Steve Harley.

SMUDGER   These women don't seem to care about their work; they've got no pride.

STEVE   Yes, I know what you mean, but have you tried to find out why?

SMUDGER   You must be joking! The last time I gave them a chance to discuss things they kicked up merry hell about the holiday rota. All I said was that some people would need to take their holidays in February as only four people could be away on holiday at a time, and those who'd been with the firm the longest would get first choice. They never seem to do what I want without a struggle.

STEVE   Still, you really should try to find out what they want.

SMUDGER   I know what they want. What they want is pin money; that's what all women work for and that's why I have to keep on at them all the time. All they're interested in is money.

STEVE   Well, I've got women in my section too, as you know, and they're keen as mustard. They even do unpaid overtime just to see a job through!

SMUDGER   Well I'll be blowed! You must have all the exceptions. In my experience, which I can tell you is quite considerable, all anyone works for is money. If they don't see a result in their pay packet, they don't want to know.

STEVE   Not everyone is like that, Smudger.

Problem-solving activities

i)   *Comment on Smudger's attitude to his work team and how it might affect their motivation.*

ii) *Why do you think Smudger has a problem with the holiday rota?*

iii) *What might the reasons be for Steve's work team being more highly motivated than Smudger's?*

iv) *Comment on Smudger's views on money and motivation.*

v)   *How could Steve help Smudger?*

> HELP **?**   See the information bank in **Section 2: Leadership**, page 119; **Motivation**, page 135.

4.3 Attitude

Attitude is a learned predisposition to think, feel and act in a certain way towards a person or object. A person's attitude therefore reflects the different ways in which he or she responds to the environment. Motivating people to change their *behaviour* is relatively easy compared with changing their *attitudes*.

No two individuals are the same, but often age groups share broadly similar attitudes. Research shows that the attitude of the workforce to all aspects of work is changing. The most significant changes forecast by a survey of supervisors are:

❏ shifting values and high expectations for all employees;

❏ a clear desire to participate in workplace decisions;

❏ ongoing requirements to select and train work *teams* rather than *individuals*.

Quick answer questions 4.3

i)   *Can attitudes be inherited?*

ii) *Why do attitudes tend to vary from one generation to another?*

iii) *Apart from age groups, what other groups of people might share similar attitudes?*

Comments on quick answer questions 4.2

I) No, everyone is motivated to do something, but it need not be to do with work.

ii) No, motivation needs maintaining or it may diminish.

iii) Pay is often used in situations like this, but it does not always work.

iv) In spite of what you may think, pay is not always the first on the list.

v) Lack of communication and consultation are commonly quoted as demotivating factors.

Comments on quick answer questions 4.3

i) No, although families may share similar attitudes, attitude is a highly individual but learned facet of someone's personality.

ii) The reason why attitudes tend to vary from one generation to another may reflect the changing effect of the environment which shapes our attitudes.

iii) Other groups of people who might share similar attitudes include professional and other work groups, cultural groups, political groups, social groups and family groups.

Task

Carry out an attitude survey among your fellow students to find out what their attitudes are to their current course of study.

 HELP **?** See the information bank in *Section 2: Attitude*, page 73.

Scenario: The Amos project

David Amos is a project manager. He considers himself to be a manager who treats people fairly. He believes that everyone has potential in the skills, knowledge and ideas they possess and that this potential should be utilised. A number of employees are involved in the projects David manages, but not everyone. Those who are, work in a section supervised by a section leader. Once the project has been set up and is running smoothly, the section leader takes over full responsibility and it becomes part of the normal workload.

In David's department little is done in the way of long-term planning. As a result events are reacted to rather than managed. David has been reviewing this and has decided to make some changes. As a first step he has decided to gather the opinions of his team on every aspect of the project: the work, the staff involved and all the other resources. This will give him a firm foundation for making plans.

He made a tour of his department and spoke to everyone who is involved in his current project and asked them to write him a brief report setting out their ideas, needs, concerns, etc, within two weeks. The day before the deadline, he received the following memo from Robert Day, one of the section leaders.

MEMORANDUM

To: David Amos   Date: 14 October 19X2

From: Robert Day   Ref: RD/misc

<u>Project views</u>

I understand from various members of my staff that you have requested
their written views on certain matters by 15th October. Everyone is
intrigued at your sudden interest. I am sure you did not intend this,
but as you have approached a number of individuals in this section it
has aroused considerable speculation as to the use their views might
be put and the weight management might give to one person's views
against another's.

We are having a section meeting on Monday at 3pm and I have been asked
to invite you to attend so that you can outline your reasons. The
success of our current work can be attributed largely to our team
spirit and team effort; perhaps a few words from you will help to
restore some of the balance to the team.

Problem-solving activities

i)   *Judging from Robert's attitude, what do you think is the problem?*

ii) *If you were David, how would you have set about obtaining the
     information? What problems might you encounter in your chosen method?*

iii) *What do you think the attitude of those present at the meeting will be?*

iv) *Should David go to the meeting?*

v)   *If David goes to the meeting, what should he do and say?*

HELP ?

See the information bank in *Section 2: Attitude,*
page 73; *Change management,* page 79;
Communications, page 81.

4.4 Change and stress management

There are many factors which cause an organisation to change. Whatever the cause,
change often affects the whole organisation. Employees' attitudes to change vary
according to how change is perceived. In order to minimise problems and maximise the
benefits, change requires careful management to reduce stress.

Four common reasons for change are:

- social and legal causes, such as new management techniques or new legislation;

- technological causes, such as new computer technology;

- economic causes, such as changed interest or inflation rates, or unemployment;

- policy changes, such as the introduction of a total quality management programme
  which it is hoped will change the organisational culture.

Quick answer questions 4.4

i)   *How are changes likely to affect people at work?*

ii)   *What might cause people to resist change?*

iii)   *Are some people more likely to resist change than others?*

iv)   *What is stress?*

v)   *Is stress an important factor in work performance?*

Task

List some common causes of stress for you and the physical, emotional and behavioural symptoms that usually result.

| HELP | ? | See the information bank in *Section 2: Stress management*, page 184 |

Scenario: Space Systems Ltd

Jenny Johnson is a newly qualified work study engineer. She joined Space Systems Ltd because the company had an equal opportunities policy and was expanding rapidly. Jenny is ambitious and expects to have enough experience to apply for a better job after a year or two.

Her supervisor has allocated the task of developing and improving the layout and procedures of the goods inwards department to her. It has been known for some time that action would have to be taken and relocating the department is part of the company's long-term plans.

The line management of Space Systems Ltd is as follows:

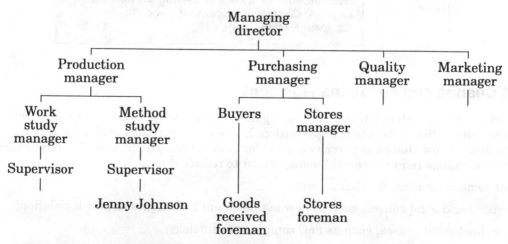

Jenny's first step was to contact the purchasing manager to get data on past and future orders to shippers and she discussed the impact the future estimates of purchases would have on his department. Armed with this information, she then consulted Dave Smith, the goods received foreman. She told him about the planned changes and developments of the department and asked for his co-operation in developing the new facility's layout and procedural system. The new system would provide him with a more efficient system to cope with the increased volume of work, she explained.

Dave is about 15 years older than Jenny and has worked for the company for about 12 years. He responded to her request with great interest, especially when he heard about the chance of obtaining additional space for his overcrowded operation. However, he was not pleased at the prospect of Jenny changing the system in his area after the move. He made it clear that his department was his responsibility and that he had recently made some procedural changes himself. Furthermore, he said, he had plans for other changes and did not feel he needed the assistance of a work study engineer who had hardly any knowledge of his operation. Somewhat reluctantly, Dave agreed to review procedures and work flows with Jenny so that she could gain enough understanding to develop a new facilities layout. After reviewing the current goods received operations and obtaining the foreman's requirements, Jenny said that she would contact him again when she had developed a plan for the proposed new facility and systems.

Over the next two weeks Jenny applied herself to the problem and developed a plan after careful analysis of all the information. She returned to Dave and presented her plan.

DAVE   That's is all very clever, but it won't work.

JENNY   Well, Dave, if you think it won't work, what do you suggest I do to make it work?

DAVE   Look, I don't need the help of any work study engineer. I know the best way to run this operation; I ought to because I've been doing it long enough!

JENNY   Dave, I'm just doing my job. I'm trying hard to work with you. I'm not against you, I hope you realise that.

DAVE   Just give me some more space, then I'll do the rest.

JENNY   Obviously I haven't met all your requirements. Do you think you could develop a better system?

DAVE   Certainly I could. And I could do it in two days, not two weeks!

Jenny left, puzzled by the foreman's hostile reaction, but determined to review her plan once more to see what she might have overlooked. Two days later they met again and Dave gave her his plan. Jenny examined it and began to ask questions.

DAVE   I'm not giving away all the information it has taken me years to collect!

JENNY   Look, Dave, I simply need to know why you have developed the system in your plan the way you have. If you don't explain it to me, how can I sell your plan to management?

DAVE   Sell my plan? I don't need anybody to sell my plan for me!

Problem-solving activities

i) *What should management do about Dave obstructing Jenny's work?*

ii) *Comment on Jenny's handling of the situation.*

iii) *How do you account for Dave's reactions?*

iv) *How would you have handled this situation?*

v) *What should happen now?*

HELP	?	See the information bank in **Section 2: Attitude**, page 73; **Change management**, page 79; **Motivation**, page 135; **Stress management**, page 184.

Comments on quick answer questions 4.4

i) Changes affect what people do at work, the way they do it and where they do it.

ii) Resistance to change may be caused by:

- ☐ self-interest;
- ☐ low tolerance of change;
- ☐ poor communications and/or lack of trust;
- ☐ contradictory assessments of benefits and disadvantages.

iii) Those with a low tolerance to change may include groups such as older workers and the unskilled.

iv) Stress is distress caused by pressure or tension. It may be caused by mechanical, physical or mental means.

v) Yes, stress is an important factor in work performance; research shows that up to 40% of absences are stress related.

4.5 Job design

Organisational change often results in changes in job design. The purpose of job design is to develop tasks which motivate and provide job satisfaction. Many people appear to be underutilised in their work and do not have enough opportunities to display talents which may remain hidden.

There seems to be a strong link between the type of job done, the level of job satisfaction and the level of motivation. However, it should be noted that there is not always a link between strong motivation and productivity. It is possible to be motivated to attain standards of workmanship far higher than those needed, resulting in lower levels of output than could be achieved at the *correct* standard of workmanship.

Organisational restructuring may necessitate job redesign and work restructuring. This is usually an opportunity to alter the work to make it more interesting and may result in *job rotation, job enlargement* or *job enrichment*.

Quick answer questions 4.5

i) *Do some people like doing boring jobs?*

ii) *If many people can do a lot more than is required, what stops them from doing it?*

iii) *Do you think many jobs are designed to meet people's needs and aspirations?*

iv) *What job would you find interesting and why?*

v) *What makes a job boring?*

Task

Write a brief description of your job or a job you have done in the past and highlight the elements which give you job satisfaction.

See the information bank in *Section 2: Job design*, page 115; *Motivation*, page 135.

Scenario: Stanley Engineering Ltd

At Stanley Engineering Ltd there are a number of machine operators who work on computer-controlled machines making engineering components. The work is very routine. Although the company pays an attendance bonus to encourage the operators to work a 39-hour week, many actually work fewer hours.

It is the operator's job to feed the instructions into the machine by punching keys on a key pad, load the metal bar and clean and oil the machine. When a new component has to be made, or if there is a machine fault, a tool setter is called. The finished components are checked by a quality control inspector who reports any faults to the operator's supervisor. The supervisor reports faults to the tool setter.

Problem-solving activities

i) *How might the operator's job be changed for the better?*

ii) *Consider your answer to (i) above. Would you change your suggestions if there were trade unions involved?*

iii) *What effects would you expect your changes to have and why?*

See the information bank in *Section 2: Job design*, page 115; *Motivation*, page 135.

Comments on quick answer questions 4.5

i) It is possible that some people like doing boring jobs, but it is more likely that they only enjoy certain aspects of the job. These might include convenience, such as an easy journey to work, flexible hours and working with friendly people.

ii) One reason why people who are quite capable are not able to do more is that the style of management may not allow it.

iii) It is fairly unusual for jobs to be designed to meet people's needs and aspiration, especially lower down the organisation.

iv) The type of job you find interesting is very much a personal choice, but often variety and control of one's own situation are key issues.

v) Among other aspects, lack of challenge and repetitive work make a job boring.

You should now be able to attempt the activities in Unit 4 of Section 3, page 232.

Unit 5: Employee relations

5.1 Objectives

At the end of this unit you should be able to:

- ❏ describe the functions of personnel management;
- ❏ list the principal employment legislation and the main duties of employers and employees;
- ❏ differentiate between a contract of service and a contract for service;
- ❏ describe the main requirements of the Health and Safety at Work Act 1974;

5.2 Personnel management

Personnel management is concerned with the management of people at work, for the benefit of both the employer and the individual employee. Although all managers are concerned to some extent with personnel management, many large organisations appoint specialist personnel managers to centralise recruitment and selection (see Unit 6), development and retention (see Unit 7), and hold responsibility for industrial relations, health and safety and other legal aspects of employment.

Changing technology and the need for increased labour efficiency and flexibility to meet the needs of growing international competition has resulted in the need to encourage growth without an expansion in personnel. Current trends in personnel management place emphasis on *staff morale* and ways of achieving consistent *job satisfaction* through variation, especially by *training* employees to do more than one job.

Quick answer questions 5.2

i)   What other specific functions might a centralised personnel department be responsible for?

ii)   What does labour flexibility mean?

iii) What examples of labour flexibility can you think of?

iv)   How might a small organisation without a specialist personnel department overcome any lack of knowledge if problems arise?

v)   What methods might a personnel manager adopt to encourage growth without increasing the size of the labour force?

41

Comments on quick answer questions 5.2

i) Other functions you may have thought of include carrying out a personnel audit, holding personnel records, manpower planning, forecasting demand and supply of labour, carrying out job analyses (drawing up person specifications and job descriptions), holding interviews, carrying out job evaluations so that jobs can be graded, establishing pay structures, designing performance appraisal forms, carrying out training, negotiating with trade unions.

ii) Labour flexibility refers to flexible work patterns.

iii) Examples include shift work, part-time work, flexi-hours, annual hours, job sharing.

iv) The organisation might consider using a consultant's services on a short-term basis or may be able to obtain advice from its legal advisers or the Institute of Personnel Managers. In addition, the business can obtain leaflets on certain issues from the Department of Employment or the Arbitration, Conciliation and Advisory Service.

v) Methods might include training and evaluation programmes, redesigning jobs for increased job satisfaction, reviewing motivating factors such as pay, productivity agreements, bonuses, company share schemes and other financial benefits, social activities, the working environment.

Task

Find out the personnel policies adopted by your organisation or the college where you are studying.

 | See the information bank in *Section 2: Personnel management*, page 154.

Scenario: Focus on the client

Paul Maidment is in charge of the personnel department at the White Star Insurance Company. They have been the shining star in the insurance industry. Starting from a small partnership fifteen years ago, a succession of take-overs and absorptions have turned the company into a major employer in the area with over 600 staff. John Star the owner and driving force has now retired and been replaced by his son Philip.

At a meeting of department managers, Philip explained that he intended an organisational review and that the watch words for this review would be 'focus on the client'. He expected every department to be affected and unless they could show they 'focussed on the client' they would not be favourably viewed.

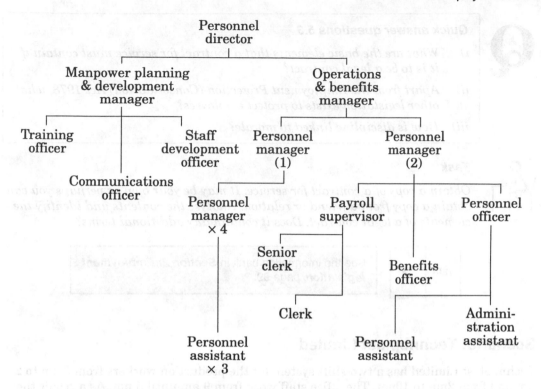

Personnel director

Manpower planning & development manager

Operations & benefits manager

Training officer

Staff development officer

Personnel manager (1)

Personnel manager (2)

Communications officer

Personnel manager × 4

Payroll supervisor

Personnel officer

Senior clerk

Benefits officer

Clerk

Admini- stration assistant

Personnel assistant × 3

Personnel assistant

Problem-solving activities

   i)   *The first step in the review is for each manager to summarise and justify his department. What should Paul Maidment say? (This report should be no longer than a single sheet of A4 paper).*

   ii)   *How might the company operate if there were no personnel department?*

> **HELP ?**
>
> See the information bank in ***Section 2: Personnel management***, page 154.

5.3 Employment legislation

There are two parties in employee relations: the employer and the employee. The details of the relationship are contained in the *contract of service (contract of employment)*. A *contract for service* is where the contractor is self-employed.

Many aspects of the duties of the parties in a contract for service are protected by law. The *Employment Protection (Consolidation) Act 1978* contains most of the employee's statutory rights in such areas as dismissal, redundancy, union membership and protection against the employer's insolvency.

In addition to the purely legal and procedural systems supervisors and managers must follow, there is the relationship between the manager and the managed. It is this relationship that very often sets the tone for employee relations in general in an organisation.

Quick answer questions 5.3

i) What are the basic elements that a contract for service must contain if it is to be a legal contract?

ii) Apart from the Employment Protection (Consolidation) Act 1978, what other legislation exists to protect employees?

iii) How is discipline linked to morale?

Task

Obtain a copy of a contract for service. It may be your own or perhaps you can obtain a copy from a friend or relation. Analyse the contents and identify the elements of a legal contract. Does it contain any additional terms?

See the information bank in **Section 2: Employment legislation**, page 99.

Scenario: Technoplast Limited

Technoplast Limited has a two-shift system for the production workers from 6 am to 2 pm and from 2pm to 10pm. The office staff work from 9 am until 5 pm. As a result there are occasions when there is no senior manager available and responsibility falls on the supervisors.

Because shift work involves working unsocial hours, requests for time off are common. The company rule book clearly states that no-one may leave the factory during working hours unless he or she has the express permission of his or her senior supervisor. Contravention of the rule is specified in the disciplinary procedure as one which leads to disciplinary action, but is not an offence leading to summary dismissal.

John Houlden has worked for Technoplast Limited for four years. He works alternate early and late shifts. John is well regarded and likely to be promoted to supervisor soon. However, recently he and the senior foreman have had a disagreement about policy at the local football club to which they both belong and at the moment their relationship is somewhat cool.

Last night John approached his chargehand, Dave Millward, with a request for permission to leave work for two hours. He is a member of the company social club darts team and they had a crucial match. Knowing that the company disliked giving time off and that the rules said permission of the senior foreman was needed, Dave said he didn't have the authority but he would ask the senior foreman and let John know.

They both went about their business and Dave completely forgot about the request until John came to him and said, 'Look I'll have to go now or I'll be late, but I should be back in a couple of hours'. Dave, who still hadn't seen the senior foreman, said 'OK, off you go, but be discreet'.

Later in the shift the senior foreman was on his rounds and Dave remembered he still hadn't cleared John's absence with him. Thinking the situation could cause them both trouble, he decided to nip over to the social club and get John to come back immediately. But before he got back with John, the senior foreman began asking where they both were.

Problem-solving activities

i) *If you were the senior foreman, what would you do? What matters would you take into consideration? Describe how you would conduct the interview / s held.*

ii) *If you were Dave Millward, what would you say in your defence?*

iii) *What disciplinary action do you think should be taken in this situation?*

HELP	?	See the information bank in **Section 2: Discipline**, page 94, **Employment legislation**, page 99;

5.4 Health and safety legislation

The Health and Safety at Work Act 1974 was a result of the Robens Report and attempts to set out a series of principles rather than specify rules. The four basic principles of the Act are:

❑ to maintain and improve standard of health and safety of people at work;

❑ to protect persons other than persons at work;

❑ to control the keeping of dangerous substances;

❑ to control the emissions of noxious substances.

One of the more important concepts of the Act concerns who is responsible for safety matters.

Quick answer questions 5.4

i) *Does the Health and Safety at Work Act mean that there is someone responsible for safety in every organisation?*

ii) *How can an employee find out what the standards of health and safety are in his or her own organisation?*

iii) *How can people become more safety conscious?*

Task

Find out the following information for your own organisation or place or study:

i) *Who is your Health and Safety representative?*

ii) *Where is your assembly point in case of fire?*

iii) *List any potential hazards in your job.*

HELP	?	See the information bank in **Section 2: Health and safety legislation**, page 109.

Comments on quick answer questions 5.3

i) The basic elements of a contract for service must contain:

☐ a specific offer of a job (advertising a job does not comprise an offer);

☐ acceptance;

☐ form and consideration (the pay);

☐ legality (the job must not require breaking the law);

☐ capacity (for example, one of the parties is not a minor);

☐ legal intent;

☐ genuine agreement.

ii) You may have also recalled the following legislation:

☐ Race Relations Act 1976;

☐ Equal Pay Act 1970;

☐ Disabled Persons (Employment) Acts 1944 and 1958

iii) The higher the morale, the less likely it is that there will be a need for disciplinary action.

Comments on quick answer questions 5.4

i) Everyone now has some responsibility for safety.

ii) An employer must maintain high standards of health and safety for employees and prepare a written statement of general policy on health and safety.

iii) The attitude of management sets the tone for health and safety matters.

Scenario: Accidents will happen

Part of the process at Marsden Limited involves soaking the sheets in large pits of solvent before they are fixed to the frames. The sheets are lifted in and out of the pits by men using long poles with hooks on. Although it is not a skilled job, it requires strength, so when Jethro (who is 6'6" and weighs 16 stone) presented himself at the gate he was ideal for the job.

Marsden Limited is a small company and employs eight process workers, three clerks and two salesmen. It is run by George Marsden, a somewhat autocratic proprietor. Much of George's business is 'No cheques, no VAT, know what I mean?'

Within 15 minutes of asking for a job at the factory gate, Jethro was working on the pits with a hook. A week later he was regarded as an experienced hand. Jethro was quite happy with his work, but did complain to the supervisor that the fumes gave him a headache. He was assured that this was because he was new and he'd get used to it. One day he fell into a pit, but his workmates hosed him down and he went home to change his clothes. George docked him two hours pay and warned him that the clothes he had been wearing would probably disintegrate.

However, that wasn't the end of it. A few days later a representative from the health and safety executive arrived. George told him quite clearly, 'OK, so Jethro's skin has gone a bit funny, but accidents will happen and no amount of paperwork will stop them.

It's up to the men to look after themselves; they always have. Anyway, we're too small a company to be affected by any regulation. They're really intended for the big firms.' Equally clear was the reply of the health and safety officer, 'You're closed until I'm satisfied that you can properly implement the Health & Safety laws'.

It seemed to George that he ought to do something. As safety was a matter for supervisors to deal with, he decided to delegate responsibility to his supervisor. 'We'll do whatever it takes,' he told him.

Problem-solving activities

You are the supervisor. Write a report to the Health and Safety Executive explaining how Marsden Limited will comply with the Act.

> HELP **?** See the information bank in *Section 2: Health and safety legislation*, page 109.

5.5 Trade union legislation

The legislation concerning trade unions is wide ranging and complex, but the following Acts certainly have had an impact on unions and their members.

- ☐ The Employment Act 1980.
- ☐ The Employment Act 1982
- ☐ The Trade Union Act 1984
- ☐ The Employment Act 1989
- ☐ The Employment Act 1990

These Acts deal with matters such as:- secret ballots, unfair dismissal, contracts of employment, closed shops.

Quick answer questions 5.5

i) *Do you know your organisation's disciplinary procedures?*

ii) *Can you think of a good reason for having a grievance procedure?*

iii) *What is ACAS?*

Task

Find out the following information about your organisation:-

i) *Are there any unions operating in the organisation, and if so, who are the officials?*

ii) *Has there been any industrial action in the past 5 years and if so, how was it settled?*

> HELP **?** See the information bank in *Section 2: Trade unions and the law*, page 192.

Comments on quick answer questions 5.5

i)   Employers are required by law to provide employees with written details of contract of employment, and they should include disciplinary procedures.

ii)   Employees have a guaranteed mechanism for handling victimisation and complaints.

iii) Arbitration, Conciliation and Advisory Service, which is run by the Department of Employment.

Scenario: Closed shop

Les Dowdy has always been very careful about the people he has hired in his firm. Les doesn't want any unions in his business and takes whatever steps he thinks are necessary to keep them out. Until recently he has been successful but now a newly employed driver (Dave) has brought with him ideas of introducing a union.

Not only is he introducing a union, but he's talking about making the firm a closed shop. At a lunch-time meeting, 128 of the 160-strong work-force voted on a show of hands to go along with the idea of a closed shop. Les Dowdy is determined to stop this, he has told Dave so. Dave's reply was 'I know my rights and unless you want a strike on your hands you'll co-operate'.

Problem-solving activities

i)   *What should Les do?*

ii)   *What are Dave's rights?*

 ? | See the information bank in *Section 2: Trade unions and the law*, page 192.

 You should now be able to attempt the activities in Unit 5 of Section 3, page 237.

Unit 6: Recruitment and selection

6.1 Objectives

At the end of this unit you should be able to:

☐ describe the main aims of manpower planning;

☐ explain the purpose of job analysis;

☐ differentiate between a job description and a person specification;

☐ list the procedures involved in recruitment and advertising, selection and induction;

☐ compare various recruitment and selection techniques.

6.2 Manpower planning

The task of managing the recruitment and selection of staff falls under the function of *personnel management* (see Unit 5.2). This may be a department headed by a personnel director or a personnel manager. In a small organisation the personnel function may be carried out by the line managers themselves or the proprietor.

Manpower, like any other expensive resource, must be carefully *planned* and *quantified*. The cost of labour is usually one of the most significant items an organisation has to pay for. It is therefore essential that it gives good value for money. Manpower planning is also concerned with the *quality* of labour. Once an employee has been recruited, he or she may be a committed member of the workforce for many years.

The manpower requirements of the organisation are estimated so that recruitment, training, promotion, transfer and retirement can be accommodated. The resulting plan usually covers a period of five years and aims to balance the *demand* for labour with the *supply* of labour.

Quick answer questions 6.2

i) *What is the purpose of manpower planning?*

ii) *What techniques might be used to forecast the future demand for labour?*

iii) *What factors should be considered when forecasting the future supply of labour?*

iv) *What balancing measures can a manager use when demand exceeds supply?*

v) *What balancing measures can a manager use when supply exceeds demand?*

Comments on quick answer questions 6.2

i) The purpose of manpower planning is to ensure that the right number of people with the right skills are in the right place at the right time.

ii) Demand forecasting techniques include statistical methods, work study and the manager's own experience and knowledge.

iii) Factors to be considered when forecasting the future supply of labour include demographic trends, skills shortages, national employment levels, local employment levels, local housing and transport developments.

iv) When demand exceeds supply, measures include increasing recruitment, improving pay, increasing training or retraining, transferring staff, amending business plans.

v) When supply exceeds demand, measures include making redundancies, offering early retirement, making use of natural wastage, transferring staff, introducing part-time working.

Task

Design a form that would help managers to analyse existing manpower in their departments.

| HELP | ? | See the information bank in **Section 2: Manpower analysis and planning**, page 133. |

Scenario: What does it mean?

Bob Carne is the Project Manager of the UB1 project, one of several large military contracts won by BPC. The Personnel Director who is based in the main factory 5 miles away has sent him the following memo:

MEMO

To: Bob Carne   From: Jim Steele

Manpower Plan

Below is the manpower plan for the UB1 Project. I'm sure you'll find it useful for managing the project.

UB1 Manpower Plan

	Present	Employees Projected Years				
		1	2	3	4	5
Final Assembly	52	120	220	220	280	160
Sub Assembly	110	180	180	170	50	70
Detail	100	150	130	50	40	25
Total	262	450	330	440	370	255
Wastage		–50	–60	–90	–120	–150
Surplus from other projects		+10	+15	+30	+10	–

Problem-solving activities

i) *What are the main conclusions that Bob could draw from this manpower plan?*

ii) *How do you think the manpower plan was compiled and how accurate do you think it would be?*

iii) *What actions might Bob take as a result of the information he has received?*

HELP ?

See the information bank in *Section 2: Manpower analysis and planning*, page 133.

6.3 Job analysis

Job analysis is the detailed study of information about a job. Such information would include any tools or equipment needed and its relation to other jobs in the organisation. The analysis can be used to draw up a *job description* and a *person specification*. In addition, it should provide guidance on the best way to do the job.

Quick answer questions 6.3

i) *What sources of information might be useful in job analysis?*

ii) *What details should be included in a job description?*

iii) *What details should be included in a person specification?*

Task

Draw up a job description and person specification for your job or a job you have held.

HELP ?

See the information bank in *Section 2: Job analysis*, page 113.

> **Comments on quick answer questions 6.3**
>
> i) Sources of information for job analysis include primary data such as interviews, questionnaire surveys, observations or work diaries, or secondary data such as performance appraisals, existing job descriptions or training manuals.
>
> ii) A typical job description might include the name of the organisation and the department, the job title, grade, reporting arrangements, overall purpose of the job, the key activities and tasks, special requirements and working conditions.
>
> iii) A typical person specification might include education, qualifications and experience, intelligence and/or aptitudes, age, status, mobility, personality and/or physical requirements, etc.

Scenario: What do your people do?

SMIGS CRISPS

MEMO

To: Packing and Transport Manager   From: Personnel Manager

Job Analysis

As you know, I am in the process of gathering job descriptions for every job in our organisation. I would like to turn my attention to your department next. Could you:

a) Confirm that your department currently employs:
   22 Packers
   4 Supervisors
   5 Drivers
   1 Manager.

b) Suggest which method of job analysis would be the most appropriate to enable us to gather the information we need for our job descriptions.

Problem-solving activities

i) *Suggest a reply to the Personnel Manager's memo.*

 See the information bank in *Section 2: Job analysis*, page 113.

6.4 Recruitment and advertising

Recruitment procedures differ from one organisation to another. They may be the responsibility of the personnel department or they may be left to the line managers. The main method of recruitment is *advertising*. Many people have personal experience of the recruitment process through their own employment.

Recruitment procedures are designed to *discriminate* between one candidate and another. However, it is unlawful to discriminate on the grounds of disability, sex or race, although there are certain exceptions which allow for the selection of candidates of one of the sexes only. In addition, employers are required to treat men and women equally in terms of pay and conditions. However, there is no direct legislation to protect job applicants from age discrimination.

Quick answer questions 6.4

i) What is the usual procedure for filling a job vacancy?

ii) For what reasons might a manager not want to fill a vacant position?

iii) What are the main methods of advertising vacancies?

iv) What information should be included in a job advertisement?

v) What information should be sent to the applicants?

Task

Design an advertisement for the job you described in Task 6.3.

> HELP **?** See the information bank in *Section 2: Discrimination and equality*, page 98; *Recruitment selection and induction*, page 167.

Scenario: The handyman

Larry McLaughlin is the managing director of Techno Ltd. The company has a large office and warehouse complex near the village of Amble, about 15 miles from the centre of the town of Winchester. Techno Ltd imports, packs and distributes electronic goods which are manufactured by a subsidiary in South Korea. Andy Burton is the site manager.

ANDY   The electrician is threatening to walk out again unless we get him some help. You know, he's got a point; there's too much work for one person alone.

LARRY   Well, we'll have to get someone then. We could do with a general handyman to help some of the other skilled men on various jobs. Aren't the stores always complaining that they're short-handed?

ANDY   Yes, but the electrician needs someone who can use hand tools and help install power and lighting systems.

LARRY   Presumably he'd want to supervise whoever it was?

ANDY   Oh yes, he'd want to supervise the electrical work, but who would be responsible for organising his other jobs?

LARRY   We'll let the electrician and your foreman sort it out between them.

ANDY   So it's okay to go ahead then and get someone?

LARRY   Yes. Send me the details and I'll advertise right away.

Problem-solving activities

Andy is more of a practical man than a man of letters and asks you to help him prepare the details his managing director has asked for.

i) *Advise him on how to set about writing a job description for this vacancy.*

ii) *Andy has not heard the term person specification before. Explain what it means and help him by drawing up a person specification for the job.*

iii) *Where would you suggest this particular job should be advertised?*

iv) *Design an application form for the vacancy.*

v) *If the company has difficulty in attracting applicants for the post because of its rural location, what measures could Andy suggest which might help the situation?*

HELP	?	See the information bank in **Section 2: Job analysis**, page 113; **Manpower analysis and planning**, page 133; **Recruitment selection and Induction**, page 167.

Comments on quick answer questions 6.4

i) The usual recruitment procedure involves seeking suitable recruits, both internally and externally, interviewing applicants, short-listing and finally selecting candidates.

ii) The reasons why a manager might not want to fill a vacant position are usually connected to measures taken to balance the supply and demand for labour.

iii) The main methods of advertising vacancies externally include the national and local press, journals, job centres, employment agencies, personnel consultants, professional institutes, educational institutions and notices posted up near places of work. Internal methods include staff newspapers, bulletins, notice boards.

iv) Normally the information contained in a job advertisement includes the name of the organisation, the job title, the main duties and details of remuneration.

v) Typical information sent to applicants might consist of an application form, a job description, details about the company and the location of the post.

6.5 Selection and induction

Whatever method of recruitment is adopted, the aim is to have a number of suitable applicants. Initial *selection* is made by inviting letters of application (or by asking applicants to fill in an application form), supported by a *curriculum vitae*. Applicants who most closely match the person specification are then listed. Screening interviews may then be held, sometimes including practical tests, so that a shortlist of final candidates can be drawn up. Second interviews are sometimes required and when appropriate psychological tests are used. The extent to which the personnel department is involved in the selection process varies from one organisation to another.

Some regard *induction* as part of the selection process since those failing to match up to requirements after induction and any period of probation may then be dismissed.

Quick answer questions 6.5

i)   What is the advantage of asking applicants to complete an application form rather than simply invite letters of application?

ii) What method would you use to decide on who to shortlist?

iii) Who should interview the applicants?

iv) What questions would you expect to be asked at an interview and for what purpose?

v)   Which is the more important: technical competence or the ability to get on with others?

Task

You are a departmental manager in an organisation of your choice. Prepare an induction programme for a school-leaver joining your department. Provide details of when and where the induction will take place, how long it will last and who would be involved in the programme.

HELP **?**   See the information bank in *Section 2: Recruitment selection and induction*, page 167.

Scenario: John Goodlad & Sons Ltd

The production lines at John Goodlad & Sons Ltd are fairly labour-intensive. There are 80 people to a line and six lines which assemble electronic components for the motor industry. The work is boring but the pay is good and so are the hours. The company encourages its employees to undertake training for self-development.

John Bonito is the general manager and he recruits the production line workers. Each applicant gets a ten-minute interview as John believes he can judge a candidate in that time. He blames the high labour turnover at Goodlads (60 per cent leave within two months) on education. He says that nowadays schools fill the kids' heads with ideas above their station.

This week John was going to interview another batch of applicants, but he has been called away to a three-day conference. You are the senior supervisor and he has left you with a list of names, addresses and telephone numbers and has told you to carry out the interviews and select three by the time he gets back.

Problem-solving activities

i) *Comment on the possible relationship between John Bonito's approach to recruitment and selection and the high rate of labour turnover.*

ii) *Write a person specification for the job.*

iii) *How will you set about selecting the three candidates? Give details of the procedures you will follow assuming that the applicants are available to attend an interview at such short notice.*

iv) *Compare your approach with John's.*

v) *Draw up a simple set of guidelines for successful recruitment and selection for future use by the production department.*

 HELP **?** | See the information bank in **Section 2: Recruitment selection and induction**, page 167.:

Comments on quick answer questions 6.5

i) The use of application forms would result in uniform information from each applicant rather than only that information that each applicant chooses to supply. This allows for easier comparison.

ii) A shortlist can be drawn up by deciding on the criteria needed and examining the application forms for those criteria, thus producing a shortlist of candidates.

iii) Interviews may be conducted by a single person or by a panel; applicants may be seen singly or in groups. Interviewing may be carried out by the personnel department with or without input from the head of the organisation/department/section and/or the person who will be directly responsible for the new employee.

iv) An interview might be described as a conversation with a purpose. Questions should be open-ended to allow the candidate to expand on the information requested. Such information should be in-depth and factual, and allow comparisons between candidates to be made. The interview is also an opportunity for the candidate to ask questions.

v) Few people work in isolation. Therefore, the ability to get on with others can be as essential as possessing the necessary technical abilities.

 You should now be able to attempt the activities in Unit 6 of Section 3, page 241.

Unit 7: Development and retention

7.1 Objectives

At the end of this unit you should be able to:

- [ ] describe the main aims of job evaluation;
- [ ] understand the importance of establishing pay structures;
- [ ] explain the relationship between job evaluation and pay;
- [ ] describe the process of performance appraisal and its relationship to promotion;
- [ ] list the benefits of training.

7.2 Job evaluation

Having made decisions concerning the recruitment and selection of staff, a manager needs to consider how such employees can be developed and retained in the workforce. Both new and existing employees need to know the level of the job to which they have been appointed, since pay and conditions often relate to this.

Job evaluation is a systematic assessment of the value and nature of jobs. It ignores the title of the job and the job holder, and concentrates on the content of the job. A *job description* is an essential requirement. Job evaluation throughout an organisation may result in a general reclassification of jobs.

Quick answer questions

i) *What techniques might be used for classifying jobs?*

ii) *Why is a job description an essential requirement?*

iii) *What is the relationship between job evaluation and pay?*

Task

Draw up a list of the advantages and disadvantages of job evaluation.

  See the information bank in *Section 2: Job evaluation*, page 117.

Comments on quick answer questions 7.2

i)   Typical techniques for classifying jobs include ranking, job classification, points rating and factor comparison.

ii) An up-to-date job description is essential to job evaluation because it contains a full description of the job which can then be used for comparison with other jobs.

iii) Job evaluation results in jobs being placed within a grading system which can be related to the organisation's pay structure.

Scenario: Pay points

At a recent meeting of the Job Evaluation Committee, the following scheme was put forward as a means of evaluating all the company's jobs.

Points system of job evaluation

Job Factor	Low	Moderate	High
Education	30	60	90
Experience	25	50	75
Physical demands	10	20	30
Totals	65	130	195

All jobs will be evaluated in terms of points and the points counts will be decided by the Evaluation Committee. Examples are given above. Salaries will be linked to points counts.

Problem-solving activities

How might the above scheme be improved?

See the information bank in *Section 2: Job evaluation,* page 117.

7.3 Pay structures

Having placed jobs within a grading system, management must establish a *pay structure*. Although the remuneration is not the only motivating factor and source of *job satisfaction*, pay is necessarily of vital concern to the majority of employees and their families. As already discussed, the process of *job evaluation* provides a fair basis for a payment system.

Q

Quick answer questions 7.3

i) *What issues might be important when deciding on levels of pay?*

ii) *Pay is related to different types of working arrangements. What are the principal patterns of work?*

iii) *Apart from basic pay, what are the main additional means of rewarding effort?*

Task

The most important piece of legislation concerning pay and conditions is the Equal Pay Act 1970. *Find out what the main provisions are.*

HELP **?**

See the information bank in *Section 2: Employment legislation*, page 99.

Scenario: Johnsons Valves

As a result of a job evaluation exercise recently carried out by the personnel department the following information has been recorded.

	Job	Evaluation Points	Present salary	Local salary equivalents	(Competitors)
1	Junior Clerk	65	6,500	6,500	
2	Clerk Typist	75	7,000	7,000	
3	General Clerk	90	8,000	8,000	
4	Shorthand Typists	120	8,900	9,500	
5	Sales Clerk	170	9,500	10,000	
6	Secretary	180	9,500	9,500	
7	Accounts Clerk	180	10,000	9,500	
8	Personnel Assistant	220	11,000	10,000	
9	Assistant Buyer	260	13,000	12,000	
10	Accounts Supervisor	295	14,000	15,000	
11	Sales Rep	330	16,000	17,000	
12	Draughtsman	360	15,500	16,000	
13	Senior Foreman	365	15,000	16,000	
14	Chief Cashier	410	17,000	17,000	
15	Buyer	430	17,000	17,000	
16	Management Accountant	500	20,000	21,000	
17	Chief Buyer	510	19,000	18,000	
18	Personnel Manager	600	22,800	21,000	
19	Work Manager	650	23,000	24,000	
20	Chief Accountant	660	22,500	25,000	
21	Chief Designer	710	25,000	25,000	
22	Sales Manager	760	27,000	28,000	

Problem-solving activities

Design a salary structure for Johnsons Valves and explain its basis.

 See the information bank in *Section 2: Salaries and wages*, page 180; *job evaluation*, page 117.

Comments on quick answer questions 7.3

i)   Issues to consider when deciding levels of pay might include the organisation's budget or plan, local and national rates, legislation and the views of employees and any unions involved.

ii) The main variations in working arrangements are full-time regular hours, shift work, flexible hours, annual hours and part-time work.

iii) The main additional means of rewarding effort are commission, bonus payments, profit sharing, performance related pay and benefits in kind.

7.4 Appraisal and promotion

Performance appraisal is concerned with reviewing an employee's performance and progress at work and assessing his or her prospects for promotion. It can be usefully applied to a fairly new member of staff to establish how successful the match has been between the recruit and the job, or to longer serving employees.

Appraisal information about the individual is methodically obtained, analysed and recorded. Appraisal can be open or closed and is often accompanied by an *appraisal interview*. Managers carrying out appraisals should be trained in the technique. The information thus collected allows the appraiser to offer guidance, agree future work and advise on how to make the best use of the employee's skills and abilities to meet both personal and organisational objectives.

Promotion within an organisation, whether in competition with outside candidates or not, can take place vertically, horizontally or by zigzagging through a series of combined vertical and horizontal routes.

Quick answer questions 7.4

i)   Who should carry out performance appraisals?

ii)   How often should appraisals be carried out?

iii) Should pay be linked to performance appraisals?

iv)   What does the employee gain from an appraisal?

v)   What are the main issues when considering whether to promote an employee?

Task

Design an self-appraisal form for your present job or for a job you have done in the past.

See the information bank in **Section 2:** **Performance appraisal**, page 145.

Scenario: A quick appraisal

Sue left college after successfully completing an intensive word processing course. Now she has found a job with the County Council and works in the typing pool. This is Sue's first full-time job and she is determined to do well because she takes pride in her work. In addition, the County Council has recently announced cuts in the workforce and consequently not all the recently appointed employees will be retained. Naturally, Sue is worried that she may lose her job.

Sue has only had one or two accidental meetings with the departmental manager, Andrew Lewis. In practice she is supervised by Joan, one of the senior secretaries. Sue is well thought of by the people she works with. When she mentioned a more senior position she had seen advertised on the notice board two months ago, Joan said that she was more than willing to give her a reference. In fact, Joan told her that she would say that she found Sue to be cheerful, highly motivated and a very useful employee.

Sue's first performance appraisal is due today. In keeping with normal practice, she has been given a copy of the evaluation sheet which will be used and has been asked to rate herself prior to her interview. The sheet has ten categories on it. These include:

1. Compliance with work deadlines and schedules
2. Attention to detail and accuracy of work
3. Reliability
4. Relations with co-workers and superiors
5. Time-keeping and attitude to work

The appraisal scheme requires that if an employee is judged to be either 'very good' or 'very bad', it must be put in writing; if he or she is categorised as merely 'satisfactory' it need not.

At 4.45pm Sue is called into Andrew Lewis' office. He hands her an identical form to the one she was given earlier, which he has completed, and asks her to sign it.

SUE: Why have you marked me as satisfactory on every point?

ANDREW: That's right. I always mark people as satisfactory on their first appraisal. A new person hasn't got the experience or knowledge to be outstanding and it's unfair to give them a low rating after such a relatively short period of time.

SUE: Well, I can't sign it. How am I supposed to know how to do my job better?

ANDREW: Look, just keep on doing as you are. This is a good appraisal. Most people here would be delighted with one like this. And this way your next one can show an improvement.

SUE: But what about my time-keeping? I'm always early. And deadlines; I've never failed to meet one, even when it's meant staying late!

ANDREW: Look, I haven't got time to discuss all that now. It's nearly 5 o'clock and I shall miss my train. I'll try and find time to talk to you about it later in the week.

Problem-solving activities

i)   If you were Sue, what would you do now?

ii) How should Andrew have handled the appraisal?

iii) What can be done to avoid this kind of situation happening again?

HELP	?	See the information bank in **Section 2: Performance appraisal**, page 145.

Comments on quick answer questions 7.4

i)   Certainly the employee's immediate superior should be involved in the performance appraisal.

ii) In most organisations appraisals are usually carried out once a year.

iii) Linking pay to performance appraisal shows that effort and pay are related.

iv) If the appraisal has been effective, the employee should gain a realistic picture of how the organisation values him or her.

v)   Promotion should be based on ability. Some abilities are difficult to measure until it is too late; for example, leadership.

7.5 Training

Having made the best possible recruitment selection, management should capitalise on the knowledge, skills and attitudes of new staff and develop potential. *Training* should start with induction and continue systematically throughout the period of employment service. This should include, where relevant, apprenticeship, instruction in semi-skilled work, technical training, training in supervision techniques and management training.

First management must identify training needs at organisational, departmental and individual levels. The next stage is to design an effective training programme which can be evaluated to find out whether it has produced the anticipated changes in the employee's behaviour.

Quick answer questions 7.5

i) Do you agree with the following sayings?

	Agree	Disagree

'You can take a horse to water,
but you cannot make it drink.'

'Learn by your mistakes.'

'You cannot teach an old dog new tricks.'

ii) What are the usual methods by which people learn?

iii) Describe your most successful and most unsuccessful learning experiences. What do you think caused the differences?

Task

Draw up a list of words that describe your attitude to learning.

> **HELP** **?** See the information bank in *Section 2: Learning*, page 124.

Scenario: Last-minute training

JPR Williams Ltd has had to struggle during the last few years because of competition from manufacturers in the Far East. The company makes components for the high technology market. Recently things have begun to improve; business is good and some expansion is planned.

In the past the company always paid top rates in order to attract labour, but recently this policy has been less successful and a training budget was established for the first time last year. With at least 50 new operators likely to be employed in the forthcoming financial year and two or three new supervisors, it is likely that the training budget will soon be increased.

Steve Knight has been given responsibility for training. He still has to spend most of this year's training budget and there are only three weeks to go before the year end. Apart from a couple of Health and Safety courses he has arranged, no training has been carried out. However, Steve has sent out a training programme with a memo to all supervisors instructing them to select a couple of courses each which will be paid for from the training budget.

Following are the *Training Programmes Summary* and details of *each* of the courses:

Training programmes

	Course title	Start date
December		
Management	Employment law – an introduction	04
	Team building	06
	Human relations for supervisors	10
Training	Instructional methods for operator instructors	03
Communication	Team briefing	17
Employment	Dismissal	06
	Redundancy	13
Computers	Lotus Symphony workshop	06
Safety	First aid at work certificate	10
November		
Management	Action Centred Leadership	19

Management: *Employment law – an introduction*

Intended for	All newly appointed or experienced supervisors who require an understanding of employment practices.
Objective	To provide a practical and informative insight into the implications of legislation of the day to day control of employee relations.
Course content	Legal aspects of recruitment
	Discrimination during employment
	Terms and conditions of employment
	Contractual obligations
	Employee protection rights during employment
	Discipline and dismissal
	Remedies for unfair dismissal.
Duration and date	One day – 4th December.
Fee	Members £105 + VAT
	Non-members £140 + VAT

Comments on quick answer questions 7.5

i)   Success in any kind of learning situation depends largely on the motivation of the learner. Because of this, training often depends on people volunteering.

ii) Learning by your mistakes may be effective, but it can be costly. It is better to make your mistakes outside the workplace, for example in a training situation, than at work. Age may be a factor in how effectively people learn, but motivation to learn is more important. Other methods of learning include attending lectures, reading relevant texts, joining in discussions, role play and practising skills through activities and exercises.

Management: *Team building*

Intended for	Managers, supervisors and team leaders who are involved in running teams or creating a 'team' organisation.
Objective	On completion of the course delegates will be capable of organising, controlling and leading a team by applying the practical team building concepts and recognising the failures and pitfalls of poor team leadership.
Course content	Introduction What is team building? Group work versus teamwork Management and leadership skills The concepts of team building Attitude of an effective team builder Selection and recruitment Training and development Setting goals Recognising priorities Problem solving Commitment collaboration and contribution Understanding and resolving conflict Feedback and praise Organisation and planning Establishing controls Developing a personal action plan
Duration and date	Two days – commencing 6th December
Fee	Members £180 + VAT Non-members £240 + VAT.

Management: *Human relations for supervisors*

Intended for	Potential, newly appointed or existing supervisors.
Objective	• To enable supervisors to recognise that their success depends to a great extent on their ability to promote good working relations, resolve workers' problems and gain commitment from the people who work for them
	• To assist supervisors to develop techniques and personal skills which are of practical value in maintaining good human relations
Course content	A supervisor's knowledge and skills. Review of the supervisor's responsibilities. Job expectations. Recognition of the individual. Individual and group behaviour in the work situation. Human relations problems and causes of poor relationships. How to handle human relations problems. Foundations and ways of improving human relations. The supervisor's relationships.
Duration and date	Three days – commencing 10th December.
Fee	Members £243 + VAT Non-members £324 + VAT.

Training: *Instructional methods for operator instructors*

Intended for	Personnel with part or full-time responsibility for training assembly, machine or process operators.
Objective	On completion of the programme course members will be able to apply an analytical and systematic approach to the training of operators relevant to the needs of their company.
Course content	Objectives of training Elements of systematic, analytical operator training. Identification of operator training needs using the Training Review System. Job Analysis – skills and knowledge. Principles and application of Faults Analysis. Writing training programmes and preparing instructor notes. Practical instruction to individuals and small groups using an effective style of on-the-job instruction. Developing operator speed and performance. Evaluating trainee performance and recording progress.
Approach	Course members will be limited to ensure delegates are actively involved in group exercises and discussion. Members will be encouraged to develop their instructional skills and technique through presentation and demonstration of individual jobs.
Duration and date	Three days – commencing 3rd December.
Fee	Members £243 + VAT Non-members £324 + VAT.

Communication: *Team briefing*

Intended for	All managers, supervisors and personnel who have a responsibility to conduct team briefings within their organisation.
Objective	To provide delegates with a structured approach in the skills of team briefing. It will provide an opportunity to prepare and present briefings in a clear, concise and accurate manner. Finally delegates will recognise the value of team briefing as a method of two way communications.
Course content	Methods of communications Introducing team briefing The briefing structure Preparing the briefing The use of language Actions before and after giving a briefing Asking and answering questions How to improve the understanding of messages Practical exercises in briefing
Duration and date	One day – 17th December.
Fee	Members £105 + VAT Non-members £140 + VAT.

Employment: *Dismissal*

Introduction	Personnel employed by a company have a right not to be unfairly dismissed. This area of employment is covered by extensive statutory and case law provisions and is subject to change in the way in which it is interpreted by the appeal courts. It is therefore important that key personnel are kept up-to-date with such legislation.
Course content	Legal aspects of fair dismissal What constitutes fair or unfair dismissal Handling different types of offence Other substantive reasons The use of a fair dismissal procedure Implications on the contract of employment Remedies for unfair dismissal Case studies
Duration and date	Half day – 6th December.
Fee	Members £60 + VAT Non-members £80 + VAT.

Employment: *Redundancy*

Introduction	Redundancy in practice results in terminating employment and if the reason for dismissal comes within the definition of redundancy then it falls within Part 6 of the Employment Protection (Consolidation) Act 1978.
Course content	What are the basic principles of redundancy? What to do about it Entitled and excluded employees Time off work What constitutes redundancy? Calculation of redundancy payments Protective awards Fair redundancy procedures and selection Alternative employment Transfer of the business Case studies
Duration and date	Half day – 13th December.
Fee	Members £60 + VAT Non-members £80 + VAT.

Computers: *Lotus Symphony workshop*

Intended for	Anyone who will be using Symphony for the first time and wishes to obtain a good overall understanding of the program.
Objective	To introduce delegates to the facilities of Symphony, and to provide 'ands-on' experience using carefully structured examples which enable delegates quickly to appreciate the potential of the program for their own requirements. Symphony is a fully integrated software package featuring spreadsheet, database, graphics, word processing and communication.
Course content	Spreadsheet – Data entry – Ranges – Copy – Move – File Save/Retrieve – Functions – Formatting – Protection – Printing Introduction to Graphics Introduction to Windows Database – Concepts – Commands Introduction to Macros Graph printing Word processing – Concepts – Workshop Communications
Duration and date	Two days – commencing 6th December
Fee	Members £180 + VAT Non-members £240 + VAT.

Safety: *First aid at work certificate*

Introduction	This course leads to the award of the statutory First Aid Certificate and complies with the Health and Safety (First Aid) Regulations 1981.
Course content	Introduction to First Aid Respiration Circulation Bleeding Circulatory Failure Duties of First Aider Unconsciousness Fractures Miscellaneous Transport Revision and Examination
Duration and date	Four days (two days a week) commencing 10th December.
Fee	£120 + VAT

Management: *Action Centred Leadership*

Intended for	Supervisors in production departments whose work involves the control and leadership of other people, also for staff about to be promoted to supervisory positions.
Course content	The role of the supervisor: importance of the 'people' part in the job of a supervisor; the need for leadership in the first line management function
	Leadership analysis: what makes an effective leader; introduction to functional leadership and concept of Action Centred Leadership (ACL)
	Practical exercises: development of a framework for ACL
	Observation exercise: delegates observe and analyse a supervisor in action
	Motivation: analysis of motivation and discussion on practical steps a supervisor can take to motivate his team
	Other techniques: a review of some of the other techniques involved in helping people to become effective as quickly as possible
	Action session: delegates prepare a specific action plan for implementation on their return to work.
Duration and date	Two days – commencing 19th November.
Fee	Members £180 + VAT Non-members £240 + VAT

Problem-solving activities

i) *You are one of the supervisors. Write a reply to Steve Knight's memo.*

ii) *If you were Steve, how would you deal with next year's training programme?*

 See the information bank in *Section 2: Training,* page 119.

 You should now be able to attempt the activities in Unit 7 of Section 3, page 266.

Section 2

The information bank

Introduction

This information bank provides a summary of the theory, principles and practice of management. You will be directed to look up items in this section from Sections 1 and 3.

You will see from the list of contents on the next page that The Information Bank is arranged alphabetically so that you can use the contents page as an index. When you look a topic up, you may see cross references to other related items in The Information Bank, and be directed to wider reading in the form of recommended texts.

Contents

	Page		Page
Attitude	73	Management theories	132
Authority	75	Manpower analysis and planning	133
Budgetary control	77	Motivation	135
Change management	79	Non verbal communication	137
Communications	81	Organisational objectives, policies	
Control	86	and strategies	142
Counselling and listening	88	Organisational structures	144
Data protection legislation	89	Performance appraisal	145
Decision-making and problem solving	90	Personnel management	154
Delegation	93	Production control	156
Discipline	94	Quality assurance	159
Discrimination and equality	98	Questionnaires and surveys	166
Employment legislation	99	Recruitment, selection and induction	167
Groups and teams	104	Redundancy action checklist	178
Health and safety	109	Responsibility	179
Job analysis	113	Salaries and wages	180
Job design	115	Stress management	184
Job evaluation	117	Time management	190
Leadership	119	Trade unions and the law	192
Learning	124	Training	199
Management by objectives	128	Work study	202
Management qualities and activities	130		

Attitude

It is useful for management to know the nature and strength of the attitudes of its employees as a guide to future policy and to show possible causes of poor industrial relations. For example, if a large number of employees were leaving the company an enquiry into attitude might reveal the reasons and indicate what could be done to retain more employees.

The chief methods of detecting attitudes are:

a) an in-depth interview usually done by outside consultants and using a sample of employees;

b) an exit interview given when an employee is leaving the company;

c) an attitude survey by questionnaire. (See Illustration: Attitude survey.)

 SEE ALSO

> *Section 2: Authority*, page 75; *Change management*, page 79; *Counselling and listening*, page 88; *Questionnaires and surveys*, page 166.

Attitude surveys

Attitude surveys. *Personnel Management Factsheet No. 21.*

303.38   Oppenheim, AN, *Questionnaire design and attitude measurement*, Heinemann, 1966.

658.314 Davey, DM, *Attitude surveys in industry*, IPM, 1970.

Attitude survey

We are all interested in maintaining sound personnel policies and practices. You can help by contributing your opinions through this questionnaire.

We would appreciate your frank, straight-from-the-shoulder answers. There are no right or wrong answers. Please read each question carefully. Then check the one answer which most nearly reflects your personal opinion.

This survey is completely anonymous. **Please do not put your name anywhere on the questionnaire.**

When you have finished, please return the questionnaire in the enclosed envelope.

Thank you for taking the time to give us your opinion.

1) How much information do you receive about what is going on in your department?

   1. ☐ I get more than enough information.
   2. ☐ I get all the information I am interested in.
   3. ☐ I get almost as much information as I am interested in.
   4. ☐ I get about half the information I am interested in.
   5. ☐ I get very little of the information I am interested in.

2) How well do you know what is expected of you in your job?

   1. ☐ I know exactly.
   2. ☐ I have a very good idea.
   3. ☐ I have a pretty good idea.
   4. ☐ I have a somewhat vague idea.
   5. ☐ I have only a vague idea.

3) When your supervisor makes decisions and commitments about your work, how is it handled?

   1. ☐ It is almost always discussed with me first.
   2. ☐ It is usually discussed with me first.
   3. ☐ It is discussed with me about half the time.
   4. ☐ It is sometimes discussed with me first.
   5. ☐ It is rarely or never discussed with me first.

4) Does your supervisor ask for your advice about changes which will affect your job?

   1. ☐ My opinion is always sought.
   2. ☐ My opinion is usually sought.
   3. ☐ My opinion is sought about half the time.
   4. ☐ My opinion is rarely or never sought.
   5. ☐ This does not apply to me.

5) How sincere is your supervisor's interest in getting your opinions and suggestions?

   1. ☐ My supervisor has a very sincere interest in my opinion.
   2. ☐ My supervisor has considerable interest in my opinion.
   3. ☐ My supervisor has some interest in my opinion.
   4. ☐ My supervisor has little or no interest in my opinion.
   5. ☐ I don't know whether my supervisor is interested in my opinion.

6) What attention or emphasis is given to the following by your supervisor?

	Too much attention	About right	Too little attention	Doesn't apply
The quality of your work	☐	☐	☐	☐
Costs involved in your work	☐	☐	☐	☐
Meeting schedules	☐	☐	☐	☐
Getting your reactions and suggestions	☐	☐	☐	☐
Giving you information	☐	☐	☐	☐
Making full use of your abilities	☐	☐	☐	☐
Safety and housekeeping	☐	☐	☐	☐
Development of subordinates	☐	☐	☐	☐
Innovations, new ideas	☐	☐	☐	☐
Effective teamwork among subordinates	☐	☐	☐	☐

Authority

Authority is a concept with a number of meanings. Managerial authority may be defined as the right to act or direct the action of others in the attainment of organisational goals. This definition explicitly states that authority is a right and as a result of possessing this right, the holder is entitled to act either directly or indirectly through the actions of others. It also implies the power to employ penalties or rewards so that the desired action is completed.

Most organisations adopt a pyramid structure in which authority and responsibility extend downwards in a hierarchical pattern. Authority is passed down the chain of command by delegation.

The *acceptance theory* of authority suggests that managers only have authority if and when their subordinates accept that situation. Usually the workforce has little choice in accepting authority, the only recourse being to leave, but the spirit in which authority is accepted influences performance.

The *institutional theory* of authority suggests that authority is derived from the law of the society in which we live.

Douglas McGregor's Theory X suggests that authority is a situational phenomenon. It exists only when the subordinates accept another person as having the authority to direct them.

One of the dilemmas confronting supervisors and managers is that they have to choose the degree to which they should rely on their authority and power rather than use good human relations practices which might provide opportunities for self-motivation. In part the approach used by individual supervisors is related to their beliefs or perceptions about people. For the purpose of comparison, McGregor stated that the extremes in contrasting attitudes could be classed as Theory X or Theory Y. However, most people's attitudes fall somewhere in the middle.

Theory X assumptions are:

❏ The average person dislikes work and will avoid it.

❏ Because of this dislike, most people must be coerced, controlled, directed and threatened to get them to put in effort towards the organisation's objectives.

❏ The average person prefers to be directed and tries to avoid responsibility, having little ambition and wanting security above all.

Theory Y assumptions are:

❏ Work is as natural as play.

❏ People will exercise self-direction and self-control to attain objectives to which they are committed.

❏ People will seek responsibility.

❏ Ingenuity and creativity in the solution of organisational problems is widespread in the population.

❏ The potential of the average person is only partially utilised.

In broad terms the holder of authority has certain rights:

❏ to make decisions;

❏ to issue orders;

❏ to insist that the orders are carried out.

Authority can be classified as:

❏ *official authority*, which is usually associated with the job;

❏ *specialist authority*, which is usually associated with an individual's expertise or specialist skills;

❏ *personal authority*, which is the result of an individual's personality and behaviour and the effect it has on subordinates.

The more personal authority a person has, the less he or she needs the other two types of authority. Developing personal authority means developing the respect of subordinates.

SEE ALSO | **Section 2: Communications**, page 81; **Delegation**, page 93; **Leadership**, page 119.

Authority

658.3   Armstrong, M, *A handbook of personnel management practice*, 4th ed, Kogan Page, 1990. pp.195–197.

658.407 Culligan, MJ, *Back to basics management*, Gower, 1983.

Budgetary control

A *budget* is a plan which is prepared in advance for a trading or operating period. It expresses the performance to be achieved during that period by each functional area of the business, and for the business as a whole, in financial and/or quantitative terms.

Budgetary control is a process of financial control. It takes the targets of desired performance as its standards, then systematically collates information relating to actual performance (usually on a monthly or four-weekly basis) and identifies the variances between target and actual performance. Whereas budgets are primarily tools of planning, the process of budgetary control is both a planning device and a control device.

The *budget setting* process needs to commence some time before the start of the budget period. A budget committee may be formed consisting of the functional heads of the organisation, chaired by the chief executive. The management accountant usually occupies the role of committee secretary and co-ordinates the preparation of the budget information provided by each organisational and/or functional budget centre.

The steps by which a budgetary control system is built are usually as follows:

1. *Forecasts* for key aspects of the business are prepared. These are statements of probable sales, costs and other relevant financial and quantitative data.

2. A *sales budget* is prepared based on an analysis of past sales and a forecast of future sales made in the light of number of assumptions about market trends. The resulting budget is an estimate of sales for a given budget period.

3. A *production budget* is prepared on the basis of the sales budget. This involves assessing the productive capacity of the business in the light of the estimates of sales, and adjusting either or both to ensure a reasonable balance between demand and potential supply. Production budgets include output targets and cost estimates relating to labour and materials.

4. A *capital expenditure budget* is drawn up to cover estimated expenditure on capital items (fixed assets) during the budget period.

5. A *cash budget* is prepared by the management accountant to ensure that the organisation has sufficient cash to meet the on-going needs of the business. This budget reduces the organisation's transactions to movements of cash at particular periods of time.

6. *Departmental budgets* are drawn up in the wake of the sales and production budgets.

7. The budgets are received by the budget committee which ensures that:
    - ❏ they conform to the policies and goals of the organisation;
    - ❏ they are reasonable and achievable;
    - ❏ they are well co-ordinated;
    - ❏ they take into consideration the conditions and constraints which are anticipated during the budget period.

8. Finally, the master budget is drawn up from the departmental and other budgets and formally approved. This is effectively a statement of budgeted profit and loss together with a projected balance sheet and becomes the policy plan for the organisation for the budget period.

9. The relevant budgets are communicated to all budget centre managers who are encouraged to operate within the approved budgetary framework of costs, sales and

performance. *Period budget statements* are produced to keep managers informed about their performance against budget in the preceding period.

10. Action is taken by the budget centre managers to rectify any negative variances.

In developing such a budgetary control system, a number of points of good practice need to be considered:

❏ Budgets should be sufficiently detailed to set clear targets for the managers responsible for carrying them out, but should not be so complex that they defeat their purpose of providing planning and control aids at the operating levels of the organisation.

❏ Budgets should not be kept to rigidly if conditions change significantly, but should permit reasonable flexibility. They are a means to an end; not an end in themselves.

❏ Responsibility for a particular budget should be clearly defined.

❏ Budgets should show variances between actual and budgeted performance (ideally in quantitative as well as financial terms).

❏ Managers responsible for carrying out budgets should participate in their formulation.

Although planning is an essential ingredient in the preparation of budgets, they are more closely related to the control process. The budget itself is the stated standard. The measure of performance is the comparison of the standard with the actual figures, which highlights the need for corrective action.

Whilst budgetary control is a very useful device for achieving motivation, responsibility, co-ordination, control and effective decision-making within an organisation, there are some limitations:

❏ Spending tends to match budget limits, regardless of needs, in order to avoid cuts in the next budget.

❏ Funds can be unavailable for *unexpected* necessities.

❏ Statements made in numeric terms often indicate a degree of precision that is not warranted.

❏ Budgetary control is only one of several control techniques.

❏ Most people have a natural resistance to any form of control. If standards are too tight or move up too often, they may be resisted.

❏ Budgets rarely reflect the effort needed.

❏ Budget pressures may unite the workforce against the management.

SEE ALSO

Section 2: Change management, page 79; *Communications*, page 81; *Control*, page 86, *Responsibility*, page 179.

Budgetary control

658.15   Crowson, P, *Economics for managers*, 3rd ed, Macmillan, 1985.

658.15   ACC   Davies, D, *The art of managing finance*, McGraw Hill, 1985.

658.15   Knott, G, *Financial management*, Pan, 1987.

658.154 Scott, JA, *Budgeting control and standard costs*, 6th ed, Pitman, 1970.

Change management

Change in an organisation can be achieved directly by changing the attitudes, beliefs and values of employees or indirectly by changing the organisational structure, technology or objectives. Reluctance to accept change is often indicative of deep-seated fears. The main cause is lack of security.

Changes in systems and improvements in methods are often considered a weapon of management, designed to create redundancy and frighten staff into higher efficiency. However, if problems can be anticipated and the process of change monitored and assessed, those affected by change are usually able to adapt.

At each level it is important for a manager implementing changes to ask questions; the answers will provide suggestions as to how the change might be carried out. Typical questions might be:

How will staff be affected?

❏ considerably

❏ moderately

Who will be affected?

❏ numbers

❏ sex

❏ age

What will the change affect?

❏ training

❏ company loyalty

❏ temperament

❏ trade unions

❏ social values/culture

What is the response to the change likely to be?

❏ supportive

❏ outright opposition

❏ general mistrust

❏ unco-operative

❏ strike action

What are the reasons for rejecting change?

❏ redundancy

❏ lower status

❏ more work for the same pay

❏ habit

❏ culture

❏ alliances

❏ distrust of management

People often fear the unknown. This can be anticipated by making the reason for the change understood. Staff should be warned how, when and why the proposed changes will affect them. There may also be some fear of loss of skills and status. Working conditions and benefits may be threatened. Existing skills should be fully utilised and any losses outweighed by new benefits.

Some individuals may feel that change carries with it some criticism of past performance. Managers should emphasise the reasons for the need for change, praising and building on employees' past performance. Sometimes change can look like the management making life difficult for the workers. However, if people are involved in the planning and implementation of the change the losses can be minimised and gains maximised.

Reluctance to accept change is often indicative of deep-seated psychological fears. The main cause is lack of security. Systems changes and methods improvements are, it is too often considered, a weapon of management, designed to create redundancy and to frighten staff into higher efficiency.

The *barriers* to change are:

❑ Fear of the unknown: People fear what they don't know.

❑ Implied criticism: Criticism of past performance or the feeling of being overlooked.

❑ Fear of loss of status and/or skills: The time taken to acquire skills has been apparently lost. There may be fear of perks/conditions being lost - the 'hygiene factors'.

❑ Nuisance value: Change looks like the boss is making life difficult.

Barriers can be broken down by:

❑ Making the reason for the change understood. Warn people how it will affect them, when and why.

❑ Emphasise the need for change. Praise and build on past performance. Use experience and suggestions from those at 'the coal face'.

❑ Use existing skills. Make sure losses are outweighed by gains. Minimise the losses and maximise the gains.

❑ Get people involved in the planning and implementation of the change.

❑ Anticipate, monitor, assess and adapt.

SEE | ALSO

Section 2: Communications, page 81; **Counselling and listening**, page 88; **Leadership**, page 119; **Management qualities and activities**, page 130; **Organisational planning, policies and strategies**, page 142; **Organisational structures**, page 144.

Change management

658   Peters, T, *Thriving on chaos*, Pan, 1989.

658.3   Leigh, A, *Effective change*, IPM, 1988.

658.406 Toffler, A, *The adaptive corporation*, Gower, 1985.

658.406 Work Research Unit, *Meeting the challenge of change*, HMSO, 1982.

Communications

It is essential for organisations to be effective in their *communications* for the following reasons:

❑ to aid decision-making;

❑ to enhance the organisation's reputation;

❑ to ensure the effective operation of the organisation's systems.

Poor communications result in lack of information, misinformation, misunderstandings and lost profits. To be effective, workplace communications must be:

❑ clear, concise and easily understood;

❑ presented objectively;

❑ in a manageable form to avoid rejection;

❑ regular and systematic;

❑ as relevant, local and timely as possible;

❑ open to questions being asked and answered.

A variety of methods are needed, both spoken and written, direct and indirect. These need not be sophisticated or expensive. The mix of methods depends mainly on the size and structure of the company, with some of the more sophisticated methods likely to be of value in large organisations.

Face-to-face communication is direct and swift. It should enable discussion, questioning and feedback to take place but ought to be supplemented by written material where information is detailed or complex and where records are important. When spoken methods are used it is important that:

❑ the chain of communication is as short as possible;

❑ the frequency and timing of meetings are carefully considered;

❑ managers are fully briefed on their subjects and able to put them across clearly and consistently;

❑ opportunities are provided for questions.

The main methods of formal face-to-face communications are as follows.

Group meetings: Meetings between managers and the employees for whom they are responsible, sometimes referred to as team briefing or briefing groups. These provide valuable opportunities for discussion and feedback on matters directly related to the work group and also on wider information about the organisation's progress.
Opportunities for employees to contribute their ideas may arise from the use of quality circles whereby small groups of employees meet regularly to identify problems, discuss and suggest possible solutions.

Cascade networks: A well defined procedure for passing important information quickly, used mainly in large or wide-spread organisations.

Large-scale meetings: Meetings involving the whole workforce, establishment, with presentations by a director or senior manager. These are good for presenting the organisation's performance or long-term objectives; they require careful preparation but allow only limited opportunities for employee response. They should be used sparingly and need to be followed up in other ways.

Conferences and seminars: Meetings of selected or specified employees to study a particular problem. Emphasis is placed on questioning and group discussion, which are suitable in any size of organisation.

Information points: An indirect method which enables employees to listen to pre-recorded and regularly changed bulletins about matters of interest on an internal telephone system. Normally appropriate only in large establishments.

Audio-visual aids: Video, film or tape/slide presentations are particularly useful for explaining technical developments or financial performance. It is important to provide opportunity for feedback. Normally only large firms can consider producing films or video tapes, but even very small firms can make their own slide presentations without professional help.

Informal channels of oral communication obviously play a major part in the passage of information and instructions in any organisation, for example in the course of daily work in face-to-face encounters or on the telephone. Inevitably there will be a 'grapevine'. This will pass news and information quickly, but it cannot be relied on and is likely to encourage ill-informed rumour. It must not be allowed to replace other methods of workplace communications.

Written communication is most effective where:

☐ the need for information is important or permanent;

☐ the topic requires detailed explanation;

☐ the accuracy and precision in wording are essential;

☐ the audience is widespread or large.

The main methods of written communication are set out below.

Employee handbooks bring together employment and job-related information which employees need to know and which does not change too often, such as holiday arrangements, company rules and disciplinary/grievance procedures. They can be given to all employees and may also usefully include background information about the company, its policies and objectives.

Employee reports inform employees about the activities and performance of their organisation. Good reports are written and presented so as to be readily understood by employees at all levels, with emphasis on their contribution and achievement. In large companies it is often desirable to produce reports for operating divisions or local units and this enhances their impact. The use of clear illustrations is helpful in such reports provided they do not distort the information.

House journals and newsletters enable factual information about an organisation to be presented on a regular basis. These usually contain a large element of social or personal news. In large organisations their production is often highly professional, but even small companies can reap benefits from well produced, attractive newsletters.

Bulletins are useful for giving information on a departmental or wider basis about specific items of general interest.

Notices placed on well situated notice-boards bring matters of general importance as well as items of specific interest to the attention of a wide audience. Care needs to be taken over location, over rights to use notice-boards and in keeping them up-to-date. Diagrammatic notices and signs can also be useful for communicating to employees, particularly those with limited reading ability.

Individual letters to all employees can be used to give information about matters of major importance accurately and simultaneously.

Where the information being communicated is particularly important, it may be beneficial to use more than one method to assist in its being received by everyone and understood. Special attention should be given to ensuring information is understood by employees within a multi-racial workforce and those who cannot read easily. Help can be provided by the National Centre for Industrial Language Training. It is equally important not to overlook isolated groups, such as those on night shifts, maintenance or sales employees working away from base, and those in remote locations. In larger organisations it is also easy to ignore individual employees, such as switchboard operators, receptionists and messengers, who may work in isolation.

The *American Management Association* offers the following guidelines for improving communications:

1. Seek to clarify your ideas before communicating. The more systematically we analyse the problem or idea to be communicated, the clearer it becomes that this is the first step toward effective communication. Many communications fail because of inadequate planning. Good planning must consider the goals and attitudes of those who will receive the communications and those who will be affected by it.

2. Examine the true purpose of each communication. Before you communicate, ask yourself what you really want to accomplish with your message. Is it to obtain information, initiate action, change another person's attitude? Identify your most important goal and then adapt your language, tone, and total approach to serve that specific objective. Don't try to accomplish too much with each communication. The sharper the focus of your message the greater its chances of success.

3. Consider the total physical and human setting whenever you communicate. Meaning and intent are conveyed by more than words alone. Many other factors influence the overall impact of a communication and the manager must be sensitive to the total setting in which he or she communicates. Factors to consider include the timing of the communication, the circumstances under which you make an announcement or render a decision; the physical setting and whether you are communicating in private or otherwise; the social climate that pervades work relationships within the organisation or department which sets the tone of communications; custom and past practice and the degree to which your communication conforms to or departs from the expectations of your audience. Communication must be capable of adapting to its environment.

4. Consult with others, where appropriate, in planning communications. Frequently it is desirable or necessary to seek the participation of others in planning a communication or developing the facts on which to base it. Such consultation often helps to lend additional insight and objectivity to your message. Moreover, those who have helped you plan your communication will give it their support.

5. Be mindful, while you communicate, of the overtones as well as the basic content of your message. Your tone of voice, your expression, your apparent receptiveness to the responses of others all have tremendous impact on those you wish to reach. Frequently overlooked, these subtleties of communication often affect a listener's reaction to a message even more than its basic content. Similarly, your choice of language, particularly your awareness of the fine shades of meaning and emotion in the words you use, predetermines in large part the reactions of your listeners.

6. Take the opportunity, when it arises, to convey something of help or value to the receiver. Consideration of the other person's interests and needs, the habit of trying to look at things from his or her point of view, will frequently point up opportunities to convey something of immediate benefit or long-range value to him or her. People on the job are most responsive to the manager whose messages take their own interests into account.

7. Follow up your communication. Our best efforts at communication may be wasted and we may never know whether we have succeeded in expressing our true meaning and intent, if we do not follow up to see how well we have put our message across. This you can do by asking questions, by encouraging the receiver to express his or her reactions, by follow-up contacts, by subsequent review of performance. Make certain that every important communication has a feedback so that complete understanding and appropriate action result.

8. Communicate for tomorrow as well as for today. While communications may be aimed primarily at meeting the demands of an immediate situation, they must be planned with the past in mind if they are to maintain consistency in the receiver's view. But, most important of all, they must be consistent with long-range interests and goals. For example, it is not easy to communicate frankly on such matters as poor performance or the shortcomings of a loyal subordinate, but postponing disagreeable communications makes them more difficult in the long run and is actually unfair to your subordinates and your company.

9. Be sure your actions support your communications. In the final analysis, the most persuasive kind of communication is not what you say but what you do. When a person's actions or attitudes contradict his or her words, we tend to discount what he or she has said. For every manager this means that good supervisory practices, such as clear assignment of responsibility and authority, fair rewards for effort and sound policy enforcement, serve to communicate more than all the gifts of oratory.

10. Seek not only to be understood but to understand. Be a good listener. When we start talking we often cease to listen in that larger sense of being attuned to the other person's unspoken reactions and attitudes. Even more serious is the fact that we are all guilty, at times, of inattentiveness when others are attempting to communicate to us. Listening is one of the most important, most difficult and most neglected skills in communication. It demands that we concentrate not only on the explicit meanings another person is expressing, but on the implicit meanings, unspoken words, and undertones that may be far more significant.

Report writing

Very few people want to read a report from beginning to end. Often they only want to know what it is about in outline and what action to take. If the reader is sufficiently interested he or she can examine the report in detail. For this reason a *summary* is often provided.

The exact *format* often depends on the subject matter, but one in common use is:

1. The *terms of reference*: A few lines specifying the scope of the report and any limitations.

2. *Acknowledgements*: A few lines if applicable.

3. *Summary*: No more than one page.

4. The *setting*: Background information should be given here so that the report can be read and understood by someone who is outside the organisation.

5. The *methodology*: A short statement of how the information has been gathered. The reader can then use his or her own judgement as to its validity.

6. The *investigation*: This is the main part of the report. It should state what the problem is, why it is a problem and what costs are involved. Detailed information should be shown here. It should be evaluated and options discussed.

7. *Conclusions*: This is an analysis of the root causes of the problems and possible solutions should be discussed.

8. *Recommendations*: A course of action related to the suggested solutions should be recommended. Potential difficulties and how to overcome them should be included in this section of the report.

9. *Summary of costs*: Detailed cost implications should be shown.

10. *Appendices*: These should comprise sample documents, such as questionnaires, tables, etc.

The means of gathering information for a report will depend on the topic. Common sources of information include

- library research
- questionnaire surveys
- observation
- interview surveys
- existing statistical data

Presentations

At some time most supervisors and managers have to give a presentation. For those who are not used to speaking to groups this can be a nerve- racking experience. Most people would like to appear to be relaxed, knowledgeable and confident when they do have to make a presentation, and this is fairly easy to achieve with a little forethought. The following points should help:

1. When you stand up in front of a group all eyes are on you and this can be unnerving, so give them something else to look at; for example, a handout of some kind or an overhead transparency or slide.

2. Avoid too many facts and figures unless you want to send your audience to sleep.

3. The chances are you will feel nervous, but remember it doesn't show. No-one else knows how nervous you are.

4. Preparation is everything. Decide what you need to say and create a logical sequence. Don't forget to rehearse, if only mentally. Sort out details such as how to switch on the projector before you start.

5. If you are using overhead transparencies or handouts, make sure that they are of a good standard.

6. Do not read from your notes: there's nothing so boring and lifeless. But do use a prompt card with a list of your main points (you don't need to hide the fact that you are doing this).

7. Look at your audience. Don't talk as if they're not there.

8. If it is appropriate, summarise your main points at the end.

9. Try to avoid distracting mannerisms, such as rattling change in your pockets or playing with jewellery.

10. When in doubt be brief. Unless the topic is particularly interesting, or wonderfully entertaining, the audience's attention will start to wane after about 15 minutes. If you need to speak for longer than 15 minutes you should provide a change of activity, such as asking for comments or providing some other opportunity for audience participation.

Remember:

☐ Prepare well and rehearse.

☐ Be brief and to the point.

☐ Summarise if appropriate.

 SEE | ALSO

> **Section 2: Delegation**, page 93; **Management qualities and activities**, page 130 **Management theories**, page 132; **Organisational structures**, page 144; **Responsibility**, page 179.

Communication

658.4   Steele, P, *It's a deal*, McGraw-Hill, 1989.

658.45   Adair, J, *The effective communicator*, Industrial Society, 1988.

658.45   Bowbrick, P, *Effective communication for professionals and executives*, Graham & Trotman, 1988.

658.45   Fowler, A, *Negotiation skills and strategies*, IPM, 1990.

Control

Control is one of the prime management functions. It is the task of measuring and correcting the activities of the individuals and groups in an organisation to ensure that their performance is in accordance with plans. All control mechanisms have some fundamental characteristics in common:

☐ to establish standards of performance;

☐ to measure performance against the standard;

☐ to take corrective action if required.

Standards of performance are not averages or states of perfection. They may be difficult to reach but not unattainable. Standards can be set for any business activity. They may be based on objective quantitative analysis, such as machine output, or set by appraisal. These are essentially value judgements, yet they can be as realistic and attainable as engineering standards.

Measuring performance relies on information. The information for control needs to be available at the right time, reliable and channelled to the proper authority.

Without the power to take *corrective action* if required, there is no control. Failure to meet expected levels of performance may require that new plans are made or standards revised. Some of the questions relating to control are listed below together with the methods or techniques commonly used to answer them.

1. Who is responsible for each section of the work and for doing the work? (*Organisation plans, division of responsibility and delegation*)

2. What is the work content? (*Job description*)

3. How is the work done? (*Method study*)

4. How long will the work take? (*Work measurement*)

5. Where should it be done? (*Method study and layout*)

6. When should it be done? (*Planning and scheduling*)

7. What is the cost of the work? (*Accounts and costing*)

8. How is the work performance regulated? (*Motivation, progress chasing*)

An organisation's control structure

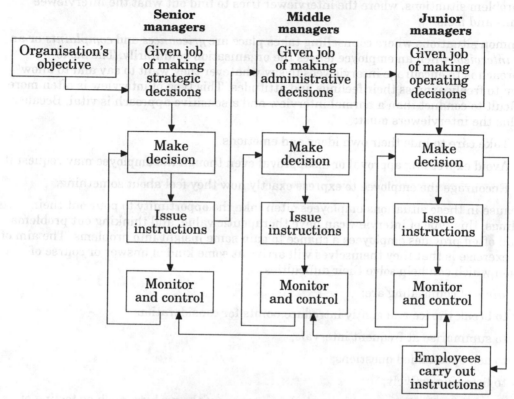

SEE ALSO

Section 2: Budgetary control, page 77;
Management qualities and activities, page 130;
Management theories, page 132; *Organisational
structures*, page 144; *Production control*, page
156; *Quality assurance*, page 159.

Control

658   De Paula, FC, *The techniques of business control*, Pitman, 1973.

658.4012   Minkes, AL, *Business behaviour and management structure*, Croom Helm, 1985.

Counselling and listening

Counselling has become recognised as an important function in management. Counselling involves an interview but the interview is often non-directive. That is to say, it is one where broad general questions are discussed in order to have the interviewee talk freely and perhaps in depth. This type of interview is most often used in problem situations, where the interviewer tries to find out what the interviewee thinks and feels.

Common situations where counselling takes place are *grievances* and *complaints* or an *exit interview* when an employee leaves the organisation voluntarily. The basic approach is to encourage interviewees to say whatever they want to say and to allow them to freely express their feelings and attitudes. This type of interview is often more difficult to conduct than a normal interview and a sensitive approach is vital. Because of this the interviewers must:

❏ Take care to hide their own ideas and emotions.

❏ Avoid expressing approval or disapproval even though the employee may request it.

❏ Encourage the employee to express exactly how they feel about something.

Because in these situations employees often take the opportunity to pour out their feelings, this type of interview can have therapeutic value, and thinking out problems aloud often provides employees a chance to gain some insight into problems. The aim of the exercise is that they themselves will arrive at some kind of answer or course of action which can help solve their difficulties.

The *aims* of counselling are:

❏ to break the ice and gently introduce points for consideration;

❏ to summarise at frequent intervals;

❏ to ask open-ended questions;

❏ to listening actively;

❏ to be alert for clues as to the underlying causes of the problem such as feeling of insecurity, false impressions of abilities, fear of loss of face.

Listening is as essential a part of conversation as talking. To achieve two-way communication, the listener must listen with understanding. This way he or she gains a view of the other person's perspective, rather than merely providing an opportunity for speech. The following *checklist* for effective listening is fairly easy to remember, but it may require some years to perfect the skill.

1. Avoid making *judgements*. Value judgements are made from the point of view of the listener rather than from the point of view of the person talking. Such a judgement places a single value on a whole series of statements and actions, and may have been made some time before or on another matter. If one party to a conversation has made his or her value judgement, for example that the other person does not understand the process under discussion or is stupid, then he or she has a closed mind and it becomes impossible to understand the other's point of view.

2. Listen to the *full story*. Put the other person at ease. Offer them a seat, a cup of coffee and make sure that adequate time is allowed for the conversation with no interruptions. Listen to all they have to say, that is, the full story. In this way you may learn the other person's motives and reasoning.

3. Recognise *emotions*. Put yourself in the other person's position. Try to find out the meaning of the feelings and emotions behind his or her statements, rather than the

meaning of the words alone. Look for signs of non-verbal communication (body language); signs of eagerness, hesitancy, hostility, anxiety or depression. At the same time, look for evasions; things left unsaid or areas of discussion consistently evaded.

4. *Restate* the other person's position. Test your understanding of the situation by summarising what the other person has said. For example, 'You believe that I'm watching you more than the others?'

5. *Question* with care. The easiest way to keep a conversation going is to use the non-committal 'uh-huh'. If this is not enough, questions such as, 'What happened after that?' or 'What did you do then?' may help the story to unfold. Occasionally restatements may be rephrased as questions. Avoid argumentative statements which result in loss of objectivity, heightened emotions and put the other person on the defensive, making it impossible for him or her to express his or her true feelings.

SEE	ALSO

Section 2: Attitude, page 73; **Leadership**, page 119; **Personnel management**, page 154.

Counselling

658.3   Attwood, M, *Personnel management*, Pan, 1987.

658.385 Megranahan, M, *Counselling*, IPM, 1989.

Data protection legislation

Under the Data Protection Act 1984, employers holding computerised data, including personnel records, need to register as 'data users'.

Employees ('data subjects') have a statutory right to access all computerised information held on them and may claim compensation for damage and distress if the information is found to be inaccurate. It should be noted that manual records are not covered by the Act provided any reference to the records is for purely factual information.

Data users are supervised by the Data Protection Registrar and they are required to disclose the nature of data held, why it is held, how and from whom it has been obtained and to whom it will be disclosed.

There are eight principles, which together form a standard against which the Registrar will seek to ensure compliance and these are as follows:

1. 'The information contained in the personal data shall be obtained and the personal data shall be processed fairly and lawfully.'

2. Personal data 'shall be held only for one or more specified and lawful purposes.'

3. Disclosure shall not be 'in any manner incompatible with that purpose or with those purposes' for which the personal data is held.

4. Personal data held shall be 'adequate, relevant and not excessive' to the purpose or purposes.

5. Personal data held shall be 'accurate, and where necessary, kept up to date.'

6. Personal data shall 'not be kept for longer than necessary.'

7. 'An individual shall be entitled:

    a) at reasonable intervals and without undue delay or expense:

        i) to be informed by any data user whether he holds personal information of which that individual is the subject; and

        ii) to access any such data held by a data user; and

    b) where appropriate, to have data corrected or erased.

8. Appropriate security measures shall be taken against 'unauthorised access to, alteration, disclosure or destruction of personal data and against accidental loss or destruction.'

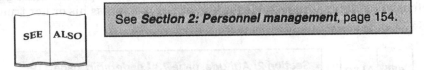

SEE ALSO   See *Section 2: Personnel management*, page 154.

Decision-making and problem solving

Whatever type of problem facing a manager, the prime consideration in the problem solving process is the gathering of information which will allow the development of possible solutions. This gathering of information is not easy and is often based on value judgements, beliefs, perceptions and attitudes. The separation of fact from opinion is often difficult and can be a basis for conflict.

Problems, no matter what their size or complexity, can usually be solved by proceeding through a sequence of steps. This ensures that everything possible will be done to apply available resources in the most effective manner, to consider a number of options, and to select the best solution.

There are many problem-solving models, and the one that follows is fairly typical:

☐ *Problem awareness* – Often this depends on the manager's motivation to be aware, although certain techniques can also help.

☐ *Defining the problem* – When feedback suggests that a problem exists it is usual then to probe and question. This often results in the problem being precisely defined in terms of expectations.

☐ *Establishing criteria* – Which of two or more alternative decisions is best. This depends on the criteria used in evaluation. These decision criteria should be explicit, ideally in order of priority, this being done before solutions are developed.

☐ *Developing alternative and choosing solutions* – There are many aids to this process such as:

    a) *Brainstorming*. This is a creative team technique for developing ideas spontaneously. The subject, or problem, to be brainstormed should be clearly stated and fully understood by all concerned. The ideal brainstorming team consists of 4 to 8 people who have diverse backgrounds and interests. The brainstorming session should have a strict timescale placed on it to encourage a speedy thought process and ensure that the session does not go stale. As ideas occur to the team members they should call them out and they should be written down immediately.

b) *Cause and effect analysis.* There are two techniques: the structure tree and the Ishikawa diagram.

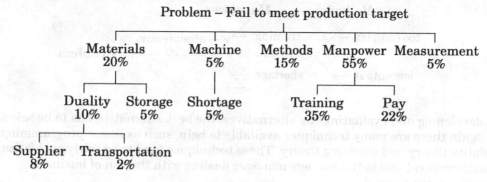

Problem – Fail to meet production target

Structure tree

The structure tree is drawn as follows:

1. Develop the problem statement.

2. Draw a tree structure showing the 5 Ms:

Materials	70%
Machines	10%
Methods	15%
Manpower	5%
Measurement	0%
	100%

3. Assign a percentage contribution to the problem for each of the 5 Ms, as above.

4. After using the 5 Ms to get the process started, list the possible causes to the highest contributing M, eg:

Materials	70%	....	quality	40%
		....	storage	20%
		....	shortage	10%

5. If needed, the tree can now be developed to another level.

6. Once the root cause has been found, corrective action can then be considered.

The *Ishikawa diagram* can be used as an alternative to the structure tree. The layout is different but the principle is the same.

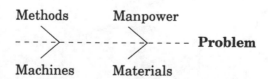

Ishikawa diagram

A partially completed diagram looks like this:

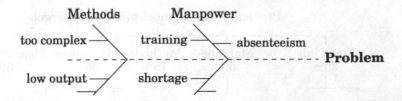

After developing and evaluating the alternatives, the best alternative has to be selected. Once again there are many techniques available to help, such as linear programming, probability theory and queueing theory. These techniques tend to be fairly sophisticated and mathematical and to the average manager dealing with the run of business problems, not very useful.

A more realistic method or at least more well used, is for the manager to rely on his or her experience, combined with the advice of experts.

 SEE | **ALSO**   *Section 2: Time management*, page 190; *Work study*, page 202.

Decision making

658.403 Adair, J, *Effective decision making*, Pan, 1985.

658.403 Francis, D, *Effective problem solving*, Routledge, 1990.

658.403 Leigh, A, *Decisions, decisions*, IPM, 1983.

658.403 Richards, T, *Creativity and problem solving at work*, Gower, 1990.

Delegation

Delegation is the act of passing authority or power, but not ultimate responsibility, to another person. Examples of reasons for doing so are:

- ❏ to free the delegator from certain tasks;
- ❏ to reduce delays in decision-making;
- ❏ to train subordinates;
- ❏ to reduce bottlenecks.

Delegation is generally accepted as being a three-step process:

1. Assign the work, giving the subordinate responsibility for doing the work.
2. Delegate the authority, which should match the responsibility.
3. Create accountability whereby the subordinate accepts that he or she is accountable to the delegator for the work.

Delegation may fail to take place for a number of reasons. For example:

- ❏ potential delegators might think that no one else can do the job as well;
- ❏ they like doing the job and do not want to give it up;
- ❏ they think it would be quicker to do it themselves.

Conditions for effective delegation are:

- ❏ parity of authority and responsibility: too little authority usually results in managers having to consult their superiors before making routine decisions;
- ❏ absoluteness of accountability: responsibility can be assigned and authority delegated, but accountability can be neither assigned nor delegated;
- ❏ unity of command: subordinates should be accountable to one superior only.

Checklist for effective delegation:

- ❏ Decide what you can delegate.
- ❏ Tell your subordinates *what* to do, and *why*, but do not tell them *how* to do it.
- ❏ Expect a few mistakes. Remember that people often learn best by their mistakes.
- ❏ Delegate to the lowest possible level; it is an excellent motivator.
- ❏ Make sure you delegate authority to match the responsibility.
- ❏ Give praise for a job well done.
- ❏ Don't just delegate the things you don't want to do yourself.
- ❏ Don't forget that some decisions can only be made by you.
- ❏ Don't forget that no one is indispensable.

SEE ALSO | *Section 2, Authority*, page 75; *Communications*, page 81; *Leadership*, page 119; *Responsibility*, page 179.

Delegation

658   Carlson, D, *Modern management*, Macmillan, 1982.

658   Cole, GA, *Management: theory and practice, 3rd ed*, DP Publications, 1990.

Discipline

Maintaining *discipline* among employees is an integral part of managing and the way that it is done sets the scene for employee relations in general. Discipline often is understood to mean punishment. Another interpretation, however, is to consider it to be a state of affairs, a condition of orderliness, in which the people concerned conduct themselves according to standards of acceptable behaviour. Discipline can be good, when employees willingly follow the rules, or bad when employees either follow the rules reluctantly or actually disobey the regulations.

Discipline is not the same as morale, but the level of morale influences problems of discipline and normally there will be fewer problems of discipline where morale is high.

The best discipline is *self-discipline* and this is based on the normal human tendency to do what needs to be done, to do one's share, to do the right thing and to follow reasonable standards of acceptable behaviour. Very often the working group itself will enforce rules by reminding members of the rules; for example, not to smoke in a particular area or to wear safety glasses.

Most employees know they will have the support of management as long as they follow the rules. Credibility for management means discipline starts at the top and requires that management themselves obey the rules.

Disciplinary situations

Although the vast majority of employees exercise self-discipline, for one reason or another there are those who don't. Common problems are lateness, absenteeism, poor standards of work, poor attitude, breaking rules on break times, improper dress, safety etc.

A supervisor is placed in a difficult position when taking disciplinary action. In spite of the use of normal sensitivity and judgement, imposing disciplinary action tends to generate resentment because it is an unpleasant experience. The challenge to the supervisor is to apply the necessary action so that it will be least resented, and in this connection the so-called *hot stove rule* is often advocated.

This rule compares touching a hot stove with experiencing discipline. When one touches a hot stove the effect is *immediate, consistent, with warning* and *impersonal*. The burn is *immediate*, with no questions of cause and effect. The effect is *consistent*: one *always* suffers a burn when touching a hot stove. There is *warning* since everyone knows what happens if you touch a hot stove: you get burnt. The result is *impersonal*: anyone touching a hot stove is burned, no matter who they are. The comparison with discipline is obvious and following the *four rules* will help supervisors and managers to reduce the resentment inherent in all disciplinary action.

The exact disciplinary procedure followed will of course depend on the procedures and needs of the organisation concerned as well as the relevant legal requirements but there are some key steps which should be considered.

Checklist for handling a disciplinary matter

This checklist sets out the key steps which employers should consider when handling a disciplinary matter. All employers, regardless of size, should observe the principles of natural justice embodied below:

1. Gather all the relevant facts promptly before memories fade. Take statements and collect documentary evidence. In serious cases consider suspension with pay while an investigation is conducted.

2. Be clear about the complaint. Is action needed at this stage?

3. If so, decide whether the action should be advice and counselling or formal disciplinary action.

4. If formal action is required, arrange a disciplinary interview. Ensure that the individual is aware of the nature of the complaint and that the interview is a disciplinary one. Tell the individual where and when the interview will take place and of their rights to a companion or representative. Try to arrange for a second member of management to be present.

5. Start by introducing those present. Explain the purpose of the interview and the nature of the complaint.

6. Allow the individual to state his/her case. Consider and question any explanations put forward.

7. If any new facts emerge decide whether further investigation is required. If it is, adjourn the interview and reconvene when the investigation is completed.

8. Except in very straightforward cases, call an adjournment before reaching a decision. Come to a clear view about the facts. If they are disputed, decide on the balance of probability what version is true.

9. Before deciding the penalty consider the gravity of the offence and whether the procedure gives guidance, the penalty applied in similar cases in the past, the individual's disciplinary record and general service, any mitigating circumstances and whether the proposed penalty is reasonable in all the circumstances.

10. Reconvene the disciplinary interview to clearly inform the individual of the decision and any penalty, explain the right of appeal and how it operates. In the case of a warning, explain what improvement is expected, how long the warning will last and what the consequences of failure to improve may be.

11. Record the action taken. If other than an oral warning, confirm the disciplinary action to the individual in writing and keep a simple record of the action taken for future reference.

12. Monitor the individual's performance. Disciplinary action should be followed up with the object of encouraging improvement. Progress should be monitored regularly and discussed with the employee concerned.

Holding a disciplinary interview

1. Prepare carefully and ensure you have all the facts.

2. Tell the employee of the complaint, the procedure to be followed and that he or she is required to attend a disciplinary interview.

3. Tell the employee that he or she is entitled to be accompanied at the interview.

4. Find out if there are any special circumstances to be taken into account. For example, are there personal or other outside issues affecting performance or conduct?

5. Exercise care when dealing with evidence provided by an informant who wishes to remain anonymous. Take written statements, seek corroborative evidence and check that the informant's motives are genuine.

6. Are the standards of other employees acceptable or is this employee being unfairly singled out?

7. Consider what explanations may be offered by the employee and, if possible, check them out beforehand.

8. Allow the employee time to prepare his or her case. In complex cases it may be useful and save time at the interview if copies of any relevant papers are given to the employee in advance.

9. If the employee concerned is a trade union official ensure that no disciplinary action beyond an oral warning is taken until the circumstances of the case have been discussed with a trade union representative or full-time official. This is because the action may be seen as an attack on the union's function.

10. Arrange a time and, if possible, a quiet place for the interview with adequate seating, where there will be no interruptions.

11. Ensure that all the relevant facts are available, such as personal details, disciplinary record and any current warnings, other relevant documents (eg absence or sickness records) and, where appropriate, written statements from witnesses.

12. Establish what disciplinary action was taken in similar circumstances in the past.

13. Where possible arrange for a second member of management to be present to take notes of the proceedings and to act as a witness, particularly if the employee is to be accompanied.

14. Where possible ensure that any witnesses who can do so attend the interview, unless the employee accepts in advance that the witness statements are statements of fact.

15. If the witness is someone from outside the company who is not prepared to attend the interview, try to get a written statement from him or her.

16. If there are likely to be language difficulties consider whether a friend of the employee can assist as an interpreter or other arrangements can be made.

17. Consider how the interview will be structured and make notes of the points which need to be covered.

Interviews rarely proceed in neat, orderly stages but the following guidelines should help.

❐ Introduce those present to the employee and explain why they are there.

❐ Explain that the purpose of the interview is to consider whether disciplinary action should be taken in accordance with the company's disciplinary procedure.

❐ Explain how the interview will be conducted.

❐ State precisely what the complaint is and outline the case briefly by going through the evidence that has been gathered. Ensure that the employee and his or her representative is made aware of witness statements and of the contents of any relevant records

❐ Remember that the object of the interview is to discover the truth, not to catch people out. Establish whether the employee is prepared to accept that he or she has done something wrong. Then agree the steps which should be taken to remedy the situation.

❐ Give the employee the opportunity to state his or her case, ask questions, present evidence and call witnesses. Listen attentively and be sensitive to silence as this can be a constructive way of encouraging the employee to be more forthcoming. If it is not practical for witnesses to attend, consider proceeding if it is clear that their evidence will not affect the substance of the complaint.

There should then be time for general *questions* and *discussion*. Use this stage to establish all the facts. Adjourn the interview if further investigation is necessary or if requested to do so by the employee's representative.

- [ ] Ask the employee if he or she has any explanation for the misconduct or failure to improve or if there are any special circumstances to be taken into account.

- [ ] If it becomes clear during this stage that the employee has provided an adequate explanation or there is no real evidence to support the allegation, stop the proceedings.

- [ ] Keep the approach formal and polite but encourage the employee to talk freely with a view to establishing all the facts. A properly conducted disciplinary interview should be a two-way process. Use questions to clarify all the issues and to check that what has been said is understood. Ask open-ended questions to get the broad picture. Ask precise, closed questions requiring a yes/no answer only when specific information is needed.

- [ ] Try not to get involved in arguments and do not make personal or humiliating remarks. Avoid physical contact or gestures which the employee might regard as threatening.

After the general questions and discussion, *summarise* the main points concerning the offence, the main points raised by the employee and any matters that need to be checked. This will ensure that nothing has been missed and will help demonstrate to the employee that he or she has been given a fair hearing.

It is generally good practice to *adjourn* the meeting before a decision is taken about a disciplinary penalty. This allows proper consideration of all the matters raised. This is a chance to carry out any further checking that is necessary and come to a clear view about what took place. Where the facts are in dispute consider which version is the most probable. If new facts emerge, consider whether the disciplinary interview needs to be reconvened.

Problems

Not every disciplinary interview goes smoothly. Where problems are expected it is particularly important to ensure, wherever possible, that a second member of management and, where requested, an employee representative are present. If the employee becomes emotionally distressed during the interview, allow time for the employee to become composed before continuing. The issues however cannot be avoided. If the employee continues to be so distressed that the interview cannot continue, it should be adjourned and resumed at a later date.

During the interview a certain number of emotions may surface. This can be no bad thing and may be helpful in finding out and understanding precisely what happened. However, if misconduct or gross misconduct such as abusive language or threatened physical violence takes place, the interview should be adjourned and reconvened at a later date when this offence can be considered as well. Consider suspending the employee with pay to allow time for him or her to calm down and to allow a full investigation.

SEE	ALSO

Section 2: Communications, page 81; *Counselling and listening*, page 88; *Employment legislation*, page 99

Discipline

658.3 ACC Torrington, D, *Face to face in management*, Prentice-Hall, 1982.

658.314   ACAS, *Discipline at work*, ACAS, 1987.

Discrimination and equality

Discrimination can be either direct of indirect. In recent years legislation has had a considerable effect on employment policies and practice. It is unlawful for an employer to discriminate against an employee for reasons of race, sex or marital status or disability in any of the following areas:

❑ recruitment;

❑ appointing a candidate;

❑ the terms on which the job is offered;

❑ promotion, transfer to a better job or training;

❑ fringe benefits offered by an employer;

❑ imposing short-time working, laying off, dismissal and redundancy.

Sex discrimination occurs when a person of one sex is treated less favourably than someone of the opposite sex. There has been a large increase in working women in recent years, and women currently form over 40% of the national workforce. The vast majority are employed in poorly paid, low level jobs in the clerical and service industries. Because women tend to bear the main burden of domestic responsibilities, they are often unable to accept training, transfer and promotion. In Britain, despite legislation on equality, women still suffer from inequality in employment.

Racial discrimination occurs when a person of one race is treated less favourably than someone of another race. Many racial minority groups live in parts of Britain where there are acute housing and educational problems and high rates of unemployment. Despite social programmes and legislation, a person from a racial minority group is far more likely to be unemployed or in low level, poorly paid work with little chance of promotion or training.

In addition to sex and racial discrimination, employers must also avoid discriminating against disabled people. Although there is no direct legislation in the UK to protect job applicants against age discrimination, employers need to prove that they have acted responsibly when selecting applicants.

Equality means ensuring the same opportunities are available to everyone. Inequality results in some people being treated less favourably than others. There will always be some inequalities at work which cannot be avoided. However, it is essential that there is a legally sound justification for them. The following checklist will help you find out if the law has been broken:

1. What are the facts? Just receiving a complaint does not necessarily give you all the facts of the case, so find out everything.

2. Find out who has suffered from differential treatment.

3. Find out what disadvantage has occurred as a result of any differential treatment.

4. Identify what legal justification exists for any unfavourable treatment.

Women and racial minority groups are the most disadvantaged groups in the workplace. Many employers claim to operate *equal opportunities* policies. The *Commission for Racial Equality* was established to work towards the elimination of racial discrimination and to promote equality of opportunity.

The problem with inequality in the work place is that it usually creates problems with morale, motivation and relationships between members of the work team. It can affect productivity and efficiency through absenteeism, wastage or the under-utilisation of workers' abilities. Legal action against an organisation can also affect its standing with its stakeholders.

 SEE ALSO — *Section 2: Employment legislation*, page 99.

Discrimination and equality

344.01133 Bourn, C, *The law of discrimination and equal pay*, Sweet & Maxwell, 1989.

344.01133 Palmer, C, *Sex and race discrimination in employment*, Legal Action Group, 1987

658.3128 EOC, *Code of practice*, HMSO, 1985. (Pamphlet)

Employment legislation

The *Data Protection Act 1984* set up a data protection register. Employers (and other data users) are required to register details of computerised information held. Individuals are entitled to be given details of certain personal data held on them within 40 days of requesting it. Compensation can be claimed for distress caused by disclosure of such information to others, although an employee can authorise his or her employer to make such disclosure. (See Data Protection Legislation, page 89).

The *Disabled Persons (Employment) Acts 1944 and 1958* contains the main legislation making it unlawful to discriminate against disabled people.

Those who work under a contract *of* service are employees. Those who enter a contract *for* service are self-employed. Only the former are covered by the *Employment Protection (Consolidation) Act 1978* which contains most of an employee's statutory rights.

Most employees sign a written *contract of employment* to show their agreement with the terms of their employment. However, a contract of employment can be either written or verbal, apart from certain seamen and apprentices who must be given written terms. The terms and conditions of the contract of employment are often both express and implied. The express terms and conditions may be contained in the letter of appointment, rule books and collective agreements, and information given at the interview, whilst the implied terms and conditions may emanate from common law and statute.

The *duties of an employer* are:

❑ to pay wages (if the amount is not fixed, the employer must pay a reasonable amount);

❑ to provide work (but only for those who are paid by results, for example salesmen on commission);

❑ to take reasonable care of the employee by providing safe working conditions;

❑ to indemnify the employee where he or she necessarily incurs expenses and liabilities in the performance of his or her duties;

❑ to treat the employee with courtesy.

The *duties of an employee* are:

☐ to render a personal service and be willing and able to do so;

☐ to take reasonable care in the performance of his or her duties;

☐ to obey reasonable and lawful instructions from the employer;

☐ to act in good faith towards the employer, for example, not to work for two employers at the same time;

☐ not to impede the employer's duties;

☐ to maintain secrecy regarding information obtained while employed, providing he or she is told it is secret;

☐ not to use position to gain benefits for him or herself.

Under the *Employment (Consolidation) Act 1978* employers are required to provide a written statement to the employee of specified particulars of employment. These particulars must include:

☐ the scale of remuneration or the method of calculating remuneration (piece rates, over-time rates etc);

☐ the intervals at which remuneration is paid (weekly, monthly etc);

☐ the hours of work;

☐ holiday entitlement, holiday pay, sickness arrangements and sick pay, pension arrangements;

☐ the length of notice to be given by both parties;

☐ the title of the job the employee is employed to do;

☐ the disciplinary rules which apply to the employee or reference to a reasonably accessible document, such as a company handbook, which specifies the disciplinary rules and procedures;

☐ the grievance procedure applicable to the employee.

Some employers also include mobility clauses, details on the use of a company car, payment of expenses for petrol, mileage and other forms of travel, etc.

If any particulars of employment which are required to be in writing are altered, written notification must be given to the employee within one month of the change. A contract of employment can only be changed if both parties agree to the changes. For example, if wages paid to an employee were unilaterally reduced from £200 to £150 per week, it is quite likely that the employee would not agree to the change. If the employee carried on working and accepted the payment of £150 each week over a long period of time, it might be demonstrated that the employee had agreed to the change in the contract.

The *Equal Pay Act 1970* requires an employer to treat men and women equally in terms of pay and conditions. To claim equal pay the employee, usually a woman, must show that he or she is doing the same work or broadly similar to a person of the opposite sex. The job must be rated by a job evaluation scheme as having the same value as that of a job done by a person of the opposite sex. The comparison may be made with a job done in the same department or in another in the same firm.

The Act covers collective agreements and employers' pay structures if they contain any provisions which only apply to one sex. It covers all matters included in the contract of employment including hours of work, basic pay, including overtime, shift allowance, night work premium, bonuses, sick pay, holiday entitlement and terms of notice; fringe benefits such as luncheon vouchers, health and medical insurance.

Under the *Health and Safety at Work Act 1974* every employer has a duty to ensure, so far as is reasonably practicable, the health, safety and welfare of employees at work. In general the employer's duties include:

- making the workplace safe and without risks to health;
- keeping dust, fumes and noise under control;
- ensuring plant and machinery are safe and that safe systems of work are set and followed;
- ensuring articles and substances are moved, stored and used safely;
- providing adequate welfare facilities;
- giving employees information, instruction, training and supervision necessary for their health and safety.

In addition the employer must:

- draw up a health and safety policy statement if there are five or more employees, including the health and safety organisation arrangements in force, and bring it to the attention of the employees;
- provide free any protective clothing or equipment specifically required by health and safety law;
- report certain injuries, diseases and dangerous occurrences to the enforcing authority;
- provide adequate first aid facilities;
- consult a safety representative, if one is appointed by a recognised trade union, about matters affecting employees health and safety;
- set up a safety committee if asked in writing by two or more safety representatives.

Employers also have a duty to take precautions against fire, provide adequate means of escape and means for fighting fire. In many workplaces employers may have other specific duties. For example:

- to take adequate precautions against explosions of flammable dust or gas when welding and soldering containers which have held an explosive or flammable substance;
- to maintain a workroom temperature of at least 16°C after the first hour of work where employees do most of their work sitting down;
- to keep the workplace clean;
- to provide, maintain and keep clean washing and toilet facilities and accommodation for clothing and to supply drinking water;
- to see that workrooms are not overcrowded and that they are well ventilated and lit;
- to ensure that floors, steps, stairs, ladders, passages and gangways are well constructed and maintained, and not obstructed;
- to take special precautions before allowing employees to enter and work in a confined space;
- to ensure that employees do not have to lift, carry or move any load so heavy that it is likely to injure them;
- to guard securely all dangerous parts of machines;
- to see that employees, especially young people, are properly trained or under adequate supervision before using dangerous machines;

- ❑ to ensure that lifting equipment and steam boilers, steam receivers and air receivers are well constructed, well maintained and examined at specified intervals;
- ❑ to give employees suitable eye protection or protective equipment for certain jobs;
- ❑ to take proper precautions to prevent employees being exposed to substances which may damage their health;
- ❑ to take precautions against danger from electrical equipment and radiation.

Employees' duties include:

- ❑ taking reasonable care of their own health and safety and that of others who may be affected by what they do or do not do;
- ❑ co-operating with the employer on health and safety;
- ❑ not interfering with or misusing anything provided for their health, safety and welfare.

Those protected by the Act include:

- ❑ employees including casual workers, part-time workers, trainees and subcontractors;
- ❑ tenants and lessees using the premises and/or equipment;
- ❑ visitors such as customers and contractors;
- ❑ neighbours and members of the public;
- ❑ customers using the products and/or services.

Other related legislation includes:

> *Factories Act 1961*
>
> *Mines and Quarries Act 1954*
>
> *Offices, Shops and Railway Premises Act 1963*
>
> *Nuclear Installations Act 1965*
>
> *Agriculture (Safety, Health and Welfare Provisions) Act 1956*
>
> *Fire Precautions Act 1971.*

The *Race Relations Act 1976* makes it unlawful to discriminate on the grounds of race.

The *Sex Discrimination Act 1975* makes it unlawful for employers to discriminate on the grounds of sex or marital status. Exceptions are:

- ❑ employment in a private household;
- ❑ employment in a small firm employing five or less people;
- ❑ employment mainly or wholly outside Great Britain (Northern Ireland has its own sex discrimination law);
- ❑ employment with a church which has a sex bar for religious reasons;
- ❑ retirement ages;
- ❑ employment of men in midwifery;
- ❑ employment of women in active underground mines;
- ❑ employment in the armed services;
- ❑ jobs where sex is a genuine occupational qualification;
- ❑ discrimination which is necessary to comply with an Act of Parliament passed before the Sex Discrimination Act or regulations made under an Act.

Employees' rights to time off work

Perform public duties [1]

- Reasonable[3] time off must be given for the following public positions: Magistrates, members of local authority, education, health and water authority.

- Each case is decided separately.

Notice of redundancy [2]

- To qualify, employee must be employed for not less than 2 years when dismissal takes effect. Time must be given off for search of alternative work/ training.

Carry out duties of safety representatives

- Time off with pay must be given for them to carry out their duties and undergo reasonable training.

- A Code of Practice by the Health and Safety Commission is available to give practical guidance for employer and employee.

Receive antenatal care

- Reasonable[3] paid time off must be given to expectant mothers. She must have an appointment and a letter to confirm the pregnancy and appointment.

- *All* part time employees are entitled to this.

Employees' rights to time off work

Carry out union activities

- Must be an official of a union recognised by employer for purpose of collective bargaining.

- Time, purpose, occasion and conditions relating to time off, are those that have regard to the Code of Practise issued by ACAS.

- Officials may have time off to meet with workers in negotiation with their employers provided those employees are associated with the officials own employees.

- To qualify for paid time off, duties/actions must relate to industrial relations between staff and employer. This does not include union meetings relating to legislation against the industry.

Participate in union activities

- Any member of a recognised union can have unpaid time off during working hours if it complies with arrangements agreed or consented by employer.

- If the above agreed, and the employee dismissed, dismissal automatically unfair. If a tribunal finds time ought to have been given when it was not and dismissal occurs, unfair dismissal provisions apply.

- Time off should be given for union meetings, elections and voting.

- An employer may dismiss an employee for taking time off without permission for planning industrial action. The dismissal would not be unfair.

---

[1] Merchant seamen excepted

[2] Dockworkers excluded

[3] 'Reasonable' is measured by:
     how much time required;
     circumstances of business and effect of absence on its running.

In addition, the protective laws covering the working hours and conditions of manual women workers are not affected by the Sex Discrimination Act.

Section 2: Discrimination and equality, page 98; **Health and safety**, page 109; **Personnel management**, page 154; **Recruitment selection and induction**, page 167.

Employment legislation

344.01   Selwyn, NM, *Law of employment*, 6th ed, Butterworth, 1988.

344.01   Thomas, C, *Employment law*, Hodder, 1984.

344.01   Tolley, *Tolleys employment handbook, 7th ed,* Tolley, 1991.

Groups and teams

Recognition of the existence of *informal groups*, and the impact that they might have on the work situation resulted from the research of Professor Elton Mayo at the Hawthorne plant of the Western Electric Company in Chicago between 1927 and 1932.

Mayo's study of the relationship between productivity and working conditions revealed that people naturally form into informal groups, with special characteristics, and that these groups can be highly influential in terms of production.

One group of women were studied as they worked in differing physical conditions. The changes were discussed with the women before being implemented. It was observed that their productivity increased *regardless* of their conditions, suggesting that they were responding to being consulted, and were enjoying being the subject of so much attention.

The women involved were reported to have:

❏ felt special because management showed an interest in them;

❏ liked the fact that working practices and policies were explained to them;

❏ felt united and had a common purpose;

❏ helped each other and developed friendships outside of work.

This could be said to show that there is a social side of work, which needs to be considered if employee behaviour is to be fully understood.

Other experiments, this time on a group of men, revealed:

❏ They all worked to an unofficial level of output, even though they were on piecework.

❏ They helped each other despite rules to the contrary.

❏ The official supervisor was not regarded as the leader of the group.

This set of experiments shows that not only are there important social factors at work, but also that the informal groups which form have rules, and these rules may be in conflict with the company's objectives.

The Hawthorne experiments revealed some general problems relating to the human relations side of work:

☐ Problems relating to social structure;

☐ Problems of control and communication;

☐ Problems for individuals adjusting to the situation.

A work group is influenced by several factors. These include:

☐ The people in the group (ages, interests)

☐ The type of work done (team work?)

☐ The technology used (judgement needed?)

☐ The way they are paid (salary, piecework, hourly)

Groups might have some of the following characteristics:

☐ They may not take much interest in what they do;

☐ They may demand changes or improvements;

☐ They may take offence easily;

☐ There might be conflict between group members;

☐ There might be conflict between the group and management.

Any of these characteristics might have an influence on the group's output.

The difference between a *group* and a *team* could be said to be that a group is a number of people with shared interests or ties; a team is a small group who work together to achieve the same thing. Effective teams tend to be small, perhaps because people lose sight of how their work relates to others in big groups.

Whenever people are collected together at work, there will be two types of structure. The formal structure as required by the formal organisation, and informal groups formed by the individuals according to their needs. As the Hawthorne experiments showed, these informal groups can be highly influential. The informal groups will be within or across the formal boundaries.

Being a group member gives a person:

☐ Friendship and support;

☐ Self respect due to their group role;

☐ Satisfaction from being with people with similar ideas and attitudes.

Teams and groups are, of course, made up of individuals, and their behaviour at work and anywhere else for that matter, is influenced by psychological factors.

☐ *personality*

☐ *motivation*

☐ *perception*.

They are also influenced by social factors such as school, family, friends and the groups they identify with. These in turn affect values, attitudes and beliefs, which affect behaviour.

Individuals interact within their groups and this results in group behaviours, called *norms* and *roles*.

Group norms are the expected ways of behaving in an informal group.

For example:

❑ The way people talk to each other;

❑ The way people dress;

❑ Attitudes (co-operation or rivalry)

Norms can also affect how much work is done and how any changes will be received. Anyone not conforming to the group norms will find themselves under considerable pressure to do so. This may be subtle, or perhaps even violent.

For example:

❑ making jokes at the expense of the nonconformist;

❑ using criticism or ridicule;

❑ sending him/her to Coventry;

❑ physical violence.

Group members are likely to conform because they want to be group members. Often a non-conformer is just left alone and so doesn't get the benefits of being in the group, such as shared problems, jokes, support, a sense of achievement.

Everyone in a group contributes something to it, and each person tends to take on a role. These include a spokesperson, mediator, ideas person, leader. A manager needs to be aware of the roles in his work teams. Sometimes it is easier to identify negative roles (trouble makers!). People may use the group for their own purposes, and these may well be contrary to the company's objectives.

Informal groups:

❑ modify individual's behaviour;

❑ select unofficial leaders;

❑ have group norms;

❑ work for *or* against the company's objectives.

Developing teams from groups

There are said to be four stages in the development of groups:

1. *Forming* – finding out about matters such as 'what do others expect?' 'how do I behave?';

2. *Storming* – conflict, while the sorting out of roles and positions takes place;

3. *Norming* – co-operation develops, and new 'norms' are developed;

4. *Performing* – operating as a team.

Groups are not static as people are changing jobs, equipment, management, all the time. Selection of an official work team by management needs, therefore, to take account of informal groups.

Work teams, once formed, need constant maintenance, otherwise conflicts will occur. For example:

❑ personality clashes;

❑ conflicts due to what is best for the team not necessarily being best for the individual;

❑ conflicts between the demands of domestic and work life.

Conflict may be within groups, or within individuals. Managers need, therefore, to be aware of potential conflict situations and the possible effects of them.

All groups are different, but in general terms the ones that are open and frank will be the ones where conflicts are most easily resolved. Conflicts may be positive or negative.

Negative conflicts get personal, are frequent and intense and drag on.

Conflicts between groups can lead to lack of co-operation, unreasonable attitudes and complacency.

When dealing with conflicts, it might be useful to consider:

❑ Doing nothing and let the group sort the problem out, ie smoothe things over, compromise, both sides lose something;

❑ Take action which allows both sides to win something.

The best performing work teams have strong group cohesion. To encourage this:

❑ Make sure all are involved and informed.

❑ Look at roles; are they adequate?

❑ Give feedback often.

Effective and ineffective work teams

Effective work group	Ineffective work group
Quantifiable factors	*Quantifiable factors*
1. low rate of labour turnover;	1. high rate of labour turnover;
2. low accident rate;	2. high accident rate;
3. low absenteeism;	3. high absenteeism;
4. high output and productivity;	4. low output and productivity;
5. good quality of output;	5. poor quality of work;
6. individual targets are achieved;	6. individual targets are not achieved;
7. there are few stoppages and interruptions to work.	7. much time is wasted due to disruption of work flow;
	8. time is lost due to disagreements between superior and subordinates.

Qualitative factors	Qualitative factors
1. there is a high commitment to the achievement of targets and organisational goals;	1. there is no understanding of organisational goals or the role of the group;
2. there is a clear understanding of the group's work;	2. there is low commitment to targets.
3. there is a clear understanding of the role of each person within the group;	3. there is confusion and uncertainty about the role of each person within the group;
4. there is free and open communication between members of the group and trust between members;	4. there is mistrust between group members and suspicion of the group's leader;
5. there is idea-sharing;	5. there is little idea sharing;
6. the group is good at generating new ideas;	6. the group does not generate any good new ideas;
7. group members try to help each other out by offering constructive criticisms and suggestions;	7. group members make negative and hostile criticisms about each other's work;
8. there is group problem solving which gets to the root causes of the work problem;	8. work problems are dealt with superficially, with attention paid to the symptoms of trouble but not the cause;
9. there is an active interest in work decisions;	9. decisions about work are accepted passively;
10. group members seek a united 'consensus' of opinion;	10. group members hold strongly opposed views;
11. the members of the group want to develop their abilities in their work;	11. group members find work boring and do it reluctantly;
12. the group is sufficiently motivated to be able to carry on working in the absence of its leader.	12 the group needs its leader present to get work done.

Teamwork is often associated with *morale*, but the two terms do not mean the same thing. Morale refers to the attitudes of employees, whereas teamwork implies co-ordination and activities achieved by a closely knit group of employees. Certainly, good morale is helpful in achieving teamwork, but it is possible that teamwork can be high and yet morale be low. Such a situation might exist in times when jobs are scarce and when the employees will tolerate close, authoritarian supervision for fear of losing their jobs. Conversely, good teamwork may be absent when morale is high. For example, employees might prefer individual effort and therefore might find their satisfaction in individual performance rather than group performance.

Most supervisors generally believe that *high morale* will be accompanied by *high productivity*. Much research has been done in this area. Although there are some contradictions in the research results, there is substantial evidence to suggest that in the long run high-producing employees do tend to have high morale. That is to say, highly motivated, self-disciplined groups of employees tend to do a more satisfactory job than those from whom the supervisor tries to force such performance. Aside from the fact that higher morale tends to be related to higher long-run productivity, a high level of morale also tends to make work more pleasant for the members of a department, including the supervisor. Where pleasant attitudes exist, better productivity is more likely to occur.

SEE ALSO

Section 2: Leadership, page 119; **Management theories**, page 132; **Motivation**, page 135; **Responsibility**, page 179.

Groups/teams

Teambuilding. *Personnel Management Factsheet No. 34.*

302.3   Douglas, T, *Groups*, Tavistock, 1983.

302.3   Johnson, DW, *Joining together, 2nd ed,* Prentice-Hall, 1982.

302.3   Sallis, E, *People in organisations, 2nd ed,* Macmillan, 1990.

658.402 Adair, J, *Effective teambuilding*, Pan, 1987.

Health and safety

Supervisor's duties

A supervisor should ensure he or she is:

- ❏ familiar with company safety policy;
- ❏ providing adequate employee training and is aware of work-place hazards;
- ❏ aware of first aid and fire precautions;
- ❏ providing adequate supervision;
- ❏ ensuring safety rules are observed;
- ❏ making frequent inspection of machinery and equipment;
- ❏ reporting defects and rectifying them promptly;
- ❏ maintaining house-keeping;
- ❏ regularly reviewing safe working practices;
- ❏ investigating accidents and incidents;
- ❏ making recommendations for prevention of accidents.

Operator's checklist

Check every time that ...

- ❏ you know how to stop the machine;
- ❏ guards are working properly;
- ❏ materials are clear of working parts of the machine;
- ❏ the area around the machine is clean, tidy and free from obstruction;
- ❏ you advise your supervisor if machine is not working properly;
- ❏ you are wearing appropriate protective clothing and equipment.

> *Never ...*
>
> ❏ use a machine unless you are authorised and trained;
>
> ❏ use a machine which has a danger sign;
>
> ❏ wear clothing etc which could get caught in machines;
>
> ❏ distract people operating machinery.
>
> *But always ...*
>
> ❏ switch off and unplug machines before cleaning.

Reporting accidents and disease

All injuries should be reported to management and recorded in the *Accident Book*. Some injuries, diseases and dangerous occurrences must also be reported to your Inspector.

RIDDO Regulations 1985 (Reporting of Injuries, Diseases and Dangerous Occurrences) apply to all employers and the self-employed, and cover everyone at work and *require you to*

❏ report immediately by telephone if as a result of (or in connection with your work):

1) someone dies, receives a major injury, or is seriously affected by, for example, electric shock or poisoning;

2) there is a dangerous occurrence (or near miss);

❏ send a written report to:

1) confirm a telephone report of the incident;

2) notify any occurrence which stops someone doing their job for more than three days;

3) report certain diseases suffered by workers;

4) report certain events involving flammable gas in domestic and other premises;

5) have copies of the report form ready for use.

First aid

Immediate and proper examination and treatment of injuries may save life.

Therefore all organisations must:

❏ *have* an appropriate level of first aid treatment available;

❏ *appoint* someone to take charge in an emergency;

❏ *provide*, and keep clean, a first aid box containing only first aid material;

❏ *display* notices giving the locations of first aid equipment and the name and location of the appointed person or first aider;

❏ *re-assess* the Health and Safety requirements as the Organisation grows in size;

❏ *have* copies of the report form ready for use.

Noise

❏ Noisy machines/processes must be identified by warning signs.

❏ Only those employees involved in the process need work there.

❏ All employees must be warned of the dangers of excessive noise and use hearing protectors provided by management, which must give adequate protection for the level and type of noise.

❏ The noise level must be monitored so that the regulations regarding how long people can stay within the noisy area are identified and employees do not exceed the 90 decibel (A) dose average over a day.

COSHH – Care of Substances Hazardous to Health

This is the latest regulation to be passed by the Government and relates to all substances both used in the process and resulting from the process (i.e. chemical reactions), that can affect the health of an employee in their place of work.

The requirements for safety are that:

❏ All employees must be aware of the regulations with regard to the safe handling and storage of substances that are hazardous to health.

❏ Protective clothing and equipment must be provided and worn where a potential hazard is identified.

❏ Where there is uncertainty with regard to the contents of a substance, the labelling on the package should be read.

❏ Where doubt still occurs the manufacturer's recommendations for storage and use should be sought.

Controlling an incident

❏ Plan for reasonably foreseeable incidents;

❏ Plan for what might go wrong ...

accidents? – explosion? – flood? – poisoning? – electrocution? – fire? – release of radioactivity? – broken bones? – chemical spills?

❏ Tell people:

    ❏ what might happen and how the alarm will be raised;

    ❏ what to do, including how to call the emergency services;

    ❏ where to go to reach safety or get rescue equipment;

    ❏ who will control the incident, the names of other key people such as the first aiders;

    ❏ essential actions such as emergency plan shut down or making processes safe.

Supervisor's checklist

❑ keep any access ways for emergency services and all escape routes clear;

❑ clearly label important items like shut off valves, electrical isolators and fire fighting equipment;

❑ make sure emergency plans cover night shift working, weekends and (possibly) times when the premises are closed, eg holidays;

❑ train everyone in emergency procedures, eg fire drills, and don't forget the special needs of disabled people;

❑ test emergency equipment regularly – disposable eyewash bottles should not have been opened and used, for example;

❑ assist the emergency services by clearly making your premises from the road. Consider drawing up a simple plan marked with the location of hazardous items;

❑ have a system to account for staff and visitors in the event of an evacuation.

Questions to ask yourself

Ask yourself some questions about the jobs – regular, irregular and the 'one-offs' – in your firm:

❐ who is in charge of the job?

❐ do their responsibilities overlap with those of anyone else?

❐ is there anything which is not someone's responsibility?

❐ are there any established safe ways of doing the job?

❐ are there any relevant Codes of Practice or Guidance Notes?

❐ are there safe working procedures laid down for the job?

❐ what protective clothing or equipment is necessary?

❐ have people been instructed in its use and limitations?

❐ has anyone assessed whether equipment, tools or machines have the capacity for the job?

❐ what will be the consequences if you are wrong?

❐ how will the person in charge deal with any problem?

❐ if things do go wrong, would your people know what to do?

Could emergency services get to the site?

❐ if the job cannot be finished today can it be left in a safe state? Are clear instructions available for the next shift?

❐ are your production people aware of what maintenance staff are doing, and vice versa?

❐ is there a system for checking that jobs are done safely in the way intended?

Enforcing the law

Health and safety laws relating to your organisation will be enforced by an inspector either from HSE (Health and Safety Executive) eg a factory inspector or an agricultural inspector or from your local council (usually an environmental health officer).

Inspectors may visit workplaces without notice but you are entitled to see their identification before they come in. They may want to investigate an accident or complaint, or examine the safety, health and welfare aspects of your business.

They have the right to talk to employees and safety representatives, take photographs and samples and even, in certain cases, to impound dangerous equipment. They are entitled to co-operation and answers to questions.

If there is a problem, they may issue a formal notice requiring improvements, or, where serious danger exists, one which prohibits the use of a process or equipment. If you receive an Improvement or Prohibition Notice you may appeal to an Industrial Tribunal.

Inspectors have powers to prosecute a firm (or an individual) for breaking health and safety laws.

 SEE | ALSO

Section 2: Employment legislation, page 99; *Responsibility*, page 179.

Health and safety at work

363.11   Goodman, MJ, *Health and safety at work*, Sweet & Maxwell, 1988.

363.11   Ridley, JR, *Safety at work, 2nd ed*, Butterworth, 1986.

363.11   Tolley, *Tolleys health and safety at work handbook, 3rd ed,* Tolley, 1990.

Job analysis

In personnel management it is often necessary to obtain and record a description of a job. The description must then be kept up to date to take account of changes in organisation or technology. Job analysis is the process by which a description of a job is compiled.

There are many difficulties in job analysis, some practical, some concerned with the attitudes of employees. The following are the most common methods used:

1. *Direct observation* – this is always necessary, but has several drawbacks:

    ❏   a skilled worker can make his job look easy;

    ❏   an experienced worker can make his job look difficult;

    ❏   mental processes are not revealed;

    ❏   some manual work is too fast or intricate to be observed accurately, unless film is used.

2. *Interview with the job-holder* – this is nearly always necessary but difficulties often occur, largely because the worker may be suspicious of the job analysis. He may decide to exaggerate the importance of the job or occasionally try to make it seem unimportant. The main problems with these interviews are:

    ❏   the worker's attitude may influence his account of the job;

    ❏   he may, even if co-operative, forget some details of the job, and emphasise the most recent events;

    ❏   he may not be able to express himself clearly.

3. *Interview with the supervisor* – this again is an inevitable occurrence, although its value varies for the following reasons:

   ❏ supervisors are surprisingly often out of touch with the details of the job.

   ❏ they frequently have never done the job themselves.

   ❏ they sometimes allow their description of the job to be influenced by their opinion of the job-holder.

   ❏ they may exaggerate the duties and responsibilities of the job in order to increase their own importance.

4. *Materials of work* – a study of the tools, working materials, machines, documents, communication media, etc., frequently provides a useful check on information obtained in other ways, and may suggest questions to be asked.

5. *Previous studies* – eg work study records, training manuals and accident reports are sometimes available and can be brought up to date or added to other information.

6. *Do-it-yourself* – in some jobs it is feasible for the analyst to spend some time actually performing the work himself.

7. *Questionnaires* are sometimes used, but are highly unreliable. The job-holder is asked to fill in answers to written questions about his job, but he may be suspicious of the questionnaire, may not understand the questions, and feel unduly restricted by them.

8. *Work diaries* are sometimes used, chiefly for managers and clerical workers. The job-holder records his activities in detail throughout the day over a period of about a month. The diary is then analysed to obtain a list of duties and their frequency. If kept conscientiously and accurately, a work diary can be very helpful.

In order to analyse a job with some degree of accuracy it is obviously necessary to use a combination of several of the above methods, each checking the other.

SEE | **ALSO** **Section 2: *Job design*, page 115; *Job evaluation*, page 117; *Workstudy*, page 202.**

Job analysis

658.306 Boydell, TH, *A guide to job analysis*, BACIE, 1970.

658.306 Pearn, M, *Job analysis: a practical guide for managers*, IPM, 1988.

658.321 McBeath, G, *Salary administration, 4th ed,* Gower, 1989.

Job design

Job design is concerned with maximising the use of employees' abilities, and increasing job satisfaction as a result. There are a number of ways of restructuring jobs in order to increase motivation, productivity and satisfaction: two main approaches are *job enlargement* and *job enrichment*.

Job enlargement

Job enlargement as the name suggests is the attempt to widen a job by increasing the number of operations in which a job holder is involved at the same level. This lengthens the 'cycle time' of repeated operations in the hope of reducing the dullness of the job. Job rotation (switching from one operation to another of the same level) is a form of job enlargement. What it does not achieve is any increase in responsibility.

Example: Volvo at one of its plants in Sweden introduced a modified form of the division of labour to try to overcome problems of over specialisation by some of its workforce. They use teams where groups of workers become responsible for producing a car from start to finish. Volvo has found the output per worker compares favourably with other plants and absenteeism, staff turnover and strikes have all declined whilst quality has improved.

Job enrichment

Job enrichment is the process of extending vertically the responsibilities of the job holder, and may involve the job holder taking on some tasks from above and below in the company hierarchy.

A job may be enriched by:

a) giving greater variety;

b) allowing the employee to decide how to do the job;

c) encouraging the employee to participate in planning and decisions;

d) ensuring the employee gets regular feedback on performance.

Example: A job enrichment program at ICI concerning sales representatives examined efforts to build up a representative's job so that it became more complete. The representatives were no longer required to write reports about every call, but just to pass on any information they thought relevant. They were also given the responsibility for deciding when to call, and were given authority to deal with certain complaints and prices. The result of these changes was an increase in sales of near to 20%.

Job enrichment can apply in some way to virtually any job. Most people will take the chance to enrich their jobs if it is offered, and the result is often increased job satisfaction and reduced costs. Can changes be made to get the benefits of job enrichment?

It might then be worth considering:

❐ will the employees affected take up the chance of enrichment?

❐ will enrichment result in benefits for the company?

Managers often assign the most difficult (and interesting) jobs to their best employees. The others may be left with the dull and routine work. Obviously it is preferable to provide opportunities for all employees. Sometimes this can be done by involving them in work such as committee work, or special one-off tasks.

Job design - what actions can you take?

1. Look at responsibility levels. Can they be increased?
2. Can operations be added to the job so that it is complete?
3. Give feedback on how well staff are doing.
4. Can you provide a challenge?
5. Give opportunities for individual initiatives.
6. Present changes as opportunities.
7. Encourage people to be experts in an activity.
8. Measure the results of any changes made.

Guidelines

It is still fairly rare for jobs to be designed with people in mind rather than production, though in the final analysis this amounts to the same thing. When re-designing jobs, it should be remembered at individual level that:

1. each job should contain enough elements to make it interesting, but not so many that efficiency is reduced or training becomes difficult;
2. tasks should be related and interdependant so that the completion of one leads on to the next;
3. the work cycle should be long enough to allow a rhythm of work;
4. some scope should be given for self checking quality;
5. feedback on performance should be available;
6. there should be enough skill, knowledge, or effort, required to allow the employee to take a pride in his work;
7. the job link with the whole operation should be made clear, so that workers can see the importance of their individual contribution.

For groups

1. Jobs should be designed to allow communication within the group.
2. Job rotation should be encouraged to give variation and equal experience, although later, individuals may choose to specialise.
3. Jobs which have little obvious contribution to the product or service should be grouped with tasks that do, in order to give a sense of purpose.
4. When a number of jobs are linked together they should form a coherent task which makes a clear contribution to the end product. There should also be some scope for setting and checking standards.

SEE ALSO *Section 2: Job analysis*, page 113; *Job evaluation*, page 117.

Job design

658.306 Davis, L, *The design of jobs*, Goodyear, 1979.

658.306 Robertson, IT, *Motivation and job design*, IPM, 1985.

See also

658.3   Armstrong, M, *A handbook of personnel management practice*, Kogan Page, 1977.

Job evaluation

Definition

It is the name given to a set of methods designed to compare jobs systematically with a view to assessing their relative worth.

The job is assessed on a number of key factors in the context of a job hierarchy. This leads to a 'rank order'. The purpose of establishing such a rank order is to enable a rational pay structure to be established according to the position of that job within the rank.

Job evaluation has several key points:

☐ it is concerned with relative positions;

☐ the holder of the job is not under assessment;

☐ the process of job evaluation is performed by a group;

☐ the concepts of logic, fairness and consistency are employed;

☐ it is a subjective procedure;

☐ it only provides a basis upon which decisions can be taken. It does not make the decisions.

The advantage of a job evaluated pay structure is that it provides a firm basis on which to defend the decision to differentiate the wages of different groups of employees. In unionised industries this system allows both unions and management to participate in the drawing up of wage scales.

Methods

1. Non-analytical methods.

    1.1 *Job ranking*

    Non-analytical methods compare whole jobs and then rank them. Each job is given a 'job description' and then these descriptions are ranked in order of importance as perceived by the evaluators. This ranking is then discussed by the committee and a final rank is agreed.

Advantage	this system is simple.
Disadvantage	because it is so subjective it can only be effective in a relatively simple and well-structured organisation.

1.2 *Job grading / job classification*

This method is a complete reversal of the above. The pay/salary structure is pre-determined and the jobs are then classified into their appropriate grade.

Advantage   easy to operate.

Disadvantage   the pay/salary arrangements must be reasonable

it does not allow sufficient distinctions to be made between jobs, especially in complex organisations.

Non-analytical methods are crude and are not suitable for complex organisations. Hence, analytical methods should be used.

2. Analytical methods.

Analytical methods break the job into component parts and allocate a points system which is related to the pay structure.

2.1 *Points rating method*

Points are allocated to job factors:

Skill	Education/training required; experience; initiative and creativity
Responsibility / decision making	Complexity of work; supervision of others
Effort	Mental; physical
Working conditions	Pressures of the job; difficult, dangerous, hazardous conditions.

Other factors taken into consideration are 'is the work manual', 'white collar', 'unionised'. The points are set out in a points rating matrix. The job factors are set up against the conditions of the work.

2.2 *Factor comparison*

This method involves monetary sums being allocated to the factors. It is not in use nowadays.

The *advantages of job evaluation* in management decision making:

❑ it focuses on job content, and provides a defensible basis on which to decide upon pay;

❑ it provides a rational basis for devising or improving grading structures;

❑ it reduces the effects caused by other systems;

❑ it encourages management/employee co-operation with regard to pay settlements.

The *disadvantages of job evaluation*:

❑ it can be costly and time consuming to implement;

❑ it is still subjective;

❑ it is unable to introduce the established grades into the labour market.

Job evaluation can be defined as a management technique in which jobs are compared systematically to assess their relative worth and ranking them on the basis of this assessment which then leads to the setting up of wage/salary scales.

SEE ALSO **Section 2: Job design**, page 115; *Salaries and wages*, page 180.

Job evaluation

658.306   ACAS, *Job evaluation*. (Pamphlet)

658.321   Armstrong, M, *Reward management*, 2nd ed, Kogan Page, 1988.

658.3225   Greenhill, RT, *Performance related pay for the 1990s*, 2nd ed, Director Books, 1990.

Leadership

A *leader* is one who achieves results through people. Leaders are not born. We have potential, but no gift of leadership. The skills mix needed for a good leader depends on many variables, such as the nature of the work, and the group concerned.

All managers are leaders of a sort, but not all leaders are managers. Production orientated organisations tend to want managers first and leaders second.

Leadership theories

There have been many studies of leadership in management, and many different theories about what makes the best leader. An awareness of the various theories can:

❏   make a manager more aware of what style predominates in his or her own industry.

❏   help a manager identify his/her own style;

❏   help distinguish between more effective and less effective styles.

However, changing one's own style is not easy, and managers are still left with the problem of turning theory into practice. In addition, followers can have a considerable influence on the leader. Consider the following questions:

❏   how many followers can you manage?

❏   how well do they work together?

❏   how mature is the leader/follower relationship?

❏   is there a tradition of following in your organisation?

Other variables to consider are:

❏   the source of authority: A manager may have a legal right to manage but it is not a qualification to lead. Influence is merited and gained, not coerced or demanded;

❏   the organisational climate or culture: task power and authority systems, political structure, work mates.

Communication is central to the leadership process but the nature of the work, the size of the work group and the type of people involved are all important.

Theories of leadership can be grouped into categories: we will consider those that fall into the two most relevant categories for modern managers – *contingency* and *style* theories.

Contingency theories

These theories of leadership see the need for the leader to adapt his or her style of management in the light of particular situations. An important example of contingency theory, *Action centred leadership,* was developed in the UK by *Professor John Adair*. It is based on the theory that leadership is more a question of *appropriate behaviour* than of personality or being at the right place at the right time. Adair's model of leadership incorporates concern for task, people and groups, and stresses that effective leadership lies in what the leader *does* to meet the needs of task, group, and individuals.

Analysis of the effective leader – Adair

1. *Achieving the task*

   The efficient leader:

   ❐ is clear in what his task is and understands how it fits into long and short-term objectives of organisation;

   ❐ plans how to accomplish it;

   ❐ defines and provides the resources needed;

   ❐ ensures that each member of the group has clearly defined targets for improving performance;

   ❐ plugs any gaps in the abilities of the group by training and development;

   ❐ constantly evaluates results and monitors progress towards the goals.

2. *Getting the best out of each individual*

   He will see that each person:

   ❐ gets a sense of personal achievement in his/her job;

   ❐ feels he/she is making a worthwhile contribution;

   ❐ if his/her performance is unsatisfactory is told in what way and given help to improve;

   ❐ feels that his/her job challenges him/her and capabilities are matched by responsibilities;

   ❐ receives adequate recognition for his/her achievements.

3. *Keeping high group morale*

   The leader:

   ❐ provides regular opportunities for briefing the group;

   ❐ provides regular opportunities for genuine consultation before reaching decisions affecting them;

   ❐ accords the official representative of the group the facilities he/she needs to be its effective spokesman;

   ❐ ensures that there is a formal and fair grievance procedure understood by all.

Integrated concept of a leader

A person with certain qualities of personality and character, which are *appropriate* to the general situation, and supported by a degree of relevant technical knowledge and experience, who is able to provide the necessary functions to guide a group towards the further realisation of its purpose, while maintaining and building its unity as a team; doing all this in the right ratio or proportion with the contributions of other members of the team.

The functions of leadership – John Adair's action centred leadership

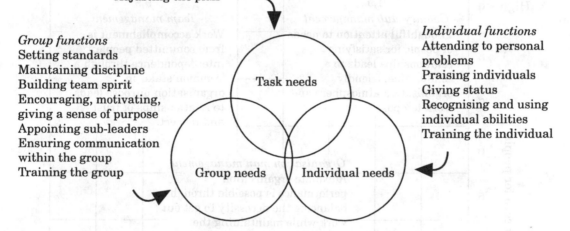

Task functions
Defining the task
Making a plan
Allocating work and resources
Controlling quality and tempo of work
Checking performance against the plan
Adjusting the plan

Group functions
Setting standards
Maintaining discipline
Building team spirit
Encouraging, motivating,
giving a sense of purpose
Appointing sub-leaders
Ensuring communication
within the group
Training the group

Individual functions
Attending to personal
problems
Praising individuals
Giving status
Recognising and using
individual abilities
Training the individual

Task needs

Group needs   Individual needs

Style theories of leadership

These theories focus on leadership as an aspect of behaviour at work, and make distinctions between authoritarian, democratic, etc. ... styles.

The Michigan studies

Although many studies have been made relating to leadership, perhaps the most direct series of studies which focused on employees needs and expectations, supervisory leadership, and productivity, were those carried out by the University of Michigan, whose researchers looked to office employees, rail road workers and factory employees. The studies established that a similar type of supervisory leadership pattern was consistently associated with high productivity and a high degree of job satisfaction. This pattern included:

❏   general supervision rather than close detailed supervision of employees;

❏   more time devoted to supervisory activities than in doing production work;

❏   much attention to planning of work and special tasks;

121

- ❏ a willingness to permit employees to participate in the decision-making process;
- ❏ an approach to the job situation described as being employee centred (that is, showing an interest in the needs and problems of employees as individuals) as well as being interested in high production.

The management grid

The grid is based on the ideas of Robert Blake and Jane Mouton, who suggested that a manager's two main concerns were production and people. If these two dimensions form the axes of a grid, an individual manager's behaviour can be plotted on it. The worst behaviour will score low on both counts (1,1), the best behaviour will score high on both counts (9,9). The object of the training programme based on these ideas is to develop 9,9 managers.

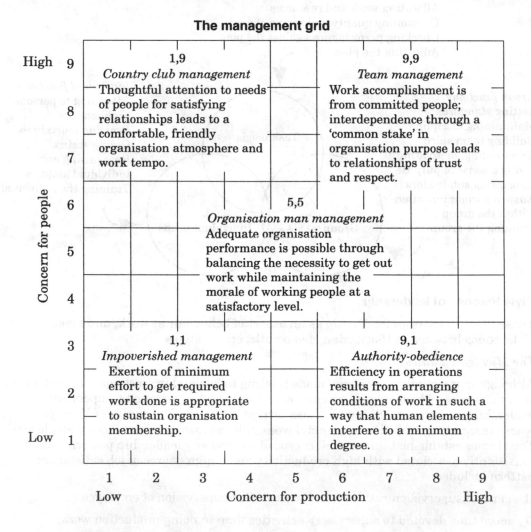

The management grid

1,9
Country club management
Thoughtful attention to needs of people for satisfying relationships leads to a comfortable, friendly organisation atmosphere and work tempo.

9,9
Team management
Work accomplishment is from committed people; interdependence through a 'common stake' in organisation purpose leads to relationships of trust and respect.

5,5
Organisation man management
Adequate organisation performance is possible through balancing the necessity to get out work while maintaining the morale of working people at a satisfactory level.

1,1
Impoverished management
Exertion of minimum effort to get required work done is appropriate to sustain organisation membership.

9,1
Authority-obedience
Efficiency in operations results from arranging conditions of work in such a way that human elements interfere to a minimum degree.

Concern for people — High 9, 8, 7, 6, 5, 4, 3, 2, Low 1

Concern for production — Low 1 2 3 4 5 6 7 8 9 High

Another way of classifying leadership behaviours

Leadership behaviour	Action taken	Underlying beliefs
Tell	Leader identifies the problem, considers alternative solutions and announces the final decision to subordinates for implementation.	Leader feels subordinate participation in the decision is unnecessary, unwarranted or not feasible. Hence no opportunity to participate is provided.
Sell	Leader takes responsibility for identifying the problem and determining the final decision. But rather than simply announcing the decision the leader takes the added step of trying to persuade subordinates to accept the decision.	Leader recognises the potential for subordinate resistance from merely announcing the final decision and therefore seeks to reduce any resistance through persuasion.
Consult	Leader identifies the problem, consults subordinates for possible solutions and then announces the final decision.	Leader recognises the potential value of effectively culling ideas from subordinates and believes such action will increase subordinate's ownership and commitment to the final solution.
Join	Leader defines the problem and then joins subordinates in making the final decision. The leader fully shares decision-making authority with subordinates.	Leader believes subordinates are capable of making high quality decisions and that subordinates want to do the right thing. The leader believes human resources are best utilised when decision-making authority is fully shared.

SEE ALSO

See *Section 2: Authority*, page 75; *Communication*, page 81; *Groups and teams*, page 104; *Management theories*, page 132; *Motivation*, page 135.

Leadership

303.34   Adair, J, *Effective leadership*, Rev ed, Pan, 1988.

303.34   Roberts, W, *Leadership secrets of Attila the Hun*, Bantam, 1989.

658   Massie, JL, *Essentials of management, 4th ed*, Prentice-Hall, 1987.

Learning

When *training* needs have been identified, a decision then has to be made as to how these needs can be satisfied; that is, which methods of training are the most appropriate. Training is commonly classified as 'on the job' and 'off the job'; a summary of the features of some common methods in those categories follows:

'On the job' training methods

Description	Advantages	Disadvantages
On the job instruction	Relevant; develops trainee/supervisor links	Noise, bustle and pressure of workplace
Coaching	Job-related; develops boss/subordinate relationship	Subject to work pressures; may be done piecemeal
Counselling	Employee needs help and boss provides it	Counselling skills have to be developed
Delegation by boss	Increases scope of job; provides greater motivation	Employee may make mistakes or may fail to achieve task
Secondment	Increases experience of employee; creates new interest	Employee may not succeed in new position
Guided projects/action learning	Increases knowledge and skills in work situation, but under guidance	Finding suitable guides and mentors

'Off the job' training methods

Description	Advantages	Disadvantages
a) *In-company* Lectures/talks	Useful for factual information	One-way emphasis; little participation
Group discussions	Useful for generating ideas and solutions	Require adequate leadership
Role-playing exercises	Useful for developing social skills	Require careful organising; giving tactful feedback is not easy
Skills development exercises, eg manual operations, communication skills etc	A safe way to practise key skills	Careful organisation required
b) *External* College courses (long)	Leads to qualification; comprehensive coverage of theory; wide range of teaching methods	Length of training time; not enough practical work
College courses (short)	Supplement in-company training; independent of internal politics	May not meet clients' needs precisely enough
Consultants/other training organisations	Clients' needs given high priority; fills gaps in company provision; good range of teaching methods	Can be expensive; may rely heavily on 'packages'.

Whilst off the job training tends to be done in groups, on the job training is often done on a one-to-one basis. Research seems to indicate that each of us has a *learning style* and that the four main types of style classify us as *reflectors, theorists, pragmatists*, or *activists*.

The learning styles

Reflectors: People who learn through watching things and thinking them over. They enjoy the opportunities to mull over their ideas in an unhurried way and to produce carefully thought out conclusions. They learn little when they are forced into activities at short notice with inadequate information. They do not enjoy having to take short cuts to a solution.

Strengths	Weaknesses
Careful	Slow to make up their minds
Thoughtful	Too cautious
Methodical	They are not very forthcoming.

Theorists: Like to understand the concepts behind what they are learning and to explore the implications. They dislike unstructured situations where emotions and feelings run high.

Strengths	Weaknesses
Disciplined approach	Intolerant of anything subjective or intuitive
Rational	
Objective	

Pragmatists: Learn best when they can link the content of their learning to a real problem. They dislike theoretical ideas but like ideas leading to practical outcomes.

Strengths	Weaknesses
Businesslike	Tend to reject that which does not have an obvious application
Get straight to the point	
Practical	Not very interested in theory
Down to earth	
Realistic	

Activists: Value the opportunity to take an active part in their learning. They like high profile activities such as giving talks.

Strengths	Weaknesses
Keen to try out new ideas	Act without thinking
Flexible	Take unnecessary risks
Open-minded	Get bored with the implementation.

Determining a person's learning style can be done by means of a 'learning style' inventory, where on the basis of ranking words in priority, scores are compiled and these scores when plotted on an axis indicate the preferred learning style (See *Section 3, Unit 7,* page 267, for *learning style inventory*). The points of the axis each represent one of the four styles. The result of a person plotting their 'learning inventory' score on the axis will indicate which style or styles are most dominant for them. An equal distribution over the four styles shows the person is equally at home with all the styles (see over).

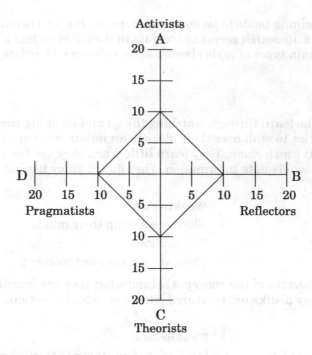

How to choose learning activities to suit your style

Just as some individuals have preference for one learning style, so, some learning activities are strongly geared to one style of learning. Where the individual's preference and the activity to which he is exposed involve the same style, he is likely to learn. If there is a mismatch, he is much less likely to learn.

If you have a preference for the *reflector style* you will learn best from activities where:

❑ you are allowed or encouraged to watch/think/chew over activities.

❑ you are able to stand back from events and listen/observe, eg observing a group at work, taking a back seat in a meeting, watching a film or CCTV;

❑ you are allowed to think before acting, to assimilate before commenting ie time to prepare, a chance to read in advance a brief giving background data;

❑ you can carry out some painstaking research, eg. investigate, assemble information, probe to get to the bottom of things;

❑ you have the opportunity to review what has happened, what you have learned;

❑ you are asked to produce carefully considered analyses and reports;

❑ you are helped to exchange views with other people without danger, eg by prior agreement, within a structured learning experience;

❑ you can reach a decision in your own time without pressure and tight deadlines;

If you have a preference for the *theorist* style you will learn best from activities where:

❑ what is being offered is part of a system, model, concept, theory;

❑ you have time to explore methodically the associations and inter-relationships between ideas, events and situations;

❑ you have the chance to question and probe the basic methodology, assumptions or logic behind something eg by taking part in a question and answer session, by checking a paper for inconsistencies;

- you are intellectually stretched eg by analysing a complex situation, being tested in a tutorial session, by teaching high calibre people who ask searching questions;

- you are in structured situations with a clear purpose;

- you can listen to or read about ideas and concepts that emphasise rationality or logic and are well-argued/elegant/watertight;

- you can analyse and then generalise the reasons for success or failure;

- you are offered interesting ideas and concepts even though they are not immediately relevant;

- you are required to understanding and participate in complex situations.

If you have a preference for the *pragmatist* style you will learn best from activities where:

- there is an obvious link between the subject matter and a problem or opportunity on the job;

- you are shown techniques for doing things with obvious practical advantages eg. how to save time, how to make a good first impression, how to deal with awkward people;

- you have the chance to try out and practice techniques with coaching/feedback from a credible expert, ie someone who is successful and can do the techniques themselves;

- you are exposed to a model you can emulate eg. a respected boss, a demonstration from someone with a proven track record, lots of examples/anecdotes, a film showing how it is done;

- you are given techniques currently applicable to your own jobs;

- you are given immediate opportunities to implement what you have learned;

- there is a high face validity in the learning activity ie. good simulation, 'real' problems;

- you can concentrate on practical issues, eg drawing up action plans with an obvious end product, suggesting short cuts, giving tips.

If you have a preference for the *activist style* you will learn best from activities where:

- there are new experiences/problems/opportunities from which to learn;

- you can engross yourself in short 'here and now' activities such as business games, competitive teamwork tasks, role-playing exercises;

- there is excitement/drama/crisis and things chop and change with a range of diverse activities to tackle;

- you have a lot of the limelight/high visibility eg. you can 'chair' meetings, lead discussions, give presentations;

- you are allowed to generate ideas without constraints of policy or structure or feasibility;

- you are thrown in at the deep end with a task you think is difficult eg when set a challenge with inadequate resources and adverse conditions;

❑ you are involved with other people, eg bouncing ideas off them, solving problems as part of a team.

❑ it is appropriate to 'have a go';

 SEE ALSO **Section 2: Attitude**, page 73.

Learning

153.15   Bower, GH, *Theories of learning, 5th ed,* Prentice-Hall, 1981.

153.15 ACC, Claxton, G, *Live and learn,* Open University Press, 1988.

153.15 ACC, Thomas, LF, *Self-organised learning,* RKP, 1985.

658.3124, Wood, S, *Continuous development,* IPM, 1988.

Management by objectives

Management by objectives (MBO) is a system which aims to improve performance and motivate, assess and train the workforce by integrating their personal goals with the objectives of the organisation. Training is usually given to explain to employees how self-fulfilment can be achieved and job satisfaction increased when the individual is involved with his or her work and participates in decision-making. Without the correct attitude, management by objectives might merely become just another method of control.

The system involves setting objectives at every level of management. It is essentially a joint setting of objectives and a joint review of their achievement or non-achievement by a manager and his or her subordinate. The steps are as follows:

1. clarification and review of the organisation's objectives by the senior management to ensure that all participants understand the system;

2. this is repeated for the departmental objectives to ensure that they are consistent with the organisation's objectives;

3. a manager (M), already included in MBO as a subordinate, interviews a subordinate (S) to discuss the purpose of S's job, the key results he or she must achieve and the performance standards he or she should attempt to achieve;

4. M and S jointly agree on the programme S should try to follow to ensure that he or she meets the objectives agreed to;

5. M arranges for control information to be available so that S's performance can be compared with his or her objectives;

6. at the end of the review period (3-12 months), M and S meet again to discuss the extent to which S has met his or her objectives so far as is possible in a problem-solving manner;

7. M advises S on how to build on his or her strengths and overcome any weaknesses;

8. key results, performance standards and an action plan are agreed for the forthcoming period. From his or her job specification, S is encouraged to pick out the tasks that are essential to the job. M and S agree on objectives or performance

standards which are challenging but not impossible and can be expressed in quantitative terms. M encourages S to suggest his or her own objectives as far as possible, but must not sanction those which are too easily achieved or are inconsistent with the organisation's objectives;

The *advantages* of MBO are:

❐ increased efficiency because employees are clear about their objectives;

❐ improved motivation because of participation in setting objectives;

❐ improved quality because of problem-solving interviews;

❐ better identification of training needs;

❐ results of training easier to assess; known standards to achieve;

❐ analysis is useful training;

❐ organisational shortcomings may be revealed;

❐ improved communications between individual managers and their subordinates;

❐ subordinates judged on performance against set objectives, rather than on personal characteristic;

❐ motivation, appraisal and training become the concern of line management instead of personnel and training specialists.

The *disadvantages* of MBO are:

❐ the problem-solving approach may not work if there has been an authoritarian style of management and objectives may be assigned rather than agreed;

❐ the system cannot work if the organisation is badly organised and directed;

❐ the system requires the enthusiasm and support of the participants as it is complicated and lengthy;

❐ it is difficult to set new objectives every year;

❐ MBO is not appropriate when jobs are structured because the employees have little control over their objectives or performance;

❐ it is not practical when the organisation cannot plan very far ahead;

❐ if a manager is less technically qualified than the subordinates, he or she may accept standards which are too easily attained;

❐ the subordinate may place too much emphasis on the measurable parts of the job and ignore the creative or innovative parts;

❐ MBO may lead to rivalry between subordinates rather than co-operation;

❐ subordinates may fail to control their objectives as a result of factors outside their control;

❐ subordinates may achieve their objectives using dubious methods;

❐ MBO encourages concentration on the short-term rather than on the long-term;

❐ MBO can be regarded by subordinates as another method of control by managers. Objectives, although supposedly set jointly, are imposed and the performance review may become inquisitorial and accusatory.

Sometimes *positive reinforcement* is combined with MBO objective-setting to increase motivation. Techniques include executives sending letters to supervisors thanking them for their contribution. The use of carefully planned reinforcement for motivational purposes has proved effective in modifying behaviour.

Section 2: Control, page 86; *Management qualities and activities*, page 130; *Management theories*, page 132; *Organisational objectives and policies*, page 142.

Management by objectives

658.302 Haimann/Hilbert, *Supervision, Concepts and practices of management*, 4th ed, South Western Publishing.

Reddin, WJ, *Effective MBO*, Pitman

Management qualities and activities

Most discussions about *management* start off with a search for the best definition for the word. In its broadest sense management is the running of an organisation, which in economic theory is sometimes regarded as a factor of production with land, labour and capital. It is carried out by the owner(s) of the business or by managers who are responsible to them. In the case of limited companies, the owners are the shareholders.

Successful management requires two main *qualities*:

❏ *Organisational skill* This involves the principles and techniques of management which are taught at colleges and business schools.

❏ *Entrepreneurial ability* This is the ability to recognise and make use of opportunities, predict market needs and trends, and achieve goals through sustained drive, skilful negotiation and argument. Entrepreneurial ability is not taught as easily as the organisational skills, but inherent ability can be developed given the right encouragement.

Management involves the following *activities*:

❏ *planning*, which is concerned with the future and involves consideration of people as well as other resources;

❏ *controlling*, which is concerned with making sure that plans are met and corrective action taken if necessary;

❏ *organising*, which is concerned not only with getting things done, but with getting them done by the right people at the right time;

❏ *motivating*, which is concerned with getting the best out of people and requires attention to the needs of the workforce as well as work needs.

In addition, questions of authority, leadership, appraisal, training, delegation, decision-making, objective-setting and many other issues can be part of a manager's job.

The time spent on these functions normally depends on the position held in the organisation. Usually first line managers spend most of their time organising and controlling, whereas top level managers tend to spend more time on planning.

The supervisor's position in management is unique. It is the only level of management with responsibility for directing the work of non-managerial staff. The staff may view the supervisor as being the management, since he or she may be their only contact with management.

Management qualities and activities

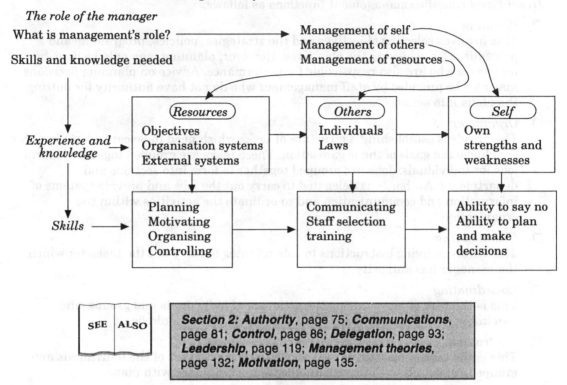

The role of the manager

What is management's role? ──────────► Management of self
                                       Management of others
Skills and knowledge needed   Management of resources

Experience and knowledge →

(Resources)	(Others)	(Self)
Objectives Organisation systems External systems	Individuals Laws	Own strengths and weaknesses

Skills →

| Planning
Motivating
Organising
Controlling | Communicating
Staff selection
training | Ability to say no
Ability to plan
and make
decisions |

SEE ALSO

Section 2: Authority, page 75; *Communications*, page 81; *Control*, page 86; *Delegation*, page 93; *Leadership*, page 119; *Management theories*, page 132; *Motivation*, page 135.

Management qualities and activities

658.4   Farnsworth, *On the way up*, McGraw Hill,

658.302 Haimann/Hilbert, *Supervision (4th ed.), Concepts and practices of management*, South Western Publishing,

Management theories

The general view is that *management* is a process which can be understood by close study of the management functions. The study of management, therefore, should lead to the development of principles of good management which can be put into practice.

Henri Fayol classifies management functions as follows:

☐ *Planning*
This involves selecting objectives and the strategies, policies, programme and procedures for achieving the objectives. However, planning may only be done by managers who are also responsible for performance. Advice on planning decisions may also be provided by staff management who do not have authority for putting the plans into action.

☐ *Organising*
This involves establishing a structure of tasks which need to be carried out in order to achieve the goals of the organisation. These tasks are grouped together to form jobs for individuals. Jobs are grouped together to form into sections and departments. Authority is delegated to carry out the jobs and provide systems of information and communication and co-ordinate the activities within the organisation.

☐ *Commanding*
This involves giving instructions to subordinates to carry out the tasks for which the manager has authority.

☐ *Co-ordinating*
This is the task of harmonising the activities of individuals and groups who inevitably have different ideas about what their goals should be.

☐ *Controlling*
This is the task of measuring and correcting the activities of the individuals and groups to ensure that their performance is in accordance with plans.

Peter Drucker classifies management functions as follows:

☐ *Setting objectives*
These are set for the organisation and then communicated.

☐ *Organising work*
The work to be done in the organisation is divided into manageable amounts and jobs. The jobs are integrated into a formal structure and people selected to do the jobs.

☐ *Motivating employees*
This includes communicating information to them to enable them to do their work.

☐ *Measuring performance*
Management must establish measures of performance for everyone and analyse actual performance with objectives set. The results are communicated and their significance acted upon.

Charles Handy suggests that a definition of a manager's role is likely to be so broad that it would be meaningless. In his view, managers' jobs are divided into three aspects:

1. *The aspect of general practitioner* The manager identifies problems and diagnoses the cause, decides how to deal with it and starts the treatment. Typical strategies for 'health' include:

    ☐ *people*: hiring/firing, reassigning, training;

    ☐ *work*: job enlargement/enrichment, redefinition of roles;

- *systems and procedures*: amend or introduce communication systems, reward systems and information systems.

2. *The aspect of managerial dilemmas* Managers are paid more than the workers because they must face constant dilemmas which must be resolved.

3. *The aspect of the manager as a person* Management is a developing science. As individuals develop skills, they should be able to apply them in any management situation.

Section 2: Management by objectives, page 128;
Management qualities and activities, page 130;
Motivation, page 135.

Management theories

658   Proctor, T, *Management: theory and principles*, Macdonald & Evans, 1982.

658.00973 Peters, T, *In search of excellence*, Harper & Row, 1982.

Manpower analysis and planning

Manpower analysis is concerned with the collection and interpretation of data relating to manpower both inside and outside the organisation. An analysis of existing manpower might typically involve asking the following questions:

- What type of staff do we have?
- How many?
- What skills and qualifications do they have?
- Are there any staff suitable for promotion or redeployment?
- How successful are we at recruiting particular types of staff?
- Are we attracting suitable external recruits?
- Can we count on filling vacancies from outside the organisation?
- Are some posts harder to fill? If so, what can be done about this?
- Why do members of staff leave the organisation?

Manpower planning involves preparation for future growth and survival. It is better to have some form of plan, even if it is inaccurate, than no plan at all. A plan provides a framework for achieving organisational goals. However, manpower plans must be continuous, not isolated. This is usually achieved by using five-year rolling plans. Plans for the first two years are set in some detail; the following three years are more broadly based. A short time-scale cannot accommodate any restructuring or long-term training which will have an impact on future manpower requirements.

Manpower analysis and planning is centred around:

- forecasting future demand;
- considering changes in manpower utilisation and the effect on manpower demand;
- analysing current manpower;
- forecasting internal manpower supply;
- forecasting external manpower supply;

- [ ] reconciling forecasts and feedback;
- [ ] making decisions and plans in relation to the budget and the external labour market.

Manpower demand is forecast from the organisation's corporate plans. It is related to the forecast production figures and sales forecasts. It is concerned with finding out how many employees are required and of what type. Forecasting manpower demand may require some work measurement techniques, job analysis or the use of statistical information.

Changes in *manpower utilisation* can affect the demand for manpower. Forecasting manpower utilisation involves looking at how tasks are performed, how long a task takes to complete, the level at which a task is carried out and on whose job description the job occurs. A variety of factors can be responsible for changing manpower utilisation.

- [ ] Changes in materials, equipment or technology.
- [ ] Changes in work organisation such as the introduction of quality circles, job redesign.
- [ ] Changes in the organisation's development.
- [ ] Changes in the organisation's structure.
- [ ] Changes in productivity such as the introduction of a bonus scheme.
- [ ] Changes in staff flexibility.
- [ ] Changes in overtime, work hours etc.
- [ ] Changes in training and performance appraisal.
- [ ] Managerial changes such as the introduction of management by objectives.

The current supply of manpower is analysed by number of employees in each occupation, age and their skills, education and training assets. This is important as it forms the base on which to plan future internal supply in relation to career succession and redundancy.

The internal manpower supply forecast attempts to predict the internal manpower in relation to future demand. Analysis is required of the reasons why employees leave the organisation and the trends. In addition, retirement numbers and future vacancies need to be assessed.

The external manpower supply forecast is needed if the internal supply is unlikely to meet future demand. It should take account of demographic trends, skills and local and national wage levels.

Reconciliation attempts to identify any shortages or surpluses in the supply and demand forecast in putting forward a manpower plan.

SEE ALSO | **Section 2: Control**, page 86; **Job design**, page 115; **Personnel management**, page 154.

Manpower planning

658.301 Bramham, J, *Human resource planning*, IPM, 1989.

658.301 Bramham, J, *Practical manpower planning, 4th ed*, IPM, 1988.

658.301 Walker, JW, *Human resource planning*, McGraw-Hill, 1980.

Motivation

Abraham Maslow, the influential American psychologist, suggested that people have a hierarchy of needs that must be satisfied, which fall into five groups:

1. *Physiological* – air, food, water.
2. *Safety* – freedom from attack.
3. *Social* – friendships.
4. *Ego* – a need for recognition.
5. *Self-actualisation* – self-fulfilment.

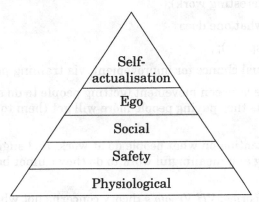

Maslow's hierarchy of needs

According to this theory, once the lower needs are satisfied, the next level needs become the motivators. For example, if you have enough air, food and water, more air, food and water will not motivate you. You will only be motivated by the next level of needs: safety needs. However, should the lower level needs become unsatisfied, for any reason, they once again become the motivators. Thus, if your air supply suddenly runs out, restoring it is the only thing that motivates you.

Efforts have been made to link these ideas to the workplace.

Need	Workplace reward
physiological	pay
safety	job security
social	sympathetic colleagues
ego	praise/promotion
self-actualisation	satisfying job

This is a well-known theory, but is perhaps a simple answer to a complex problem, as people seem to have many motivations, and these change continually, often relating to age and situation. It does however point out that money, whilst important, is not the sole motivator.

Frederick Herzberg suggested that there are two groups of factors important to motivation. He called them *hygiene factors* and *motivators*. He said that both are important to motivation, and one is not more important than the other. Hygiene factors only have the power to demotivate if they are not adequate, but increasing them will not motivate. For example, working conditions are hygiene factors because if they are not at an acceptable level they will demotivate, but once they are at the required level, improving them will not motivate people. Examples of *hygiene factors* are pay, conditions, security. *Motivators* according to this theory are:

☐ achievement at work;

☐ recognition of work done;

☐ the work itself (interesting work);

☐ responsibility for what one does;

☐ advancement (prospects);

☐ growth: the continual chance for improvement, via training perhaps.

Herzberg differentiates between movement (getting people to do something) and motivation. He suggests that paying people more will get them to move, but does not motivate.

This theory focuses attention on what people do at work, and suggests that unless people have interesting and meaningful work to do they cannot be motivated, only moved.

Unlike the previous theories, *VH Vroom's* theory concerns not what needs have to be satisfied, but what is the process of motivation. Behaviour is said to be based on perceptions, and everyone's perceptions are at least slightly different, so that any situation will be viewed differently by different people.

All individuals have goals which may well be unrelated to their jobs, so social and working lives are not separate in terms of motivation. The strength of an individual's motivation depends then on the extent to which a person expects his efforts will result in helping to reach his personal goals.

The link between effort – performance – reward, has to be established and maintained if a person is to be motivated. As every individual will have different goals this then is difficult, though it may help just to be aware of this.

A person, perhaps a stamp collector, might be motivated to work overtime in order to get enough money to buy a particular stamp. If, however, the overtime is not going to generate enough money in time, or if the stamp ceases to be available for sale, the motivation may cease too.

This theory suggests that in order to motivate a work force, a supervisor needs to know his work team well, so that he can establish links between work, and their own goals.

It seems that there is no one answer to the problem of motivation, but from the theories it is possible to draw the following general *guide-lines*:

❏ Different people seek different rewards, so get to know your team and learn what they want from work.

❏ Be aware of how their circumstances change.

❏ People must be able to influence the rewards they get by the efforts they make. Establish a link.

❏ The effects of their efforts should be made known to them as soon as possible.

❏ All supervisors can provide some personal rewards for their work teams.

❏ Organise work to take account of individual needs.

❏ Improve social relationships in the work team.

❏ Communicate well with the work team.

These guidelines can be translated into specific actions, but just what these actions are will vary with individuals and circumstances.

SEE	ALSO	**Section 2: Job design**, page 115; **Management theories**, page 132; **Performance appraisal**, page 145; **Training**, page 199.

Motivation

Incentive programmes, *Personnel Management Factsheet No. 33.*

658.314 Martin, P, *Creating a committed workforce*, IPM, 1987.

658.31423 Taylor, LK, *Not for bread alone*, Business Books, 1980.

Non-verbal communication

A recent survey by British Telecom revealed that communication is more dependent on gesture than on anything else. It was found that 80% of communication between individuals was by non-verbal means; 16% by tone of speech; and 4% by the actual words used in speech. Clearly, non-verbal communication (or body language) is important for managers to appreciate.

Following are some examples of typical body language gestures:

Unsure/apprehensive
Slight frown, eyes shifty. Looks anxious but is trying to hide it.

Interested
Looks at speaker intently – a half-smile indicates he likes what he hears.

Protectiveness
Often an unconscious signal when entering a meeting is to cross the arms across the body protectively. It may be disguised by another action such as checking bracelet or cufflinks etc.

Critically evaluating situation
Holds hand over mouth signalling he is thinking hard before speaking. Slight frown indicates giving matter serious thought before giving opinion.

Stalling for time

Looks down at papers on desk, fiddling with papers as if looking for something, to avoid eye contact.

Superiority

Tilts head back to 'look down nose' at the speaker, so she distances herself without actually moving back and appears taller (ie "draw oneself up to one's true height").

Tough customer

Head rests on clenched fist: the fist indicates determination and stubbornness, and the resting head shows boredom and lack of interest. The frown suggests a negative opinion of the situation.

Authoritative ⟹

Holds the hands behind the back in an almost military stance, showing confidence (ie by opening up the body). She has a straight posture and is making direct eye contact.

⟸ Appeal for help

'What can I do' signalled by outstretched arms and worried expression.

Anticipation ⟹

A physiological symptom of excitement or stress is a dry mouth, and a natural physical reaction is to lick one's lips.

Holding back or withdrawing from the situation

Folded arms indicate non-participation. Leaning back away from the speaker and a deadpan expression also show a desire not to get involved.

Threatening

Stabbing or pointing with one finger, often to emphasise words and 'nail' the 'victim'.

Is it true?

Hand to mouth to prevent speaking out of doubts. Raised eyebrows and head inclined away from speaker.

Sincere

Clenched fist shows conviction and leaning forward towards listener indicates he is not trying to hide anything.

Organisational objectives, policies and strategies

An organisation's *objectives* are desired states or results. If they can be measured and relate to specific time scales, they become *targets*.

Organisations are likely to have multiple objectives which may not be concerned with *maximising* profit and growth, for example, but with achieving *satisfactory levels*. Many organisational objectives now include elements of social and environmental responsibility, in excess of statutory requirements.

A well-formulated objective should meet the following criteria.

1. It starts with the word *to* followed by an action verb.

2. It specifies a single key result to be accomplished.

3. It specifies a target date for its accomplishment.

4. It specifies maximum cost factors.

5. It is as specific and quantitative (and hence measurable and verifiable) as possible.

6. It specifies only the *what* and *when*: it avoids venturing into the *why* and *how*.

7. It is readily understandable by those who will be contributing to its attainment.

8. It is realistic and attainable, but still represents a significant challenge.

9. It provides maximum payoff on the required investment in time and resources, compared with other objectives being considered.

10. It is consistent with the resources available or anticipated.

11. It is consistent with basic organisational policies and practices.

The following list of corporate objectives is taken from a large, diverse manufacturing and service organisation. It may be useful to consider how these compare with the goals of your organisation. Note that many of them are *not* stated in measurable terms which makes them *less* useful.

1. To achieve a level of profit about average in the industries in which we operate.

2. To grow as rapidly as possible.

3. To achieve the highest possible return on investment.

4. To gain a reputation as a socially concerned corporation.

5. To create an environment which employees find stimulating and challenging.

6. To make a substantial contribution to the resolution of environmental and ecological problems.

7. To identify and exploit new markets and technologies.

8. To increase substantially earnings per share.

9. To become a significant multinational company.

10. To respond to today's needs without possible detriment to the future.

11. To grow primarily through internal development.

12. To foster an environment offering long-term opportunities and security to all employees.

An organisation's *policies* are the principles or courses of action set by top management; in the case of a company, the board of directors. They emerge from the basic objectives which can be divided up into:

- ❏ marketing and sales policies;
- ❏ production policies;
- ❏ financial policies;
- ❏ personnel policies.

When policy decisions are set out in the form of a *policy statement*, they provide standard answers to all the main questions that are likely to be raised. In this way all employees are able to find out exactly what is expected of them in most normal circumstances. Thus, situations which arise regularly can be dealt with automatically by referring to these rules which have been made in advance. This ensures that:

- ❏ all action taken will be in accordance with the organisation's objectives;
- ❏ uniformity of action is achieved throughout the organisation;
- ❏ consistency of action is achieved throughout the organisation;
- ❏ tasks can be delegated since all below can be expected to know the rules;
- ❏ co-ordination is simplified.

Policies can be set out in the form of manuals of procedures, rule books, office instruction and memoranda providing that adequate provision is made for them to be kept up to date. They also need to be flexible enough to cope with special or local circumstance. In addition, there may be unwritten rules which are well appreciated and observed within the organisation.

Whatever policies are formulated, they must be the result of *deliberation* and *decision*. Making the right decision is fundamental to good management practice. Although policy decisions emanate from top management, they can originate at any level of management in the form of recommendations to the board. Such policy decisions are usually broad in scope and may be described as guidelines; their interpretation is often the responsibility of those managers at the point of impact.

SEE ALSO

Section 2: Decision-making and problem-solving, page 90; *Management by objectives*, page 128; *Organisational structures*, page 144.

Organisational objectives

658.4   Dawson, S, *Analysing organisations*, Macmillan, 1986.

658.402 Morgan, G, *Creative organisation theory*, Sage, 1989.

Organisational structures

A successful business needs to build an *organisational structure* through which it aims to achieve its objectives. Organisational structures can be classified as follows.

❏ Entrepreneurial structures which are based on the owner/manager.

❏ Functional structures which are based on functional tasks such as finance, marketing and production.

❏ Multi-divisional structures where each division is a decentralised profit centre.

❏ A matrix which is a combination of structures.

These *formal structures* are concerned with the co-ordination and grouping of related activities. The responsibilities of each division of the business must be defined and authority delegated. Formal structures are built to ensure that all workers within an organisation can identify their position, their responsibilities and know to whom they are accountable . An advantage of a formal structure is that it allows management to develop specialist areas and areas of expertise within the organisation.

Informal structures can be the result of informal rules and conventions. For example, managers may refer to one another at work as Mr, Miss, Ms or Mrs ... in front of junior staff, but by their first names when subordinates are not present. In some organisations managers may tend not to socialise with their staff at work, for example over lunch, but break this convention when it comes to old school friends or graduates from their old college regardless of their position in the firm.

Other contributory factors in the building of informal management structures may be based on common interests outside work, such as lifestyle, families, sports interests, and networks of informal communications.

An *organisation chart* shows the line authority or functional authority in an organisation.

Functional organisation structure diagram

Production workers	Senior staff	Management
7 ——	Head wood trades	
7 ——	Head trowel trades	Assistant manager (Development)
11 ——	Head mechanical & electrical services	
14 ——	Head gas services	Assistant manager (Deputy) —— Director
13 ——	Head motor vehicle	
13 ——	Head interior furnishing	Assistant manager (Quality)
3 ——	Head health & safety	
14 ——	Head technician	

Section 2: Authority, page 75; **Communications**, page 81; **Organisational objectives policies and strategies**, page 142; **Responsibility**, page 179.

Organisation structures

658.3 ACC   Armstrong, P, *People in organisations, 4th ed*, Elm, 1988.

658.3   Epps, S, *Selecting and managing personnel*. Telegraph Publications, 1988.

658.4   Jaques, E, *Requisite organisation*, Cason Hall, 1989.

Performance appraisal

There are a number of reasons for systematically carrying out a *scheme of appraisal* or *performance review*.

1. Probably the most important reason is to inform staff of their progress and weaknesses. Often assessments are made during a person's probationary period, but this is not then continued, and so many people are not made aware of their later progress, and perhaps more importantly, they are not given an opportunity to discuss their progress with the person carrying out the appraisal.

2. Once deficiencies have been identified then in many cases something can be done about it, and often this means training. Appraisal and assessment also serve the function of showing whether training which has been carried out has been successful.

3. Suitability for promotion is often decided on the basis of appraisals. A distinction should be made here between a person's suitability in their present job and predictions about their potential performance at higher level. The best workers are not necessarily the best supervisors.

4. In some companies where annual increments are not automatic, or where further payments can be made for increased performance, then the basis of these merit payments is likely to be an appraisal scheme.

How to appraise

Performance can be appraised by describing the best aspects of the employee's work and suggesting areas for improvement. This is usually done at an interview.

A formal appraisal interview needs to be planned so that over and under emphasis can be avoided. It is usual to agree a procedure which will apply to all such interviews, and the employees should be given adequate notice of both the time and the form of the interview. The framework below might be a useful model from which to work.

1. Outline the *purpose* of the interview.

2. Ask the employee to *report* and *comment* on the previous period's work.

3. Refer to *targets previously agreed* and give an assessment of performance against these targets.

4. Discuss any *shortfalls* in performance and agree what action should be taken.

5. Check *understanding* and record agreements which both parties should sign.

6. *Inform* anyone else who may be involved or should be notified.

Not surprisingly, appraisal interviews can raise problems.

1. Many people are likely to see their own appraisal as being criticism. Criticism can constitute a threat to a person's self esteem and result in defensiveness and so disrupt rather than improve performance.

2. A negative appraisal, that is telling someone that they are not doing well, is always going to be difficult, and obviously the reactions and remedies will vary with situations and individuals. Particularly difficult are those situations where the individual is only a few years from retirement, after many years service.

3. Often the biggest difficulty for the appraiser is developing listening skills, particularly when the appraiser's perceptions are not the same as those of the person being appraised. If a manager is dissatisfied with performance and says so without giving the individual a chance to put his/her case, the result is often an aggressive reaction. If the individuals feel that they cannot reach their targets, reassurance is not much use. Only constructive help such as training is likely to be useful.

There is no doubt that in order to be successful appraisals must be conducted in the right 'climate'. This needs to be that of sincere open discussion, with a problem-solving rather than blame allocating approach. The timing of the appraisal is a difficult decision. Once a year may not be enough. On the other hand there is the danger of overloading employees with criticisms. It is also worth remembering that the appraisal process is very time-consuming, and so for this reason, both parties should have done the maximum preparation prior to the interview to avoid unnecessarily prolonging it. The actual discussion should then be a useful discussion of what went wrong, why and what should be done in the future. This will follow earlier agreement as to what he/she has been expected to do and the standards to be reached.

Promotion

Many organisations depend on the promotion of existing employees as a source of trained and proven people. The policy of promoting from within is a widely practised one with benefits not only for the organisation but also for the employees, for whom it provides a powerful incentive to perform better. Clearly, where employees have worked for an organisation for some time, more is known about them than would be revealed by even the most sophisticated selection procedures, and equally the employee knows more about the organisation than he/she would learn at an interview.

Generally speaking, an internal promotions policy should be applied whenever possible. There will be occasions though where because the appropriate skills are not available, or because of a need to bring in 'new blood', promotion from within would be harmful. It needs to be remembered too that not everyone wishes to be promoted. Many are satisfied with their present situation.

In order to maximise the benefits from a promotions policy, it needs to be clear to employees just what the criteria for promotion are. Often productivity, quality and skill are considerations, but it is also important to remember that perhaps the most important, and the least measurable, is a person's potential. A commonly-used criterion, which is said also to eliminate favouritism, is seniority or length of service. The draw-back here though is that this discourages younger employees and sometimes loyalty is confused with ability. Good practice probably results from decisions being made on a balance of merit and ability on one hand, and length of service on the other.

Any organization with a performance appraisal system should issue detailed guidelines on how the system should be implemented.

Example of guidelines on performance appraisal

ANZAC Banking Group

Guidance notes on performance appraisals

Performance appraisals of
supervisory and managerial staff

Introduction

The Appraisal Scheme described in this booklet is intended to be responsive to the Bank's business and staff development requirements.

The Scheme meets a number of needs, among which are:

- to enhance the understanding of the objectives of the organisation, and of those of the job in question;
- to form part of the communications process between a member of staff and the supervisor/manager;
- to inform staff of 'how they are doing';
- to identify any training/development needs;
- to provide a comparative means of assessment for succession/manpower planning purposes;
- to complement overall personnel policies and procedures.

The Guidance Notes are intended to be of assistance to all involved in conducting appraisals thereby contributing to the achievement of the above aims.

The basis of the scheme

Assessing performance

From an examination of the content of people's jobs it has been found that the skills and requirements necessary to fulfil the respective functions fall into three broad categories.

- The need to meet business or other pre-set objectives (ie what is to be achieved).
- Managerial or other job related skills (ie what methods are used to meet those objectives).
- Skills which stem from a member of staff's personal characteristics (ie what personal skills have been displayed in tackling those objectives).

The appraisal sequence

The sequence of events leading up to the annual appraisal process may be summarised as follows.

At the beginning of the operational year

a) After consultation with the Appraisee and having regard to the discussions held in respect of budget preparation, the Appraiser completes the Recording of Job Objectives Form. A completed copy is then to be given to the Appraisee.

Throughout the year

b) Both copies of the Recording of Job Objectives Form are up-dated as necessary to reflect any fresh or amended objectives.

c) The Appraiser and the Appraisee make their own notes on their respective forms of achievement against those objectives. This should not detract, however, from the on-going process of management informing staff of how they are doing as part of the normal working relationship.

At the end of the operational year

d) The Bank's Personnel Department sends out the Appraisal Report Form to the Appraiser who, in turn, reminds the Appraisee that an interview is shortly to be held.

e) The Appraiser and Appraisee, after referring to the Recording of Job Objectives Form and examining other data compiled during the year, individually make provisional assessments using draft forms. The measured and considered views of the Appraisee's performance are to be in respect of the preceding year's work relative to the objectives of the post.

f) Appraiser and Appraisee arrange a mutually convenient interview and exchange copies of their provisional assessments some time in advance of the interview date.

g) Appraiser and Appraisee each individually consider the two assessments and make notes for discussion at the interview.

h) The interview takes place where the two provisional assessments are discussed, amended by agreement and finally entered onto the actual Annual Appraisal Form.

i) The Appraiser provides an overall assessment and summarises the Appraisee's training needs and career development position.

j) The Appraisee makes an overall comment on the Appraisal and the form is then signed by both parties.

k) The Appraiser and Appraisee discuss future objectives and a fresh Recording of Job Objectives Form is completed. A copy of the Form is then kept by both parties for up-dating through the operational year.

l) The Appraisal Report Form and the used Job Objectives Form are returned under confidential cover to the Bank's Personnel Department. Appropriate action can then be taken on such matters as identified training needs, the up-dating of manpower plans, etc.

The frequency of appraisals

Whilst in normal circumstances appraisals will be conducted annually, it is recognised that there is a need to measure performance against objectives on an on-going basis throughout the year, with fresh objectives being set as necessary.

Persons authorised to conduct appraisals

Any officer authorised to conduct performance appraisals must be in a position to monitor personally the Appraisee's performance over the period in question and have access to any necessary information from other Departments, e.g. Marketing, Inspection, Personnel, etc. However, the Appraiser should at least be of the status of an Assistant Branch Manager.

The appraisal format

Personal details

So that the comments and assessments that will appear in the Appraisal Report Form are seen in context, the Form requires that the member of staff's age, grade and date of appointment are stated.

The Form also provides for any change since the last Appraisal in the Appraisee's duties, qualifications or training position to be recorded.

Objectives

Whilst a number of the requirements of the Appraisal Scheme are listed in the Introduction, the need to provide management with a reliable means of assessing performance in relation to objectives is seen as being of major significance.

The objectives of each job should relate to the overall objectives of the Bank and have regard to the discussions which took place at the time that budgets, for the relevant year, were being prepared. It follows that management will be the major contributor to the setting of objectives. However, discussions must take place with the Appraisee to ensure that those objectives are reasonable, achievable and a fair reflection of the duties of the post in question.

Objectives could be job related and for example specify the number and type of visits required to customers or potential customers.

Some objectives could be of a more personal nature and relate to the acquisition of new skills.

When considering objectives, therefore, each major component of the Appraisee's job should be examined and related to a standard of achievement that is required by management. Where possible, objectives should carry numerical values.

In addition to the regular review of objectives and standards it will be necessary to undertake a special review following organisational change or a change of manager. Such a special review will be particularly necessary where business objectives are to change.

Appraisals should have regard to the future direction that the Officer's career might take in order to give maximum assistance to the Bank in the completion of manpower and succession plans.

The Career Development Section of the Report Form is also used as the means whereby Appraisers consider whether members of staff with high potential are to be recommended for inclusion within the management development process.

Appraisees so recommended may be asked to complete a separate, additional form and may be invited by management to attend a special assessment interview. Being recommended does not automatically mean that the member of staff will be included within the management development process.

In considering whether members of staff should be recommended, Appraisers should bear in mind that it would be expected that probably no more than five per cent of Appraisees would fall into this category.

In addition, Appraisers should have regard to the fact that not all officers who are performing very well in their current job would necessarily be promotable. Alternatively, members of staff could be regarded as promotable yet not be performing exceptionally well in undertaking their present role.

It is anticipated that senior management's requirements for nominations under the management development process may change each year. Further guidance will be given to Appraisers before the annual interviews are commenced.

Summary of appraisee's comments

Although as part of the scheme Appraisees provide written assessments at each stage of the process, this section enables the member of staff to comment on the Appraisal as a whole and in particular the Overall Assessment Factor given by the Appraiser.

The assessment process

The general style

In order to provide for in-depth assessments which are indicative of the Appraisee's performance, the Appraiser is required to express those assessments in the narrative form.

In showing the reasons for the assessment, Appraisers should specify the standard against which the Appraisee has been assessed. In this way, the Appraisee's performance can be viewed in relation to that of other members of staff with similar jobs.

Similarly the Appraisee is asked to comment in writing on each set of criteria.

As an aid to the assessment process, each of the headings has been defined and that definition is followed by a list of prompting questions.

Whilst this list is not exhaustive, it has been designed to cover almost all of those points that would be considered necessary by the Bank/Appraiser.

As with any system of appraisal, the Appraiser is required to collect information throughout the preceding period about the member of staff's performance and development. Dependent upon the Appraisee's duties and responsibilities, data should be collected from other Divisions, eg. Business Development, Inspection, Personnel, etc.

Assessing performance against objectives

As objectives will, as far as possible, have been set by the Bank/branch in the form of numerical targets, performance must be similarly gauged. However, when the Bank/branch is supplementing this by provision of narrative, the Appraiser may find it helpful to ask and respond to a number of questions. Wherever possible, those questions should be put in a form requiring more than a 'yes' or 'no' answer.

If, for example, a primary objective of Branch Manager was to maximise the number of mortgages given by the branch and the standard of say 24 in the year was adopted, the prompt questions might be:

– how many new mortgages have been secured in the past year?
– what evidence is there that the Appraisee is actively pursuing market opportunities?

Managerial skills

Management of staff

To ensure that staff are fully aware of what is required of them and equipped to meet those requirements. To ensure that effective monitoring and control are exercised. To give a sensible and balanced approach to the needs of the organisation and the individual.

– What evidence is there that the Team is well led?
– How far are the Appraisee's staff aware of both individual and team objectives?
– To what extent do the staff appear to be well motivated?
– How well have appropriate monitoring and control techniques been maintained by the Appraisee?
– What level of in-unit training takes place?
– How well does the Appraisee appraise and counsel his/her own staff.

Organisation of the unit

To ensure that the correct level of resources is deployed at all times in order to maximise efficiency and effectiveness in meeting workloads.

– How well is the work planned and allocated?
– To what extent is work returned accurately and on time?
– How effectively is job rotation operated?
– Are the units systems safe and secure?

Servicing of customers

To provide customer services in an efficient, effective and courteous manner. To operate in a way likely to promote further business.

– How successful is the Appraisee in portraying the Bank's required image?
– To what extent is the Bank's objective of minimising queue lengths met by the Appraisee and the support staff?
– Is the customer appointments procedure operated effectively?
– What evidence is there that queries are successfully dealt with?
– To what extent are complaints received and effectively handled?

Evaluating personal skills

Judgement

To make correct decisions consistently by utilising all available knowledge and data.

- To what extent is the Appraisee able to make effective use of available data when making decisions?
- To what extent are such decisions sound?

Initiative/enterprise

That full use be made of experience and knowledge to respond to all situations requiring imagination and the use of creative skills.

- How well does the Appraisee respond to unaccustomed situations?
- What degree of innovation has been demonstrated to create or improve systems and services?

Technical competence

To apply technical skills and abilities to the full. To take every opportunity to develop knowledge and skills.

- To what extent does the Appraisee possess the necessary professional skills and expertise?
- How effectively are these utilised?

Planning

To assess future requirements correctly and adopt the best methods of approach to each activity.

- How much emphasis does the Appraisee put on the planning function?
- What methods or approaches are employed in the process?

Communication

To receive and convey information in the most effective and efficient way.

- To what extent is the Appraisee able to express himself clearly and concisely:
    a) Orally?
    b) In writing?

Application

To make full use of all attributes to see all tasks successfully through to completion and in accordance with the Bank's objectives.

- What degree of enthusiasm for the job is demonstrated by the Appraisee?
- How determined is the Appraisee to meet both Bank and personal objectives?

Interpersonal skills

To develop and maintain successful professional relationships.

- How well does the officer relate to:
    a) Customers?
    b) Colleagues?

Overall assessment

Having assessed performance in relation to each of the preceding criteria a consideration of 'the total job' is required in order to produce an overall assessment factor. That factor is to be expressed as a numerical value so as to provide a means of comparative analysis.

It is anticipated that in most circumstances there will be general agreement between Appraiser and Appraisee on the assessments for each of the criteria within those sections. However, where this is not the case, the Overall Assessment should be a reflection of the Appraiser's conclusions, although the Appraisee has the opportunity to express an alternative viewpoint, if necessary, at the end of the Form.

General points

Setting future objectives

Having established the relationship between objectives and actual performance, it will be easier to set future objectives.

The objectives to be set for the coming year should again be reasonable, achievable and a fair reflection of the postholder's duties.

Where the Appraisee exceeded the objectives set for the previous year over a number of areas, and also demonstrated career aspirations, this could have a material bearing on the Appraiser's comments under the Career Development Section of the Form.

Where a gap between the stated objectives and the level of performance has been identified, Appraisers would then need to consider whether this gap could be narrowed by training or re-training.

Future actions/improvement targets

The Appraiser may also use the Future Objectives section to summarise any action that management may wish to take, eg. to follow up a suggestion for improving a service that arose out of the appraisal interview.

In such circumstances the Appraiser should also make a separate note and undertake to inform the Appraisee of the outcome of this as soon as is reasonably practicable.

Disputes

Should an officer wish to dispute any point in the performance appraisal, he or she must first inform the Appraiser of the grounds on which the complaint is being made.

If an irreconcilable difference of opinion still exists, the matter may be dealt with under the appropriate machinery.

Disciplinary situations

Where employees are reported as performing unsatisfactorily, remarks made within the Appraisal Report Form will not be sufficient in themselves, to act as a disciplinary warning or a notice of termination of employment. Such action must only be taken in accordance with the Disciplinary Procedure.

Example from 'Notes for Appraisers', County Council

Ensuring commitment

Commitment comes from having a clear understanding of what is expected of you and why, and accepting it as reasonable and achievable.

Once these stages have been satisfactorily accomplished both appraisee and appraiser will have established a clear common understanding of what is to be achieved by the job holder over the next year. Commitment to these objectives stems naturally from a process involving participation and understanding.

However, appraisers should never lose sight of the fact that the quickest way to bring any appraisal system into disrepute is for successive levels of management to *tell* subordinate levels what 'their' (subordinate's) objectives are to be. Of course, the organisation needs to be able firstly to survive, and secondly to grow. Of course, this must happen through the attainment of corporate objectives; but the organisation needs committed, enthusiastic people if its objectives are to be achieved. Unless people are encouraged to contribute, to participate and to be party to the organisation's objectives, misunderstandings and missed opportunities will arise.

Setting objectives is a two-way process; matching the needs of the organisation with the contribution each manager *believes* he can make to those objectives. Imposing objectives which are *seen to be* unrealistic is demotivating. The subordinate will not 'own' the objectives – he will see them as belonging to his superior – and he will not be committed to them.

The following steps need to have taken place during the process of establishing the job-holder's objectives if he is to be committed to the attaining of them.

1. *Clarifying the job*

   Both parties must have a clear, common understanding of the key task areas of the job-holder's job.

2. *Identified standards of performance*

   The standards of performance, related to the key task areas, will have been identified, agreed, recorded and converted to job related objectives.

3. *Organisational objectives*

   The superior will have explained to his subordinate what his (the superior's) objectives are. This enables the subordinate to see the broader picture and increases the subordinate's awareness of the fact that he is one of a team striving for organisational objectives.

   The subordinate will have been invited to put forward his views on what contribution he can make to the attainment of his manager's objectives. (Managers achieve things through people – without that help and support they are unlikely to be very successful.

4. *Priorities and external conditions*

   Skills and knowledge will have been discussed and help offered by the appraiser to the appraisee in developing them. Real discussions will have taken place on what the subordinate can realistically achieve. This will have involved consideration of opportunities and conditions affecting the job holder as well as the identification of support and resources available to him or her.

   Priorities will have been established and the objectives will have been recorded in a clear manner.

   The purpose of this stage is to increase or re-affirm the job-holder's belief in the importance of the objectives and of their realistic nature, and to establish the objectives against which his or her performance will be measured. Unless the job holder believes in the objectives – ie if they are imposed – he or she will not be committed to achieving them.

   Without commitment, there is no motivation; without motivation there is little chance of success. If the subordinate fails to meet his or her objectives the superior is unlikely to be able to meet his or hers. The appraisal at the end of the period will then centre around arguments about the 'ownership' of the subordinate's objectives, and will do little to bring about improved performance and growth in the next period.

SEE ALSO | **Section 2: Management by objectives**, page 128; **Motivation**, page 135; **Personnel Management**, page 154.

Performance appraisal

Appraisal, *Personnel Management Factsheet*, No. 3.

658.3125   *Effective appraisal interviewing*, HMSO, 1985.

658.3125   Landy, FJ, *The measurement of work performance*, Academic Press, 1983.

658.3125   Randell, G, *Staff appraisal, 3rd ed*, IPM, 1984.

658.3125   Steward, V, *Managing the poor performer, 2nd ed*, Wildwood House, 1988.

Personnel management

The role of the personnel function is to provide advice, guidance and services which will enable management to deal effectively with all matters concerning the employment of people.

Personnel managers advise management on the solution to any problems affecting people. But they also have the more positive role of advising on personnel policies and procedures. These will, of course, vary considerably, depending on the type of organisation, but the main areas covered are summarised below.

The main personnel policy areas are:

a)   *organisation*. The basis upon which the organisation should be structured and developed;

b)   *social responsibility*. Treating people fairly and equitably; taking account of individual needs; providing as far as possible for a good quality of working life;

c)   *employment*. The level, in terms of quality, of people the company wishes to employ; the provision of equal opportunity; the provision of reasonable security and continuity of employment; the terms and conditions of employment offered to staff;

d)   *pay*. The level compared with market rates; the type of pay structure preferred; methods of fixing and reviewing rates of pay; the extent to which pay policies are revealed;

e)   *career and promotion*. The degree to which the organisation is prepared to offer long-term career prospects; the extent to which promotion should take place from within the organisation;

f)   *training and development*. The scope of training and development schemes;

g)   *industrial relations*. The extent to which unions or staff associations should be recognised; the preferred unions and bargaining units; the approach to negotiations and joint consultation; the scope for participation and industrial democracy; the approach to dealing with grievances, discipline and redundancy;

h)   *health and safety*. The way in which the organisation intends to achieve a healthy and safe working environment;

i)   *welfare*. The amount of help the organisation is prepared to give to employees to overcome their personal problems; the scale of social and sporting facilities the company wishes to provide.

The main personnel procedures upon which advice is given are those concerned with:

a) *manpower planning.* Techniques of forecasting and budgeting for manpower needs; methods of improving the use of manpower and reducing labour turnover;

b) *recruitment and selection.* Procedures for preparing job specifications, advertising, interviewing and testing;

c) *employment.* Induction, transfer, promotion, grievance, disciplinary and redundancy procedures;

d) *training.* Procedures for identifying and meeting needs; the training techniques used on courses;

e) *management development.* Procedures for identifying managerial potential and for career planning;

f) *performance appraisal.* Procedures for assessing levels of performance and potential;

g) *pay.* Systems for fixing and adjusting rates of pay; job evaluation and salary administration procedures;

h) *industrial relations.* Procedural agreements with unions and staff associations covering recognition, bargaining units, union facilities, the rights and duties of shop stewards, and grievances; constitutions for joint consultation committees;

i) *health and safety.* Procedures for medical examinations, health and safety inspections; accident prevention.

The personnel function interprets and helps to communicate personnel policies. It provides guidance to managers which will ensure that agreed policies are implemented.

Personnel managers may apply sophisticated techniques such as psychological testing, performance appraisal and job evaluation. But the job is much more than the development of these techniques. Care is required to ensure that appropriate systems are introduced, and persuasive and administrative abilities must be deployed to see that they are accepted and applied.

SEE ALSO

See *Section 2: Employment legislation*, page 99; *Job evaluation*, page 117; *Manpower analysis and planning*, page 133; *Performance appraisal*, page 145; *Recruitment selection and Induction*, page 167; *Trade unions and the law*, page 192.

Personnel management

658.3   Cole, GA, *Personnel management, 2nd ed,* DP Publications, 1988.

658.3   Cowling, AG, *Managing human resources, 2nd ed,* Arnold, 1990.

658.3   Cuming, MW, *Theory and practice of personnel management, 6th ed,* Heinemann, 1989.

Production control

In general, there are three types of production system.

Job production is used where the item is a one-off, such as a ship or a building. Many small firms are engaged in this type of work. The buyer usually puts out a specification and requests an estimate of cost or a quotation. A contract is agreed and the firm accepting the contract makes the item according to the specification.

Batch production is used where a range of products are made in insufficient quantities to justify mass production. Often the amount produced is more than the actual orders received and the surplus is held in stock.

Mass production is used where demand for a product is high and is expected to last for long enough to justify the cost of setting up a production line. It results in a continuous flow of identical or similar products. Work is done in a strict sequence. The speed of manufacture is decided by the slowest operation. Goods such as cars, televisions and chemicals are produced in this way.

The purpose of *production control* is to make sure that the right goods are made at the right time, in the right amount, by the most economical method. Production control can be defined as the direction of the production activities according to the planned programme in the most economic way. This planning and controlling of production depends on many factors according to the industry concerned.

The six main components of production control are:

1. scheduling;
2. stock control;
3. manufacturing order control;
4. machine and labour usage;
5. progressing;
6. dispatching.

The process of *scheduling* involves listing all the items needed for production such as raw materials, components or sub-assemblies. These are then placed in the right sequence for production, taking account of production times, delivery times and allowances for waste. Finally, the materials must be routed from one section to another. Effective scheduling requires such information as:

- sales orders;
- delivery dates;
- layouts;
- parts lists;
- machine loadings;
- labour utilisation;
- scrap and waste rates;
- progress as the work takes place;
- storage and dispatch facilities;

Stock control is concerned with both materials control and stock. Material control involves the purchasing and cost of material, and the material flows into the organisation. Stock control is the method of controlling the amounts and quality of the materials as required by the production plan. It ensures that:

❑   materials are available at the right time and in the right quantities;

❑   stock is properly cared for;

❑   accurate records are kept.

Manufacturing order control concerns the provision of the documents which give the authority to the various departments to produce according to the plan.

Machine and labour utilisation aims to minimise the idle time of both the workforce and machinery.

Progressing is concerned with co-ordinating the production programme by checking the actual against the planned schedule. This often involves:

❑   taking responsibility for all the production orders once issued;

❑   ensuring variances are investigated;

❑   providing alternatives when bottlenecks occur.

Dispatching is the process of authorising the operator to carry out work allocated. The dispatching section is responsible for:

❑   assigning the work to the section or machine;

❑   preparing and issuing materials, tools, etc;

❑   co-ordinating the progress of the work.

A number of aids and techniques are used in production control: these include *Gantt charts*, *network analysis* and *work study*.

A *Gantt chart*, devised by Henry Gantt, is a master plan showing the dates when each stage of production must be ready and when each phase is completed, so that it can be seen whether delivery dates agree with estimates. There are many variations on the Gantt chart theme and the chart is so versatile it can be adapted to any control system in which a number of functions are linked to time.

Example of a Gantt chart

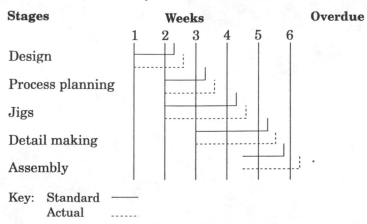

Key: Standard   ——
         Actual   ------

Network analysis covers a number of techniques used to plan and control complex projects. These include *critical path analysis (CPA)* and *programme evaluation and review technique (PERT)*. CPA assumes an accurate time for an activity, whereas PERT estimates the time. Network analysis results in a diagram which shows the sequential relationships between activities in a job. The various activities are linked to minimise the overall time spent on the project. The optimum route through the network is called the critical path. Events which take place at a significant point in time and mark the start and finish of an activity are represented as circles. Lines represent activities which take time to complete.

Example of a simple network: Making tea

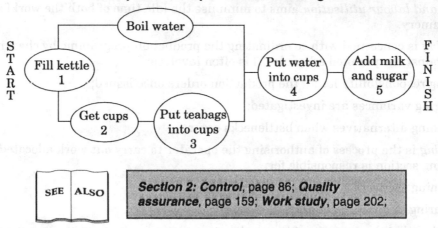

SEE ALSO

Section 2: Control, page 86; *Quality assurance*, page 159; **Work study**, page 202;

Production control

658	Lock, D, *The Gower handbook of management, 2nd ed,* Gower, 1988.
658.51	Hall, RW, *Zero inventories*, Business One Irwin, 1983.
658.51	Reinfeld, NV, *Production and inventory control*, Reston Publishing Co, 1982.

Quality assurance

Quality assurance is a term used to refer to all the activities and functions concerned with the attainment of quality. The principles of quality assurance cross all industrial boundaries and professional disciplines. The management task is to persuade the workforce to adopt the desired attitude towards quality. This means ensuring adequate definition and communication of the organisation's objectives. Most organisations which have a reputation for quality have not done so simply by appointing a manager with a range of techniques, but with a total corporate commitment to quality.

Quality control is the systematic inspection of product or samples of products on a production line at various stages of production. The purpose of quality control is to ensure that standards are being maintained. In mass production the statistical analysis of parameters measured on a random sample of the end product is most important. The larger the sample tested, the higher the manufacturer's reputation for manufacturing goods of a high standard.

Quality control charts may be used, particularly in mass production. The horizontal axis of the graph shows units of time; the vertical axis shows the value of such variables as the percentage of defective products. The cause of any sustained rise in the variable must be found and corrected immediately.

Quality circles are small groups of workers, usually from the same section or department, who meet regularly to discuss work problems. Quality circles were first used to advantage by the Japanese, but are now in widespread use. Quality is only one of the issues discussed and usually any work problems are considered. The meetings are held on a voluntary basis in working hours. The group identifies the problem, analyses it and proposes solutions. The most suitable solution is selected and agreement obtained from management to implement it. The main aims of quality circles are:

❑ to improve productivity by participation;

❑ to improve quality;

❑ to exploit the knowledge and ingenuity of the workforce.

Quality circles are usually found on the shop floor and group members examine the work that they do themselves, whereas project teams or value analysis groups look at work they do not necessarily do themselves.

Quality circles only work if:

❑ the group consists of volunteers;

❑ there is management commitment to the scheme;

❑ there is union support and involvement;

❑ training programmes are available for the group members;

❑ all members of the group except the leader do similar work.

Standards

Standard specifications are the backbone of any quality assurance programme. Standards for sampling, gauging and measuring lay down the methods of testing and calibration which are the basic tools for assessing quality. There has been a move away from reliance on incoming inspection and towards a more rigorous assessment of the supplier's ability to satisfy the purchaser's needs. This cannot be done solely by checking a small sample from a batch. It is also achieved through continuous surveillance of the supplier's quality organisation and procedures. British Standard 5750 lays down the standards for a quality system. It includes organisation, reviews, planning, work instructions and records, and can be applied to any organisation.

Conventional views on quality have generally been limited to the product being made to a specification which is monitored by quality control techniques. A more recent approach is that of a *quality culture* which aims to give the customer a product or service of high quality and good value. Poor quality often starts before the product reaches the shop floor because of defective raw materials, design, scheduling, maintenance or working conditions. Adopting a quality culture to solve these and other problems starts at board level and throughout the organisation emphasis is put on:

❏   an aggressive strategy to overcome quality problems;

❏   putting the customer first;

❏   finding out what the customer wants;

❏   making sure that all the activities of the various departments give priority to quality;

❏   continual updating;

❏   continually establishing projects to improve quality involving all employees.

There are various forms of quality culture. These range from a situation where a supervisor puts forward an idea worth trying, receives permission to form a group of volunteers to pursue the issue, to a full-scale version involving all employees in training and implementing the quality culture.

British Standard 5750 specifies requirements for three basic levels of system for the assurance of quality of material and/or services. These are given in three parts as follows:

1. *Specification for design, manufacture and installation*

    This specifies the quality system to be applied when the technical requirements of material and/or services are specified principally in terms of the performance required, or where design has not been established.

    In these circumstances, the supplier is frequently responsible for design, development, manufacture, installation work and field trials. Reliability and other characteristics can be ensured only by control of quality throughout all phases of this work. Comprehensive guidance on the reliability of systems, equipment and components is provided in BS 5760.

2. *Specification for manufacture and installation*

    This specifies the quality system to be applied when the technical requirements of material and/or services are specified in terms of established design and where conformity to specified requirements can be ensured only by inspection and testing during manufacture and, as appropriate, installation.

3. *Specification for final inspection and testing*

    This specifies the quality system to be applied when conformity to specified requirements of material and/or services can be adequately established by inspection and tests conducted on the finished material or services.

The level of system necessary to assure quality in a rational and cost effective manner depends on the nature of the material or service required.

The following series of questions may be found useful as a guide when auditing a system established in accordance with BS 5750: Part 1. The questions invite a *yes* or *no* answer.

The questions are intended only to serve as indicators and reminders of important points.

1. *Quality system*

   Has the supplier established and documented a formal system of quality management?

2. *Organisation*

   ❏ *Personnel responsible for functions affecting quality*

   a) Has the supplier identified, and assigned responsibility for, the functions and activities directly affecting quality?

   b) Are there any gaps?

   c) Is there overlapping or conflict of responsibilities?

   ❏ *Management representative*

   d) Has a 'management representative' been appointed?

   e) Has the representative the necessary authority, responsibility and ability to perform his functions effectively?

   ❏ *Purchaser's representative*

   f) When applicable, is the Purchaser's Representative afforded reasonable access and facilities?

3. *Review of the quality system*

   a) Does the supplier's management carry out periodic reviews?

   b) Do these reviews make use of the findings of internal audits?

   c) Does the supplier have a programme for auditing his quality system?

   d) Are procedures for audit documented?

   e) Are written audit procedures sufficiently comprehensive to provide objective evidence of the system's effectiveness?

4. *Planning*

   a) Has the supplier obtained all the information needed to execute the contract?

   b) Has the supplier conducted a complete review of his contract to identify and provide for special or unusual contract requirements?

   c) Has the supplier initiated quality planning prior to starting work?

   d) Does the supplier's quality planning include identification of the need for developing new testing and inspection techniques?

   e) Does quality planning provide for identifying material characteristics, or new or unique manufacturing processes, that affect end product quality?

   f) Are the plans and practical equipment compatible, for example, tool precision and inspection and measuring instruments?

5. *Work instructions*

   a) Are documented instructions available for work operations where lack of instructions would adversely affect work performance?

   b) Are such work instructions clear and complete?

   c) Do they establish acceptable quality standards for the work operations covered?

   d) Are they compatible with associated inspection and testing?

e) Is proper use made of the work instructions?

f) Are the work instructions systematically reviewed?

6. *Records*

   a) Are these records of essential quality assurance activities?

   b) Are there effective means for assuring the currency, completeness and accuracy of records?

   c) Do inspection records contain all essential data?

   d) In instances of rejection, do records show resulting action?

   e) Are records analysed and used for the purpose of management action?

   f) Are there satisfactory arrangements for the storage and retrieval of records?

7. *Corrective action*

   a) Does the system provide for prompt detection of inferior quality and for correction.

   b) Is adequate action taken to correct the causes of defects in material, facilities and functions, e.g. design, purchasing, testing?

   c) Are analyses made to identify trends towards material nonconformity?

   d) Is corrective action taken to arrest unfavourable trends before nonconformities occur?

   e) Does corrective action extend to sub-contractor material?

   f) Is corrective action taken in response to user data?

   g) Are data analysis and material examination conducted on scrap or rework to determine extend and causes of defects?

   h) Is the effectiveness of corrective action reviewed and subsequently monitored?

8. *Design control*

   a) Does the supplier's system provide for a planned programme of design and development?

   b) Does this system cover the aspects of reliability, maintainability, safety, design review, value engineering, standardisation, interchangeability and documentation control?

   c) Are design and development responsibilities clearly assigned?

   d) Are design reviews carried out as part of the supplier's system of design control?

   e) Does design review provide for assurance that the technical data created by design reflect contract requirements?

   f) Is there an adequate system for controlling the issue and recall of this data?

   g) Is there a procedure for proposing, approving and implementing design changes?

   h) Is there appropriate control of design changes requiring approval by the purchaser?

9. *Documentation and change control*

   a) Does the system provide for clear and precise stipulation of responsibilities in documentation issue and change control?

   b) Are changes made in writing?

   c) Is the system of recording changes satisfactory?

   d) Are obsolete documents promptly removed from all points of issue or use?

10. *Control of inspection, measuring and test equipment*

   a) Are necessary gauges, testing and measuring equipment available and used?

11. *Control of purchased material and services*

   ❐ *Purchasing*

   a) Does the system ensure that material and services supplied by sub-contractors meet contract requirements?

   b) Does the system provide for the selection of sub-contractors on the basis of their quality capability?

   c) Does the supplier review his sub-contractors' performance at intervals consistent with the complexity and quality of the product?

   ❐ *Purchasing data*

   d) Do the supplier's purchasing documents clearly describe requirements?

   e) Are requirements for any necessary tests and inspection of raw materials specified in purchasing documents?

   ❐ *Receiving inspection*

   f) Does the supplier inspect incoming material to the extent necessary upon receipt?

   g) Does the supplier adjust the extent of receiving inspection on the basis of objective data?

   h) Does the supplier assure that material conforms to the applicable physical, chemical and other technical requirements, using laboratory analyses as necessary?

   i) Is tested, approved material identified and carefully segregated from that not tested or approved?

   j) Does the supplier have effective controls for preventing the use of nonconforming incoming material?

12. *Manufacturing control*

   a) Are all production processes accomplished under controlled conditions?

   b) Does control include necessary documented work instructions, adequate production equipment and appropriate working environments?

   c) Do necessary work instructions provide criteria for determining whether production, processing and fabrication work is acceptable or unacceptable?

   d) Does the quality system provide for monitoring both the issue of necessary work instructions and compliance with them?

   e) Are physical examinations, measurements or tests of materials provided for each work operation where appropriate?

f) When direct inspection is not practicable, does the system provide for indirect control by monitoring of processes?

g) Are both physical inspection and process monitoring used when either alone would be inadequate, or when required by the contract?

h) Is inspection and process monitoring accomplished systematically and are records kept?

i) Are unsuitable inspection or monitoring methods corrected promptly?

13. *Purchaser supplied material*

a) Does the supplier examine 'supplied material' upon receipt for damage, quantity, completeness and type?

b) Are there precautions and inspections during storage against damage and deterioration and to check on storage life limitations?

c) Is all 'supplied material' properly identified and protected from unauthorised use or improper disposal?

d) Have procedures been established for notification to the purchaser of any loss, damage, malfunction or deterioration of 'supplied material'?

14. *Completed item inspection and test*

a) Are completed items given a final inspection and test to establish overall quality?

b) Does the final testing meet the requirements of the relevant specification?

c) Are inspection and test problems or deficiencies promptly reported to the appropriate authority?

d) Is there re-inspection and re-test of all items that are re-worked, repaired or modified after initial and product testing?

15. *Sampling procedures*

a) Are recognised standards on sampling being utilised or are supplier-designed sampling plans available for review by the Purchaser's Representative?

b) Are proper records maintained of sampling procedures and results?

c) Is there a clear identification of characteristics to which sampling is applied?

16. *Control of non-conforming material*

a) Does the supplier have an effective system for controlling non-conforming material?

b) Does the supplier properly identify, segregate and dispose of non-conforming material?

17. *Indication of inspection status*

a) Does the supplier employ an effective system for indicating the inspection status of material?

b) Is the inspection status of material readily apparent?

c) Is batch or lot identity maintained throughout the manufacturing process where necessary?

18. ☐ *Protection and preservation of product quality*

a) Does the system provide for the identification, as necessary, of the material from the time of receipt until the supplier's responsibility ceases?

b) Are adequate work and inspection instructions prepared and implemented for the handling, storage and delivery of material?

c) Are handling, storage and delivery procedures and methods monitored as part of the quality system review?

❏ *Material handling*

a) Has the supplier instructions or procedures, where necessary, to control handling and transport operations?

b) Are special crates, boxes, containers, trucks or other transportation vehicles provided for handling material?

c) Are handling devices periodically inspected for cleanliness and suitability for use?

❏ *Storage*

a) Are there procedures and regular schedules for the inspection of products in storage and are these procedures adequate to prevent deterioration or damage?

b) Are all required critical environments maintained during storage?

❏ *Delivery*

a) Is all material to be stored or shipped properly identified and labelled?

19. *Training*

a) Are arrangements for personnel training satisfactory?

b) Are training records maintained?

| SEE | ALSO | *Section 2: Communications*, page 81; *Control*, page 86; *Production control*, page 156; *Quality assurance*, page 159; *Responsibility*, page 179; *Training*, page 199. |

Quality assurance

Total quality, *Personnel Management Factsheet No. 29.*

658.562 DTI *BS 5750/ISO 9000: 1987; A positive contribution to better business*, DTI, 1991.

658.562 DTI *The case for costing quality*, DTI, 1991.

658.562 DTI *The case for quality*, DTI, 1991.

658.562 *Implementing TQM*, IFS Ltd, 1991.

Questionnaire surveys

Questionnaires are a widely used means of gathering information in a systematic way. Devising suitable questions can, however, be quite difficult. The paramount consideration is that the person filling in the questionnaire understands the questions and provides the information wanted.

Features of a good questionnaire

1. Do not ask the interviewee to write an essay.

    Wrong: *"State the reasons why you prefer applicants from the world of banking"*

    Instead, offer some possibilities.

2. Where possible, try to allow for *yes* or *no* answers. This type of answer is not only easier to respond to but also is much easier to analyse later.

3. Do not ask for more accuracy than is needed or is reasonable for people to know.

    Wrong:

    "On what dates were you absent from work last year?"

    People are unlikely to remember dates but may well know the number of days.

4. Where it is vital to get certain information, put check questions in your questionnaire. For example, should you need to know age, ask early in the questionnaire:

    "What is your age?"

    and then later, ask

    "What is your date of birth?"

5. Do not ask leading questions or questions which use emotional words. For example:

    Wrong:

    "Do you believe it is wrong to wilfully obstruct management objectives?"

6. Do not use technical words unless you are sure they will be understood by everyone concerned.

7. Keep the questions short and as few as is possible.

8. Do not ask questions that call for calculations.

    Wrong:

    "How much did you spend on travel to work last year?"

    Instead, ask

Did you spend ? *£0 – 200*	☐
£201– 500	☐
£501 – £1,000	☐

9. Remember, most people who fill in questionnaires are volunteers, so make the task as easy and entertaining as you can. Explain why you want the information and that confidentiality is assured.

10. Pilot your questionnaire before doing the full survey. In this way, you can iron out any wrinkles in both the collection and the analysis of the data.

SEE ALSO

Section 2: Attitude, page 73, *Communications*, page 81; *Manpower analysis and planning*, page 133.

Questionnaires/surveys

658.314 Walters, M, *What about the workers*, IPM, 1990.

658.46 Reeves, TK, *Surveys at work*, McGraw-Hill, 1981.

Recruitment, selection and induction

Because of occurrences such as skills shortages and demographic trends, many organisations carry out *manpower planning* in an effort to avoid recruitment difficulties. Usually this is done by the *personnel department*, and normally means an analysis of personnel data looking at matters such as labour turnover rates, business forecasts and age trends, to arrive at estimates as to manpower needs in the future.

Recruitment is concerned with assessing the jobs to be filled, and with attracting suitable applicants. Assessing the job is often done in the form of a job description which details matters such as main duties, who the person is responsible for, and what they are responsible for, as well as giving information on circumstances and difficulties. The detail included is of course a matter that will differ depending on organisational needs. Often, the *job description* is the basis of other personnel activities such as appraisals, and so is a fundamental document.

Once a job has been described, the person required to fill the job can also be specified. The *job specification* or *person specification* will detail matters such as skills, knowledge required, experience needed, and personal qualities desired.

At this point, it is now possible to draw up an advertisement, the purpose of which is to attract a suitable number of potential employees. Not too many, but enough to give a reasonable choice.

Once potential applicants have made contact, it is then normal to send out both an application form and more information, perhaps even the job description and specification. The completed application forms then form the first stage in the selection process.

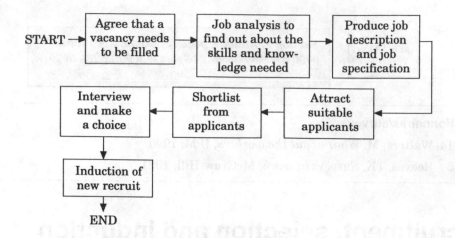

The following *checklist* offers guidance to managers responsible for recruitment and selection.Recruitment and selection checklist

Item	Consider
1.	Has the vacancy been agreed by the responsible manager?
2.	Is there an up-to-date job description?
3.	What are the conditions of employment (salary, hours, holidays, etc)
4.	Has a job specification been prepared?
5.	Has a notice of the vacancy been circulated internally?
6.	Has a job advertisement been agreed? Have details of the vacancy been forwarded to relevant agencies?
7.	Do all potential candidates (internal or external) know where to apply and in what form?
8.	What arrangements have been made for drawing up a shortlist of candidates?
9.	Have the interviewing arrangements been agreed, and have short-listed candidates been informed?
10.	Have unsuitable candidates, or candidates held in reserve, been informed of their position?
11.	Have offer letters been agreed and despatched to successful candidates? Have references been taken up, where necessary?
12.	Have suitable rejection letters been sent to unsuccessful shortlisted candidates, thanking them for their attendance?
13.	Have all replies to offer letters been accounted for?
14.	Have the necessary procedures for placement, induction and follow-up of successful candidates been put into effect?

The next stage in the process involves *selection.* There are four steps:

1. shortlisting candidates on the basis of information supplied by them, usually in the form of application forms;

2. interviewing the applicants;

3. testing (if appropriate);

4. making a choice.

The initial shortlisting usually means comparing the applicants with a list of desired qualities as well as with each other. It may be that there have not been any suitable applications and there is therefore a need to re-advertise or re-think the requirement.

Once a shortlist has been drawn up, it is then usual to hold an interview. There are a number of possibilities for the form of the interview:

Closed interviews

This type of interview follows a set pattern of asking questions which are planned to cover all the requirements of a particular job. This means that all the essential information is gathered together in the same way from each person interviewed.

Open interviews

This type of interview requires more skill from the interviewer, who puts the interviewee at ease and then steers him on to the subjects thought necessary.

Board interviews

This technique subjects the individual to a number of interviewers at one time. An alternative to this is where each member of the committee interviews the candidates privately. The opinions on each interviewee are then examined and analysed.

No matter which form is decided on there are certain basic considerations.

1. The aim of the interview should be clear. It is usually primarily concerned with identifying the best candidate, but it should also be concerned with clarifying the nature of the job to enable the candidate to judge whether he wants it.

2. Preparation is critical to success. The interviewers must review the demands of the job and study the application forms, deciding on the main question areas. The interview should have structure and continuity.

3. The conduct of the interview will need consideration of the room layout, the need to establish rapport, the use of questions to gather the required information, while at the same time encouraging the candidate to volunteer information.

4. After the interview the information gathered needs to be evaluated along with the other information from the application forms. There is a well-known classification system used for the selection process known as the seven point plan. This was developed by the National Institute of Industrial Psychology.

N.I.I.P Seven point plan		
1.	*Physical make-up*	Appearance, bearing, speech. Defects or disabilities of occupational importance.
2.	*Attainments*	Type of education, progress made educationally, occupational training and experience. How well has the candidate done occupationally?
3.	*General intelligence*	Level of general intelligence, how effectively is it used?
4.	*Special aptitudes*	Understanding of mechanical things Manual dexterity Numerical and/or written skills
5.	*Interests*	Intellectual, constructional, physically active, artistic, practical, social.
6.	*Disposition*	Acceptable to other people Capable of influencing others Steady and dependable Self reliant
7.	*Circumstances*	Domestic circumstances, children's progress What do other members of the family do?

An interview assessment form may be used or an evaluation chart.

Interview assessment form

	Actual	Desirable
Formal qualifications		
Knowledge		
Experience		

Skills   – Manual
     – Social
     – Other		

Personality/motivation		
Physical requirements		
Interests		
Circumstances		

Evaluation chart: Considerations

1. *Appearance*: Physical characteristics, carriage, posture, personal grooming, dress, features.

A	B	C	D	E
Outstanding presence, clearly recalled, very distinctive.	Creates good impression, attractive presence, well and neatly dressed, energetic.	Adequate, but indistinguishable, in most respects.	Lax, careless or overdressed, room for improvement, lacks energy.	Decidedly odd, unacceptable, well below standard.

2. *Manner*: Approach, natural self-possession, attractiveness.

A	B	C	D	E
Exceptional poise. Naturally charming and engaging manner. Great aplomb and proper dignity.	Agreeable manner, likeable, correct behaviour, self-possessed in most circumstances.	Fairly neutral, responds predictably. Neither outstanding nor colourless.	Awkward, ill at ease. Too anxious to please, over-sensitive, touchy, colourless, or indolent.	Crude, coarse, repellent, avoided by others, obsequious to superiors.

3. *Voice and Diction*: Quality, clarity, volume, timbre, accent.

A	B	C	D	E
Unusually agreeable, clear, resonant and attractive.	Pleasant and acceptable, not difficult to listen to, distinctive.	Indistinguishable, but broadly acceptable for the job. Room for improvement.	Too loud or indistinct, affected or too marked on accent, unacceptable for this job.	Disagreeable, irritating, whining or unpleasant.

4. *Self-expression*: Vocabulary, grammar, pronunciation, ability to communicate information or ideas with clarity and brevity.

A	B	C	D	E
Has a wide vocabulary and uses it with ease but without being pedantic. Can be eloquent.	Sound grammar and vocabulary. Careful and educated choice of words and phrases. Communicates clearly.	Ordinary, but acceptable range of vocabulary. Will descend to clichés. No sparkle, capable of improvement.	Makes common errors. At a loss for words. Illogical or irrelevant. Too much jargon.	Bad grammar. Limited vocabulary. Unable to communicate, confused, slip-shod.

5. *Participation*: Degree of participation, quality of contribution, adherence to relevant points.

A	B	C	D	E
Stimulating responses and a careful listener. Distinctive and educated style.	Initiates some relevant points. Has learned to listen. Neither reticent nor garrulous. Can reason closely.	Answers carefully but contributes no distinction of style.	Responds too slowly or too quickly. Conversation flags or is monopolised by one party.	Reticent, evasive or talks incessantly.

6. *Domestic/Family Stability*: Stable, well-integrated happy home environment: any evidence of undue dominating, stresses or demands?

A	B	C	D	E
A soundly-based active family background, with exceptional qualities and much mutual support and affection both now and in childhood.	A happy, stable home environment, mutual support and affection. A happy childhood and adolescence.	A stable, happy home environment, an unexceptional childhood and adolescence.	Some evidence of a dominating or demanding parent or partner, or disturbing influences.	Dominating or doting parents, over-dependency, unlikely to cope normally with crises, unhappy history.

171

7. *Maturity*: Ability to inspire confidence, breadth of views, range of interests, consistency.

A	B	C	D	E
Inspires deep confidence. Has a broad grasp of affairs. At ease with people of all ages and backgrounds. Consistent progress towards goals. Exceptional judge of character.	Consistent, gives an impression of reliability. At ease with most people of a similar age. Wide range of background activities. Sound judgement on most topics.	Mature in the accepted sense for his/her age. 'Learned the hard way.' Dependable within the limits of this job. Likely to improve.	Tends to emotional or prejudicial responses. Personal goals not clearly defined. Suspect in domestic or social stability. May improve.	Immature, emotional and irrational. Unstable and erratic progress. Easily led. Not likely to improve.

8. *Vigour and Enthusiasm*: Vitality as observed from voice or actions, animation, energy, 'attack'.

A	B	C	D	E
Immense vitality, radiates controlled energy, an attacking spirit. Infectious enthusiasm which can overcome inertia in others.	Very alert and energetic, lively manner, spirited responses, can enthuse others and re-stimulate the pessimistic.	Neither radiates energy nor appears indolent. Brightens visibly when stimulated.	Tends to droop, misses points. Fails to stimulate enthusiasm.	Listless, sluggish to the point of inertia. Dull-eyed.

9. *Attitude*: Resolution, optimism, positive approach, cheerful demeanour.

A	B	C	D	E
Resolute, sensibly optimistic. Radiates confidence. Cheerful and encouraging.	A cheerful and determined person not easily daunted. Encourages his/her colleagues.	Not particularly cheerful nor easily discouraged. Tries to get his/her facts straight. Generally optimistic.	Requires encouragement in the face of adversity, or counsels of caution when over optimistic. Needs to take a broader view.	Negative approach, pessimistic, outlook may veer wildly to overoptimism. Unpredictable, glum.

10. *Group Behaviour/Social Skills*

A	B	C	D	E
Very perceptive and tactful. Socially adroit. Entirely self-possessed.	Perceptive, tactful, well-accepted, self-possessed in most circumstances. Group Leader.	Pleasant, agreeable, not easily recalled, unlikely to create gaffes, seldom the Group Leader.	Undistinguished, colourless, uneasy outside usual environment. Prickly or inconsiderate.	Egotistical, insensitive or acutely withdrawn and self-conscious.

11. *Ambition*: Consistent progress towards goals, motivation, working philosophy, realism.

A	B	C	D	E
Has made consistent rapid progress towards set goals and plans to continue progressing to the top. Realistic without being consumed with ambition to succeed at all costs. Without undue vanity about a real flair or talent.	Has continued to make good progress and aspires to set goals. Healthy motives and ambitions, and likely to have growing potential. Consistent progress to be expected.	Healthy ambitions. Capable of doing this job. Long-term potential. Consistent progress to be expected.	Tends to over-estimate capabilities. Ambitions at this moment exceed potential, motivated by others and less predictable in a future role.	Pretentious ambitions based on vanity, fear, or other factors. Not basically a self-starter and little evidence that he/she will be.

Pitfalls in evaluating candidates

Often the chief problem in employment interviews is not that of obtaining the candidate's background, personal history or other facts, but how they are interpreted. Personal preferences and prejudices are difficult to eliminate. Some common ones are:

❏ *Halo effect*

This means basing one's overall impression of an individual on only a part of the total information, and using this limited impression as a guide in rating all the other factors. This may work for or against the candidate. For example, a man with long hair may be judged on the interviewer's dislike of long-haired employees not on what the applicant has to say. It is wrong to base an overall evaluation on one factor such as the person's hair style or ability to communicate verbally. Just because someone is not very articulate does not necessarily mean to say that he or she will be a bad employee.

❏ *Over generalisation*

Just because a person behaves in a certain manner in an interview situation, it does not mean that the person will behave the same way in all circumstances. For example, someone who dresses in worn clothes and so does not appear to be neat, should not be assumed to be a sloppy worker.

❏ *Comparison with current employees*

Will the applicant fit in? Is the person very different from those who are now working for the organisation? Not employing people for these kind of reasons can lead to uniformity and conformity which can have a detrimental effect. This should not be interpreted as meaning that you should deliberately seek out "oddballs", but it does mean that individuals should not be rejected because they do not exactly fit the mould of other employees.

❏ *Excessive qualifications*

Often candidates who are over qualified become frustrated and dissatisfied with their work.

The following checklist offers guidance to managers carrying out interviews with job applicants.

1. Be clear about what you are looking for.

2. Prepare questions to which you *need* answers.

3. Use plain language.

4. Allow thinking time for responses.

5. Look for non-verbal signals.

6. Maintain an atmosphere of friendly neutrality.

7. Listen rather than talk.

Managers may find the following step-by-step guide helpful.

Interviewing guide

Be prepared	Obtain available information e.g. job details, candidate specification and application form.
	Arrange interview room.
	Ensure no interruptions.
	Plan the interview.
Welcome the candidate	After initial courtesies, thank candidate for coming.
	Explain briefly what procedure you propose to adopt for the interview.
	Commence by asking relatively easy and non-threatening questions.
Encourage candidate to talk	Ask open-ended questions.
	Prompt where necessary.
	Indicate that you are listening.
	Briefly develop points of interest raised by candidate.
Control the interview	Direct your questions along the lines that will achieve *your* objectives.
	Tactfully, but firmly, clamp down on the over-talkative candidate.
	Do not get too involved in particular issues, just because of your own interests.
	Keep an eye on the time.
Supply necessary information	Briefly add to information already made available to candidate.
	Answer candidate's questions.
	Inform candidate of the next steps in the selection procedure.
Close interview	Thank candidate for his/her responses to your questions.
	Exchange final courtesies.
Final steps	Write up your notes about the candidate.
	Grade, or rank, him/her for suitability.
	Operate administrative procedures regarding notifications, etc.

Tests

Where testing is part of the selection process, the tests need to be used with care, and the following ground rules may help.

☐ The attribute to be tested should be defined. So, for example, typing ability is not a clear enough requirement; it should be perhaps typing at sixty words per minute with no errors.

☐ The test must be reliable and valid. A high score on the test should be associated with good job performance.

☐ The test should use standard conditions so that everyone has the same chance.

There are five types of test.

1. *Aptitude tests* – perhaps to measure mechanical or manual dexterity.

2. *Attainment tests* – to check on skills previously acquired, e.g. typing.

3. *Personality tests* – gaining in usage in recent years, though often regarded with suspicion.

4. *Medical tests* – is the candidate fit for the work?

5. *Group selection* – in some cases it is desirable to test for leadership qualities, or social skills.

Induction

Whenever new employees report for work on the first day, the way they are treated will be of crucial importance. Studies have shown that the first days on a job are for most people both disturbing and anxious. A careful and considerate introduction to the place and the people helps build confidence and increase a sense of belonging. Some of the matters to consider in an induction programme are:

☐ *Terms and conditions*

Pay, hours, bonus, shifts, overtime, holidays, rules, sickness, pension.

☐ *Department rules and procedures*

Timekeeping, absenteeism, smoking, discipline, meal and other breaks, unions, time-off.

☐ *The job and how it fits in*

Tour of the site, duties, standards and quality, colleagues.

☐ *Health and safety*

Special hazards, first aid, fire drills, accident procedures.

Groups that may need special consideration

School and college leavers

School leavers need special help when they start their first job. Most youngsters are excited and nervous about their entry into working life. Their fears must be allayed and their enthusiasm captured if they are to settle down and enjoy their jobs. It is important for them to develop a positive attitude to work, and for this to happen they need to appreciate their importance to the organisation and understand where their job fits in to the whole. Their attention should be drawn to opportunities for training, development and advancement within the organisation.

A lack of experience of work and the possible dangers of the workplace make young people vulnerable to industrial accidents. Where several young people work together, natural high spirits could have dangerous consequences. Safety requirements should be stressed at an early stage in induction and recruits should know who the safety representative is.

Women returning to work

Women returning to work after some years of caring for young children often find difficulty in once more adapting to working life. They also find that developments in the company or in their field of work leave them feeling out of date and out of touch.

Planned induction and updating training if necessary, can assist them to catch up and quickly re-establish their satisfaction in their work and their previous value to the organisation.

Disabled employees

The induction of disabled people should be given careful attention. Individual care is well worthwhile in helping to overcome from the start any problems over access, or special facilities. Advice on the employment and training of disabled people can be obtained from the Disablement Resettlement Office at the local Jobcentre.

Management trainees

Graduates and other management trainees, whether in large or small organisations, are often not immediately destined for a specific job and may be involved in further educational or training programmes. Nevertheless, their induction programme should if possible include practical opportunities to be involved in the work of the organisation. If this is not done, it is easy for their general induction to seem remote and for their interest and motivation to wane.

Minorities

Members of minority racial groups require the same induction as other employees but, in addition, there may be some social conventions or traditions of which they or the company may be unaware. Drawing attention to these differences early in their employment can help them and their colleagues to work well together.

Companies who recruit employees with only limited knowledge of English should seriously consider providing facilities for language training. The Race Relations Employment Advisory Service will advise on this and other aspects of the employment of racial minorities; local advisers can be contacted through Jobcentres.

Managers and other specialist staff

Employees often see a new job in terms of the old one. A carefully planned induction programme can help them to identify more positively with their new job and its role.

Extract from Company selection policy

Equality of opportunity in selection

It is our policy to fill any vacancy with a person who matches the requirements of the job (e.g. in ability, experience, qualifications) and is the most suitable, subject only to any rules/ agreements on giving priority to internal applicants. In accordance with legislation and our equal opportunity policy, selection will be regardless of the applicant's sex, race and marital status. Preference must be given to any registered disabled applicant, who is one of equally suitable candidates. Staff who are surplus in other units must be considered for any suitable vacancies before external recruitment takes place.

Selectors should identify a job's requirements and having done so *use only job-related criteria* at all stages of the selection process and apply them consistently. In particular:

Standards/qualifications

- ❑ Avoid unnecessary seniority, physical requirements and experience considerations.

- ❑ Equivalent foreign qualifications offered should be regarded as acceptable on the same basis as their UK counterparts. In cases of doubt the relative standing of foreign qualifications should be checked.

- ❑ Only apply age limits when these can be justified as necessary for the job.

- ❑ Do not demand a higher standard of English than is required for the safe and effective performance of the job on a clearly demonstrable career pattern.

Selection techniques

- ❑ Any tests or selection exercises used must be approved by the selection methods group and administered and marked only by trained persons. Any materials used should be related to a job's requirements and designed to measure an individual's ability to train for or perform the job.

- ❑ Shortlisting should be done by more than one person using a common process for all candidates regardless of their race, sex or marital status.

Interviews

- ❑ Job interviews should be planned and structured and the questions should seek only the ability to meet job requirements.

- ❑ Use short open questions; avoid leading questions.

- ❑ Generalised assumptions and prejudices about individuals from particular groups must not be allowed to influence selection decisions.

- ❑ Take care to avoid misunderstandings which can arise between individuals of different cultural backgrounds.

- ❑ Do not ask questions about marriage plans or family intentions.

- ❑ Only ask questions about domestic responsibilities if they are relevant and are asked of men and women alike.

- ❑ The reasons for all decisions to select or reject individual candidates should be recorded in writing.

SEE	ALSO

Section 2: Personnel management, page 154.

Recruitment selection

658.3   Hackett, P, *Personnel: the department at work*, IPM, 1991.

658.311   Income Data Services, *Recruitment*, IPM, 1990.

658.3112   Lewis, C, *Employee selection*, Hutchinson, 1985.

Redundancy action checklist

1. Make sure that redundancy is provable within the legislative definitions.

2. Decide whether employees have to be categorised within separate establishments.

3. Decide whether selection is called for.

4. Decide which descriptions of employees are to be affected.

5. If selection is needed, decide upon the method of selection but ensure observance of any customary or agreed procedures.

6. If the employees are covered by a trade union recognition agreement, follow the redundancy handling procedures as soon as possible after taking the decision on redundancy.

7. Decide whether the Department of Employment has to be notified and, if it does, make notification before the expiry of the periods prescribed.

8. Whether or not the redundancy handling procedures apply, arrange consultation with the employees likely to be affected as soon as possible after taking the decision on redundancy.

9. Examine the whole of the undertaking to determine whether any redundancies can be avoided by transfer or offers of alternative employment.

10. Decide which particular employees are to be made redundant and notify them.

11. Allow personal interviews with any employee who wishes to raise a grievance or problem arising from the redundancy.

12. Issue dismissal notices with appropriate notice and with calculation of any remuneration due and any redundancy pay.

13. Allow for employees who so request to take time off during the notice period to seek retraining or to look for other work.

14. On termination, make payments that are due.

SEE ALSO | *Section 2: Employment law*, page 99; *Trade unions and the law*, page 192.

Redundancy

Burrows, G, *Redundancy counselling for managers*, IPM,

Crowley, T, *Redundancy*, Turnstone Press,

Responsibility

Holding *responsibility* means being obliged to fulfil certain functions and being accountable for those actions. In an organisation, individuals have certain duties and responsibilities assigned to them as part of their jobs. Unlike authority, responsibility cannot be delegated. When a supervisor delegates authority, he or she still remains responsible for making sure the work is done, even though it may be done by another person.

Managerial responsibilities include:

- ❐ forecasting;
- ❐ planning;
- ❐ organising;
- ❐ co-ordinating;
- ❐ communicating;
- ❐ commanding;
- ❐ controlling;
- ❐ motivating.

Supervisory responsibilities include:

- ❐ organising;
- ❐ co-operating;
- ❐ communicating;
- ❐ controlling;
- ❐ motivating.

It is sometimes said that administration is concerned with getting things done *right* and management with getting the *right* things done. A supervisor is a manager whose job it is to make sure that the work is done. A supervisor must be a good leader of his or her team but also a competent subordinate to superiors. Supervisors are expected to keep good relations with other departmental heads and supervisors. Whether in an office or factory, a supervisor must possess a high degree of technical competence of the jobs being supervised and the ability to manage.

SEE ALSO | *Section 2: Authority*, page 75; *Communications*, page 81; *Control*, page 86; *Decision-making and problem-solving*, page 90; *Delegation*, page 93; *Groups and teams*, page 104; *Leadership*, page 119; *Management qualities and activities*, page 130.

Responsibility

658   Carnall, C, *Management: a revision aid*, ICSA, 1988

Salaries and wages

Wages

Wage payment systems consist of the pay structure and any productivity, bonus or profit sharing schemes used to motivate and reward workers for their efforts. The assumption behind most payment systems is that pay is the key factor in motivating workers. This is not necessarily always valid, but it is certainly true that in some circumstances, incentive payment systems will motivate employees, and it is equally true that the pay system as a whole will play a major part in obtaining and retaining workers. It can also be a major cause of dissatisfaction.

A pay structure is formed around the rates paid for the jobs within an organisation. The structure will incorporate pay differentials between the various jobs. These aim to reflect differences in skills and responsibility but are affected by national and local pressures, including the results of pay bargaining and the effects of changes in labour market conditions.

The two main types of pay structures are:

a) *graded structures* in which there is a hierarchy of grades into which jobs are allocated according to their relative value as determined by bargaining, tradition, or a formal system of job evaluation. Within each grade there may be scope for additional merit payments so that there is a pay bracket for each group of jobs;

b) *fixed rate structures* in which there is a fixed rate for each job, although there may also be scope for additional merit payments in this system.

Time rate systems

Time rate, also known as day rate, daywork or flat rate, is the system under which operators are simply paid a predetermined rate per week, day or hour for the actual time they have worked.

Time rates are used when it is thought that it is impossible or undesirable to apply a payment by result system. They do not provide a direct incentive relating reward to effort and for that reason some companies introduce a system of merit awards in addition to the base rates.

Payment by results schemes

Payment by results schemes relate the pay or part of the pay of the worker to the number of items produced or the time taken to do a certain amount of work. The main requirements for the success of a payment by results scheme are that:

a) it should be based on standards determined by work measurement;

b) the reward should be proportionate to achievement and the effort required;

c) the individual should be able to calculate the reward for a given level of achievement;

d) there should be the minimum of delay between making the effort and receiving the reward;

e) the scheme must contain provisions for dealing with waiting time, machine downtime and trainee labour.

These requirements are often difficult to meet, hence the problems created by many schemes which have not been based on adequate work measurement and have not included arrangements to maintain proper standards in the event of new work or changes in existing work.

Types of schemes

Three main types of individual payment by results schemes are:

a) *straight money piecework* – the payment of a uniform price per unit of production;

b) *straight time piecework* – (time allowed system) – the payment of a basic bonus rate for the time allowed to do the work, but if the worker completes the job in less time he or she gains the advantage of the time saved, as he or she is still paid for the original time allowed;

c) *differential piecework* – where, with increased productivity, the worker's bonus increases but not at the same rate as output.

Measured daywork

In measured daywork the pay of the employee is fixed on the understanding that he or she will maintain a specified level of incentive performance which is fixed and monitored by work measurement. The incentive element is therefore guaranteed in advance and puts the employee under an obligation to perform at the effort level required. If performance is consistently above or below standard over the longer term, the payment is adjusted accordingly for a further fixed period.

Group incentive schemes

Group bonus schemes provide for the payment of a bonus either equally or proportionately to individuals doing similar work on a production line or other defined area. The bonus is related to the output achieved over an agreed standard or to the time saved on a job – the difference between allowed time and actual time.

Group bonus schemes are most appropriate where groups of workers are carrying out interdependent tasks and individuals have only limited scope to control the level of their own output. Their disadvantage is that they eliminate personal incentive.

Factory-wide bonus schemes

Factory-wide incentive schemes provide a bonus for all factory workers which is related to an overall measure of performance such as output or added value (the value added to the cost of raw materials and bought out parts by the process of production). Such schemes can help to improve motivation and performance if they include arrangements for participation in planning improvements or overcoming problems. But they cannot provide a very direct incentive because the link between individual effort and reward is so tenuous.

Profit sharing

Profit sharing schemes pay a bonus to employees which is related in some way to the profits earned by the business. The bonus can be determined by a published and agreed formula or it can be issued as a sort of *ex-gratia* payment at the discretion of the management. The former method is more likely to result in improved motivation but even this will be very limited because of the impossibility of linking individual effort to reward. Profit sharing schemes cannot provide a direct incentive – they can only demonstrate the willingness of management to distribute a proportion of profits to all those who have contributed to producing them. This may improve identification and commitment if it is seen as part of a general policy of participation. In many cases, however, profit sharing is regarded as no more than a financial handout which has no long-lasting effects on morale.

Salaries

The basic aims of a salary structure are to attract, retain and motivate staff by developing and maintaining a competitive and equitable salary structure.

Salary structure is concerned with:

a) determining salary levels – by job evaluation and salary surveys;

b) designing and maintaining salary structures;

c) operating salary progression systems, including incremental payment schemes;

d) designing and operating bonus schemes;

e) providing employee benefits.

Deciding salary levels

Salary levels are affected by three factors.

1. What the job is worth compared with other jobs in the organisation – this is assessed by internal job evaluation.

2. What the job is worth compared with jobs outside the organisation (market rates).

3. The performance of the individual in the job – this may be assessed by performance appraisal.

Job evaluation schemes are often used to establish the value of jobs in a job hierarchy. So far as possible, judgements about job values are made on objective rather than subjective grounds – these judgements are based on analytical studies of the content of the jobs irrespective of the individual contributions made by job holders.

Job evaluation schemes can determine internal relativities but in themselves they cannot put a price on the job. The price will inevitably be influenced by market forces and it is necessary to establish market rates before designing the salary structure.

The choice of salary structure is between:

1. a graded salary structure which consists of a sequence of salary ranges, each of which has a defined minimum and maximum salary and into which jobs of broadly the same value are allocated;

2. a structure consisting of individual salary ranges for each job. This is less typical – it is sometimes used for more senior jobs which cannot readily be grouped together into grades;

3. salary progression curves which aim to link increases in salary over a fairly long period to increased maturity or experience.

Graded salary structures

The basic features of a graded salary structure are as follows:

a) each salary consists of a salary range or band. No individual holding a job in the grade can go beyond the maximum of the salary range unless he is promoted;

b) the mid-point of each grade represents the salary that the company believes a fully experienced and competent job holder in that grade is worth;

c) the number of grades will depend upon two main factors:

  1. the width of the salary brackets, and

  2. the upper and lower salary limits of the jobs the structure is meant to cover. The number of grades should be sufficient to enable jobs at distinct levels in the hierarchy to be graded separately and to provide for a reasonable degree of flexibility in grading jobs.

d) the salary brackets should be wide enough to enable job holders in the grade to be rewarded as their performance in the job improves;

e) there is an overlap between salary grades which acknowledges that an experienced person doing a good job can be of more value to the company than a newcomer to a job in the grade above.

Salary progression

Salary progression policies relate increases in salary to performance or experience.

Performance related systems allow for variable progression according to merit. The main problem with such systems is to provide for consistency and equity in determining merit increases.

Bonus schemes

Bonus schemes provide an award, usually in the form of a lump sum payment, which is additional to basic salary and is related in some way to the performance of the individual or group of individuals receiving the bonus. Bonus schemes aim to provide a specific additional incentive, but to achieve this they should satisfy the following criteria:

a) the amount of the award received after tax should be sufficiently high to encourage staff to accept exacting targets and standards of performance;

b) the incentive should be related to criteria over which the individual has a substantial measure of control;

c) the scheme should be sensitive enough to ensure that rewards are proportionate to achievements;

d) the individual should be able to calculate the reward he can get for a given level of achievement;

e) the formula for calculating the bonus and the conditions under which it is paid should be clearly defined;

f) constraints should be built into the scheme which ensure that staff cannot receive inflated bonuses which may not reflect their own efforts;

g) the scheme should contain provisions for a regular review, say, every two or three years, which could result in it being changed or discontinued;

h) the scheme should be easy to administer and understand, and it should be tailored to meet the requirements of the company.

Employee benefits

Employee benefits consist of any items or rewards that are provided for employees which are not part of normal pay. They include pensions, sick pay, holidays, company cars, housing assistance and medical benefits. The aim of an organisation in deciding its remuneration policies should be to look at the total remuneration package consisting of basic pay and all these benefits. This package should be adjusted according to the needs of the company and of the individual, taking into account the perceived value of the different benefits and taxation considerations. Employees should be told of the value of the total package to them and comparisons should be made of this total with that provided by other companies to ensure that remuneration policies remain competitive.

SEE ALSO **Section 2: Job evaluation**, page 117; **Personnel Management**, page 154.

Salaries and wages

Performance related pay, *Personnel Management Factsheet No. 30*.

331.21   Suter, E, *Cashless pay and deductions*, IPM, 1987.

658.32   Income Data Services, *The merit factor*, IDS, 1985.

Stress management

The business world is divided on the subject of *stress*. But there are more and more people now who consider stress a serious issue in the workplace. Managers might tend to be among the doubters, since the evidence indicates that they are the people least likely to suffer from stress, perhaps because they can pass the problems down the line, and because they have more control over their working environment. It is the middle and first line managers who seem to suffer the most.

Researchers claim that 1% of workdays are lost due to strikes, and 5% of workdays are lost due to stress related illness. Prolonged stress at first causes performance to rise and then, after fatigue and exhaustion set in, performance drops away or ceases altogether. Indications of a highly stressed workforce include high staff turnover and increased self-certificated absenteeism.

Some causes of stress

❏   A new job or boss; new technology or systems of working and controls.

❏   New colleagues/work practices or location.

❏   Unrealistic deadlines and demands.

❏   Overstretched financial commitments/work overload or underload.

❏   Redundancy.

❏   Imprecise job description.

❏   Cut-throat competition.

❏   Divorce/separation.

❏   Moving house.

❏   Loss of pet.

❏   Children failing exams or leaving home.

Physical, emotional and behavioural symptoms of stress

Physical symptoms

❏   Palpitations – an awareness that the heart is beating forcefully, irregularly, or quickly.

- Pain and tightness in the chest.
- Indigestion and abdominal distension due to wind.
- Colicky abdominal pain and diarrhoea.
- Frequent passing of urine.
- Impotence or lack of libido (sexual drive).
- Alteration of the menstrual pattern in women.
- Tingling feelings in the arms and legs.
- Muscle tension and often pain in the neck or low part of the back.
- Persistent headaches, often starting in the neck and extending forward over the head.
- Migraines.
- Skin rashes.
- Feeling a lump in the throat.
- Double vision and difficulty focusing the eyes.

Emotional symptoms

- Excessive and rapid swings in mood.
- Worrying unreasonably about things that do not matter.
- Inability to feel sympathy for other people.
- Excessive concern about physical health.
- Withdrawal and daydreams.
- Feelings of tiredness and lack of concentration.
- Increased irritability and anxiety.

Behavioural symptoms

- Indecision and unreasonable complaints.
- Increased absenteeism and delayed recovery from accidents and illness.
- Accident-proneness and careless driving.
- Poor work, cheating and evasion.
- Increased smoking.
- Increased consumption of alcohol.
- Increased dependence on drugs, i.e. tranquillisers and sleeping tablets.
- Over-eating, or, less commonly, loss of appetite.
- Change in sleep pattern, difficulty getting to sleep and waking tired.
- Impaired quality and quantity of work.

The longer stress is allowed to remain unresolved, the more the sufferer's physical health is likely to be affected.

Heart and respiratory disease kill a large percentage of the UK population and apart from smoking, the main contributory factors for this kind of illness linked with stress. Sufferers are likely to come from a bad home environment, have two occupations, or work more than 60 hours a week, and have hobbies such as DIY which can be seen as another form of work. Stress can also be brought on by physical conditions such as noise, bad lighting, vibrations and humidity.

Professional people and company directors are the least likely to suffer stress related disease, while the unskilled labourer is most at risk. At manager level, inefficient managers cause stress for themselves and their staff. Too little work, responsibility or pressure can be just as stressful as too much. Experts agree that what one person finds stressful another might find stimulating or normal. There is no way of distinguishing a *common* stress level since each person reacts differently.

Data on mortality shows that some occupations are more stressful than others.

If the standard mortality rate = 100

Clergymen	62
Accountants	88
Engineers	99
Turners	66
Foundry workers	160
Coalminers	180
Firemen	82
Publicans	147

Checklist of organisational and job pressures

Organisational pressures

☐ mismatch between responsibility and authority;

☐ size of enterprise, work group;

☐ inconsistent policy and behaviour;

☐ unpredictable, arbitrary changes;

☐ decisions forced against inadequate information;

☐ conflict of goals, expectations;

☐ inadequate/too much/inaccurate information;

☐ too many bosses;

☐ restricted social contacts;

☐ inconsiderate superior;

☐ being in boundary spanning role (e.g. project leader, supervisor).

Task and job related pressures

☐ overload;

☐ ambiguous, unclear objectives;

☐ conflicting, inconsistent tasks;

☐ mismatch   between tasks and resources;

          between capacity and expectations;

☐ lack of feedback and acknowledgement;

☐ machine pacing;

- [ ] repetitive, undemanding work;
- [ ] under-use of talents;
- [ ] high, external control.

Individual pressures

- [ ] inappropriate level of skill, knowledge;
- [ ] low adaptability;
- [ ] low tolerance of ambiguity;
- [ ] high need for structure;
- [ ] lack of support from others;
- [ ] additional non-work stress;
- [ ] inadequate strategies for coping.

Stress types

Where stress is concerned, there are two types of people:

- [ ] *type A people* – like to be under pressure, they are people in a hurry, they cram as much as possible into every day;

- [ ] *type B people* – are not to be rushed, they are 'laid back' and don't feel they need to be achieving something every minute of every day.

The nearer your score (on the questionnaire Section 3 Unit 4, page 235) is to a 100, the closer you are to a Type A person. The nearer the score is to 0 the closer you are to a Type B person.

Type A people are not necessarily always stressed, but because of the way they operate, they are more likely to put themselves under stress.

Type B people can be under major stress, but as they don't continually put themselves into stressful situations, they are less likely to be stressed.

Type A are six times more likely to have heart attacks than Type B.

Stress management

Stress management is effected both by change in the organisation and the individual. The organisational aspect is improved by acknowledging the potentially negative impact of stress.

Common sources of stress include inadequate communication, profusion of paperwork, constant pressure due to workload and lack of competent staff. Other factors are inadequate staffing, delegation problems, vague roles and areas of responsibility and excessively long hours leading to insufficient time for family or personal life. Most of the problems are linked to an unrealistically competitive, go-getting company strategy or bad organisation, and can be removed or modified.

Jobs can be redesigned, to modify the flow of work and reporting systems. This is vital if individuals are to feel that their work is recognised and that support and advice are readily available through effective feedback. Careful attention to ergonomic factors can also improve occupational well-being and morale, so vital in motivating the workforce.

Stress management programmes should not be considered as mollycoddling. They demonstrate an open and positive approach to helping individuals and endorse stress as an essential topic for consideration in a management programme.

The individual can be helped by techniques for relaxation and breathing, time structuring and appropriate self-assertion without aggression. Meditation, a sophisticated but practical skill, is also very effective. Known availability of counselling is of inestimable value following crises such as serious or unpredictable accidents and disasters and individual traumatic events, like verbal or physical violence.

Sensitive listening is the most important function in counselling at any level in the occupational health or personnel departments. Ideally, this is carried out by someone with the appropriate skills.

Change in the working environment is particularly stressful and it is no coincidence that sometimes the strategies advocated for reducing the causes of stress can also contribute usefully to the effective management of change.

Strategies for reducing pressures during change

- Do not change everything at once. Leave a stable and secure basis from which new arrangements can be explored. In particular, leave work teams together if they are working well.

- Ensure that there is adequate and direct feedback about new methods. This helps learning and encourages rapid adjustment.

- Give sufficient time for rehearsing and learning through experience, especially when alternatives and options need to be tried out.

- Involvement of people in the process of change pays off in adding important data, gives people some degree of control over their own work, and an awareness and ownership of the new arrangements. Their involvement must not be illusory, trivial, irrelevant or superficial. It must be seen as an integral and legitimate part of their job which is reflected in the rewards system.

- A stepwise, incremental sequence of changes, giving adequate time for acclimatization is worthwhile, with identifiable achievements signalled and publicised.

- Planning and feasibility testing should be as close to the users as possible.

- The project team set up to implement changes and particularly their leaders should have adequate time and resources and should not be expected to carry the task on top of existing full operational load.

- Conflict and resistance are likely to be reduced if an open, exploratory style is adopted by the project team, encouraging collaboration and help-seeking, looking at the causes of mistakes rather than looking for someone to blame, looking at how work is actually done rather than the procedures originally laid down.

- Some aspects of the process of change might specifically address the reduction of conflict and overload on people, improve the person/job fit, and perhaps loosen the boundaries between people's jobs, ensuring some degree of security but discouraging over-dependence on a narrow set of skills or one employer, or, even worse, an individual manager or supervisor.

- Stress can arise if people are overloaded or have conflicting work objectives. It is not necessarily that they have too many decisions to make but face too many constraints and pressures. However, the reverse can occur. It is a matter for judgement whether more or less responsibility for decisions is appropriate.

- Increase opportunities at every level to exercise judgement, enhancing the individual's feelings of competence, ability to cope, to use skills and make decisions.

❏ During project meetings and progress discussions, encourage open expression of doubts, difficulties, fears and feelings. This may be useful in its own right, but should also lead to remedial action.

How to reduce stress and its symptoms

1. Be gentle with yourself.
2. Work no more than ten hours a day.
3. Have at least one and a half days a week free from normal work routine.
4. Plan one 'away from it all' holiday each year.
5. Allow 30 minutes for each meal.
6. Eat slowly and chew well.
7. Examine your eating habits and balance your diet.
8. Cultivate the habit of listening to relaxing music.
9. Practise relaxation or meditation twice a day (ideally 3 times) for no less than 15 minutes.
10. Find a 'hermit' spot, use it daily and do not allow interruptions.
11. Take at least *ten* minutes daily for physical exercise preferably in the open air.
12. Have a regular massage or join a yoga class.
13. Cultivate a creative, non-competitive hobby, and spend time on it, e.g. gardening, painting, making music, etc.
14. Actively cultivate the habit of walking, talking and moving at a slower pace.
15. Smile and respond cheerfully whenever meeting anyone.
16. Remind yourself that you are an *enabler*, not a magician. You can only change how you relate to people, you cannot change them.
17. Caring and being there is sometimes more important than doing. Admit that you feel helpless when you do.
18. Give support to others and learn to accept it in return.
19. If emotional/or sexual relationships are upsetting, seek advice.
20. If you are unhappy at work – take stock and look at choices, i.e. retraining new areas of work, job agencies, etc.
21. Avoid the tendency to dwell on the past – concentrate on the present.
22. Express your feeling openly without antagonism or hostility.
23. Finish one task before moving on to another.
24. Do not accept, or give yourself, unrealistic deadlines. Most things can be done tomorrow.
25. Change your routine as often as is practicable.
26. Say "thank you" to yourself when you have finished something that you feel satisfied with.
27. Before you go to sleep, remember *three* good things that have happened during the day.
28. Use supervision or the 'buddy' system regularly as a source of support, assurance and redirection.

29. Avoid 'shop talk' during breaks and when socialising with colleagues.

30. Say "I choose ..." rather than "I should, ought to have to ...". Say "I won't ..." rather than "I can't ...".

31. Accept personal responsibility for your life.

32. If you never say "no" what is your "yes" worth?

SEE ALSO

Section 2: Change management, page 79; Counselling and listening, page 88; Personnel management, page 154.

Stress

157.3   Cox T, *Stress*, Macmillan, 1978.

157.3   ACC Fisher, S, *Handbook of life stress*, Wiley, 1988.

157.3   Fontana, D, *Managing stress*, British Psychological Society, 1989.

Time management

How your *time* is utilised will depend on the type of work that you do, and whether you work alone or in a group. There is also the influence of the organisation culture (do they expect speedy decisions?) and lastly your own personal style (an open-door style often means lots of interruptions).

It is important to realise that *activity* is not the same things as *achievement*, and being constantly busy often means inefficiency. The aim should be to be constructively active. The penalties of poor time management include poor decisions, missed opportunities, and stress, which often leads to sickness.

The core of effective time management is personal planning, based on an analysis of the situation, but surrounding this core are other considerations, such as:

☐   delegation – as well as being of benefit to subordinates, this frees the delegator's time;

☐   assertiveness – this is knowing that you have the right to say 'no' to people, and refusing to take on other's problems. Some people are also better than others at dealing with people who consume their time;

☐   meetings – these are greedy consumers of time. Questioning the worth of a meeting, its length, and proper preparation, are all important.

The two most common aids to time management are *lists* (of jobs to do) and *diaries* (for longer-term planning). The problem is not what to put on a list, but setting priorities. One way to deal with this is to classify all jobs into one of four possibilities, based on *urgency* and *importance*.

Most tasks to be done have some degree of urgency and some degree of importance. For example, returning someone's telephone call before noon, when it's eleven o'clock, may well be urgent, but may not be important. A way to analyse work then is to use the axis which follows:

Priorities axis

Very urgent

(3) In this area tasks are not very important but are very urgent	**(1)** In this area tasks are both very urgent and very important
(4) In this area tasks are not very important nor very urgent	**(2)** In this area tasks are very important but not very urgent

Not important ——————————————————— **Very important**

Not urgent

Classified in this way, it is easy then to draw up a priorities list, using the categories in the order 1, 2, 3, 4.

These can then perhaps be allotted a time slot in a daily diary such as the one below:

Daily diary

	9.00	10.00	11.00	12.00	1.00	2.00	3.00	4.00	5.00	Tasks
Mon										*1 meeting*
Tue	*1*									*2 interview*
Wed			*2*							
Thur										
Fri										

What actions should you take?

1. Analyse the way you spend your time now, and look for patterns, with a view to identifying the time wasting activities.

2. At the end of the day, draw up a list of activities for the next day.

3. Prioritise the list, and make sure your plan for the day is realistically attainable.

4. Start working on item one, and deal with each item in turn.

5. Try to deal with each item only once.

6. Inevitably new occurrences will alter your list as the day goes on. Allocate them a position in your list according to your priority method.

Tricks of the trade

Callers

❑ Find an empty room in which to 'hide away' for top priority work.

❑ See certain people by appointment only.

❑ Keep to the point in conversation/discussion. Finish as soon as usefully, and politely, possible.

❑ Without being rude, develop ways of signalling that your time is limited.

Meetings

❏ Must have a purpose.

❏ Structure them carefully if you are in charge.

❏ Only join committees that are essential to your work.

Travelling

❏ Only go if necessary. Get people to come to you.

❏ Can someone else go?

Work practices

❏ Be realistic about how long tasks will take.

❏ Delegate non-important work.

❏ Do not take on more than you can effectively do.

❏ Plan your work for the days and weeks ahead.

SEE ALSO | **Section 2: Decision-making and problem solving**, page 90.

Time management

658.4093   Adair, J, *Effective time management*, Pan, 1988.

658.4093   Fleming, S, *Manage your time*, Fontana, 1985.

658.5421   Ferner, JD, *Successful time management*, Wiley, 1980.

Trade unions and the law

The Employment Act – 1980

The Employment Act 1980 received Royal assent on 1st August, 1980. It was introduced to provide payments towards Trade Union expenditure, from public funds, in respect of ballots and also afforded the use of employee's premises in connection with these ballots. It also provided for the issue, by the Secretary of State, of codes of practice for the improvement of industrial relations: to make provision in respect of exclusion or expulsion from Trade Unions and otherwise to amend the law relating to workers, employers, Trade Unions and employers' associations.

The Act itself is relatively short because it brings in little new information but updates previous Acts. Some of the main provisions are as follows:

Secret ballots

Public money was to be made available to trade unions to offset the cost of holding secret ballots for starting and ending strikes, the election of shop stewards and national officials, changing rule books and for mergers with other unions. Employers with more than twenty members were obliged (after House of Lords amendment) to give a recognised union a place on the company's premises to carry out the poll.

Codes of practice

The Employment Secretary was empowered to issue such codes. The first two issued on 5 August 1980 covered picketing and the closed shop (see below). Under the former, the number of employees picketing an entrance to a place of work was limited to six. Under the latter, existing closed shop agreements were to be reviewed periodically.

Unfair dismissal

Onus was placed on the worker to show that an employer acted unreasonably in dismissing an employee. The industrial tribunals also had to take into account the size and resources of the company when making the decision. Companies with twenty or fewer employees were exempt from unfair dismissal rules when the employee had worked less than two years. The basic award could be reduced by the tribunal if there was evidence that the employee behaved unreasonably. Workers received a general right to stop employers taking action short of dismissal in order to make them join a trade union. The union would also be liable to pay some of the compensation if it was held to have pressured the employer into taking such action.

Maternity

A woman could be fairly dismissed if it was not reasonably practicable for her to return to her former job after maternity leave, and she turned down suitable alternative employment. An employer with five or fewer workers could be exempt from any such responsibility as he could claim that it was not even reasonably practicable to offer another job.

Repeal of schedule 11

Under schedule 11 of the previous Labour government's Employment Protection Act, unions were able to go to arbitration to secure recognised terms and conditions and in the absence of them to demand for groups of workers the general level pertaining in a particular area or industry. In addition, repeal of the remaining parts of the 1938 Road Haulage Act has abolished similar procedures specific to that industry.

Trade union recognition

The statutory procedure operated by ACAS (Advisory, Conciliation and Arbitration Service) under which unions dispute over recognition could apply for official investigation was also removed.

Coercive recruitment

This clause outlawed action by trade unionists to force workers at another company to belong to their union. It was aimed quite specifically at the abolition of recruiting tactics such as those allegedly used by SLADE (Society of Lithographic Artists, Designers and Engravers – now part of National Graphical Association) in its expansion among advertising art work studio employees.

Closed shop

A 'closed shop' is an agreement or arrangement made between a trade union and an employer that requires every employee in the appropriate jobs to be a member of the union. This Act established the right of individuals not to be unreasonably expelled from or refused admission to a trade union where a closed shop operated. The procedure for such cases lay through Industrial Tribunals and then appeal to the Employment Appeal Tribunal (EAT). If union membership was still refused, EAT would be able to award compensation of up to £16,000. New closed shops had to have the support of 80 percent of the workers involved (not just those voting in a ballot) to be immune from unfair dismissal claims if an employee lost his job through the operation of a closed shop agreement.

The statutory conscience was widened from including only religious belief to objections on other grounds of conscience or deeply held personal objection to joining any trade union or to joining a particular trade union. The exact impact of these provisions depended on how wide a view industrial tribunals took of the definition of the term 'conscience'. In addition, non-unionists employed at the time a closed shop agreement arrangement came into operation were exempt from compulsion to join the union.

A footnote to the Act absolved the Secretary of State from the duty to draw up a charter on press freedom. This duty was specified in the 1976 Trade Union and Labour Relations Act after fears that closed shops in journalism would probably pose a threat to freedom of expression.

Picketing

This section removed immunity from civil action from persons who picket at places other than their own place of work. Trade union officials and dismissed workers were allowed to join picket lines.

Sympathetic industrial action

A complex provision introduced quite late into the bill removed the statutory immunity (embodied in the Trade Union and Labour Relations Act) where there was secondary industrial action unless

a) the purpose of the secondary action was directly to interfere with the flow of goods or services to or from the employer in dispute (and the action was likely to achieve that purpose),

b) its purpose was to interfere directly with the flow of goods or services vis à vis an employer associated with the employer in dispute and the goods or services were in substitution for the goods or services normally supplied to or by the employer in dispute,

c) the secondary action involved picketing within the new and more narrow definition in section 16 of the Employers Act.

This Act formed the basis for the 1982 Employment Act and was amended and superseded by the new Act.

The Employment Act 1982

A summary of the main points in the Act:

New rights for closed shop employees

☐ The Secretary of State may pay compensation to employees dismissed for not being union members.

☐ Gives rights to workers in a closed shop environment not to be unfairly dismissed or have action taken against them.

☐ Cannot be fairly dismissed for non-membership of a trade union in a closed shop or for refusing to make payments to a trade union or some other body/person in lieu of union membership.

☐ Ballots must be held.

Employment involvement

The Act requires Directors of large (200 or more employees) companies to include a statement regarding action they have taken to develop their employees involvement in the business.

Compensation for unfair dismissal

☐ The Act has increased basic compensation given to people found to be unfairly dismissed either because of their trade union membership or activities or because of their non-membership to a union.

☐ Introduces £2,000 minimum basic award for any person unfairly dismissed for one of the reasons above.

☐ 'Special Awards' payable if a worker takes his case for dismissal to an industrial tribunal to get reinstatement/re-engagement but does not get it. For non-reinstatement decided by the tribunal an award of 104 weeks pay, £10,000 minimum and a maximum of £20,000. If upon decision of tribunal reinstatement is agreed but not taken up, the 'award' is 156 weeks pay, subject to a minimum of £15,000.

On either cases such 'special awards' are payable in addition to any compensation or basic award and can be reduced if employees conduct before dismissal is called into question.

Non union companies

This Act protects companies who do not use union labour and makes it unlawful to exclude such companies from:

☐ tender list;

☐ tendering a contract;

☐ awarding a contract;

☐ terminating a contract with them;

☐ taking any industrial action that is seen to pressure an employer to act against the provisions above.

Dismissal and industrial action

☐ Employees cannot claim unfair dismissal while on strike or during any industrial action.

☐ Employees can continue in employment until unfair dismissal has been decided upon by the industrial tribunal.

☐ Employees can take work elsewhere during a strike or lockout.

☐ Where an employer has not given adequate notice before an employee's dismissal under the Act the minimum notice will be added on from the date of dismissal.

Trade dispute

☐ Only lawful when employees are in dispute with their own employer and the dispute concerns pay, conditions or jobs.

☐ Limits lawful picketing to the workplace of those picketing.

Trade union immunities

◻ In particular section 15 of this Act has abolished the special immunities which have prevented trade unions from being sued in their own names. Companies can now sue a trade union for injunctions and damages if it gives authority to unlawful picketing, strikes, etc.

◻ Awards: The Act states an upper limit of awards for damages made against trade unions.

◻ Trade Union Property: Certain property such as personal property of a union official/member can be excluded from awards, damages, costs or expenses.

◻ Sit ins: A court decision (*Plessey PLC v Wilson and Others*) has made it possible for immunity of prosecution where sit ins occur. This is of course assuming no other law has been broken, e.g. trespass, nuisance.

The Trade Union Act 1984

The Trade Union Act 1984 is concerned with:

1. the election of trade union leaders;
2. secret ballots before industrial action;
3. trade union expenditure on party political matters;
4. assistance for trade union secret ballots.

Section I – The election of trade union leaders

To comply with Part 1 of the Act, a trade union must:

a) elect every voting member of its governing body at least every five years by a secret ballot of the voting membership;

b) keep an accurate register of its members' names and addresses.

Section II – Secret ballots before industrial action

Part II of the Act makes it a condition of trades unions' legal immunity for organising industrial action that:

a) they first hold a secret ballot in which all those due to take part in the action are entitled to vote;

b) they must establish that a majority of those voting say that they wish to take part in the action.

Section III - Trade union expenditure on party political matters

Part III of the Act makes a number of changes to the law relating to trade union political funds. In particular, it requires trade unions with political funds to ballot their members at regular intervals on whether they wish their union to continue to spend money on party political matters.

Section IV - Assistance for trade union secret ballots

Under Part IV of the Act, election ballots held to comply with Part I of the Act and political fund review ballots held to comply with Part III of the Act will qualify for the two kinds of assistance which were made available in the Employment Act of 1980.

The two kinds of assistance to which trade unions are entitled under the 1980 Act mean that they can:

a) apply for refunds of money from the Certification Officer towards the cost of postal ballots;

b) request the use of employers' premises for workplace ballots.

Provisions of the Employment Act 1989

The main purposes of the Employment Act 1989 are:

❏ removal of restrictions on the employment of women and young people;

❏ to help employers create jobs and become more competitive by easing the burden of regulation on them;

❏ to take forward the government's training strategy into the 1990s.

Key provisions of the Act

Most legislation that still discriminates between women and men in employment and training matters is repealed or amended to remove discrimination. This includes the ban on women working underground in mines and some restrictions on their working with machinery in factories. Protection is retained in special cases such as work which through exposure to radiation or lead might endanger the health of an unborn child.

Restrictions on the hours of work of young people are removed, including the prohibition of night work. Certain other restrictions on young people's employment is also lifted e.g. street trading. Burdens on employers are reduced by a number of deregulatory amendments to the Employment Protection Act (1978).

Women become eligible to receive statutory redundancy payments up to the age of 65, in line with men and they have the same retirement age. Measures are introduced to facilitate the transformation of the industrial training boards into independent bodies.

Employment Act 1990

Key measures

The key measures on industrial relations and trade union law in the 1990 Employment Act:

❏ give a remedy to anyone refused a job because he or she is, or is not, a union member;

❏ make unions properly responsible for calls for industrial action made by any of their officials;

❏ deter and discourage unofficial industrial action;

❏ make it unlawful to call for secondary industrial action;

❏ give additional protection to members; democratic rights in union industrial action, executive election and political fund ballots; and

❏ bring more proceedings within the scope of assistance from the Commissioner for the Rights of Trade Union Members.

Employers checklist

Employers should consider the following steps to help improve industrial relations and ensure compliance with the law:

☐ review recruitment procedures to ensure that jobs are not refused to applicants because they are, or are not, members of a trade union.

☐ make clear to your employees that:

    ☐ it will be unlawful for their union to call upon them to take industrial action in support of a dispute between another employer and his or her workers; and

    ☐ taking part in unofficial action puts them at risk of selective dismissal, and – if applicable – that this risk may be increased for those who also organise such action.

☐ if unballoted industrial action may be organised amongst your workers by a union committee, shop steward or other official, find out how to notify any such act to the executive, president or general secretary of any union to which such organisers belong.

☐ review your dismissal procedures to ensure that, for example, appeals procedures do not unnecessarily obstruct your ability to make dismissals to deter and discourage unofficial industrial action.

Trade union law

331.88   Dept of Employment, *A guide to the Trade Union Act 1984*, HMSO, 1984.

331.88   Jackson, MP, *Trade unions,* 2nd ed, Longman, 1988.

331.88   Statutes, *The Trade Union Acts with commentary*, Sweet & Maxwell, 1985.

658.315 Thomason, G, *A textbook of industrial relations management*, IPM, 1984.

Training

Identifying *training needs* is a key stage in training administration. What actually is the training need? The reason for care with the question is to ensure that the training is needed as well as being correctly undertaken. It is easy to assume that an operating problem can be solved by a training initiative, when a quite different solution is needed. Correct identification of training needs is achieved through asking the following four questions.

1. What are the organisations' objectives?

2. What tasks must be completed to achieve these objectives?

3. What behaviours are necessary for each job holder to complete his/her assigned tasks?

4. What deficiencies, if any, do job holders have in knowledge, skills or attitudes required to perform the necessary behaviours?

Answers to these questions show the training gap which illustrates the need for a training initiative to deal with the identified deficiencies.

Training is not simply responding to requirements; it involves being proactive by seeing training needs before they become obvious and anticipating ways in which training can make a contribution to business growth.

It is important to note that the level of training provision in companies is much lower than is needed for international competitiveness, economic performance and the reasonable expectations of employees. Indeed training is one of the first casualties of financial economies in organisations because it is very difficult to quantify the results of training. However, the benefits to both the organisation and individual in training should not be overlooked.

Benefits to the organisation

1. *Objectives*

    By considering both the short and long-term objectives of the organisation, it is possible to develop a training programme to achieve them.

2. *Competitiveness / effectiveness*

    The speed with which improvements in training are implemented in an organisation influences its competitiveness and economic performance. Training enables companies to keep pace with the continuing changes in technology.

3. *Growth / development*

    Training is a key element in any plans for organisational growth and development. Without training plans, the anticipated growth of any company could be thwarted as employees fail to keep up with new developments. Training should be seen as a long-term investment in human resources.

Benefits to the employee

1. *Motivation / commitment*

    Consider the following equation:

    $$\text{Performance} = \text{Ability} \times \text{Motivation}.$$

    Training can have an impact on this equation by increasing the skills and abilities of employees so enhancing their motivation and sense of commitment.

2. *Self-development*

Many employees appreciate learning new tasks and skills as part of being able to fulfil their potential.

3. *Job satisfaction*

Maintaining and increasing employees' skills not only increases productivity, but is likely to increase their commitment and thus job-satisfaction.

4. *Advancement*

Work is an important part of people's lives. Thus it is necessary to develop careers in which training and development can be used to achieve long-term career aims.

The following diagram illustrates a basic training cycle.

Systematic training: The basic cycle

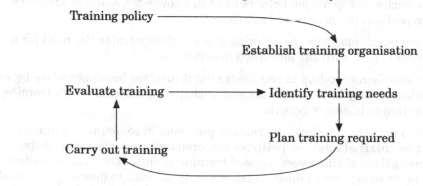

The Process of Training

The essential components of the process of training are:

☐ the identification and analysis of training needs – all training must be directed towards the satisfaction of defined needs; for the company as a whole, for specific functions or groups of employees, or for individuals;

☐ the definition of training objectives – training must aim to achieve measurable goals expressed in terms of the improvements or changes expected in corporate, functional, departmental or individual performance;

☐ the preparation of training plans – these must describe the overall scheme of training and its costs and benefits. The overall scheme should further provide for the development of training programmes and facilities, the selection and use of appropriate training methods and the selection and training of trainers;

☐ the implementation of training plans, including the maintenance of training records;

☐ the measurement and analysis of results, which require the validation of the achievements of each training programme against its objectives and the evaluation of the impact of the whole training scheme on company or departmental performance;

☐ the feedback of the results of validations and evaluations so that training plans, programmes and techniques can be improved.

Analysing training needs

The analysis of training needs aims to define the gap between what is happening and what should happen. Training needs should be analysed:

❒ *for the organisation as a whole*. Corporate needs which relate to organisational strengths and weaknesses or to the requirements arising from the manpower plan, for example apprentice training;

❒ *for departments or functions*. Group needs in areas where expertise or skill is lacking, for example, project management skills in a computer department;

❒ *for individuals*. As the needs of individuals for training to improve performance or to develop potential emerge they may be grouped together as a common training need, e.g. the understanding of financial matters for non-financial managers.

There are three basic methods of analysing training needs.

1. *General surveys* in which departmental and functional training priorities are identified by discussion with managers and supervisors. The needs and priorities should be related to any problems that exist, such as shortage of expertise or skills, gaps in knowledge or poor performance.

2. *Job analysis*, which consists of:

   ❒ a broad analysis of the requirements of the job and any special problems surrounding it as seen by the job holder, his superior and, possibly, his colleagues;

   ❒ a detailed study of the responsibilities, duties and tasks carried out which forms the basis for a job description;

   ❒ an analysis of the knowledge and skills required by the job holder which forms the basis for a job specification;

   ❒ a description of the training requirements for the job – the training specification.

3. *Performance appraisal and potential reviews*, which assess the performance of individuals against agreed objectives and job requirements and consider potential for promotion, thus establishing gaps in knowledge, weaknesses in performance, and areas to be developed if the individual is to progress. Reviews are analysed to determine individual training needs.

SEE ALSO

Section 2: Learning, page 124; *Manpower analysis and planning*, page 133; *Motivation*, page 135; *Organisational objectives, policies and strategies*, page 142; *Performance appraisal*, page 145.

Training

658.3124 Buckley, R, *The theory and practice of training*, Kogan Page, 1990.

658.3124 Coopers & Lybrand, *A challenge to complacency*, MSC, 1985.

658.3124 *Training for small and medium companies*, FEU, 1991.

658.3124 Harrison, R, *Training and development*, IPM, 1988.

Work study

Work study is a means of raising the efficiency (productivity) of a factory or operating unit by the re-organisation of work. There are two main parts to work study:

❑ method study;

❑ work measurement.

Definitions are given for work study and its constituents, method study and work measurement in the British Standard 3138 *Glossary of terms used in work study*. These are:

a) *Work study*: a generic term for those techniques, particularly method study and work measurement, which are used in the examination of human work in all its contexts and which lead systematically to the investigation of all the factors which affect the efficiency and economy of the situation being reviewed, in order to effect improvement;

b) *Method study*: the systematic recording and critical examination of existing and proposed ways of doing work as a means of developing and applying easier and more effective methods, and reducing costs;

c) *Work measurement*: the application of techniques designed to establish the time for a qualified worker to carry out a specified level of performance.

Method study is therefore concerned with how work should be done, and work measurement with how long it should take.

The main *objectives* of work study are:

❑ the analysis, design and improvement of work systems, work places and work methods;

❑ the establishment of work standards for determining requirements in labour and equipment, assessing performance, planning operations, costing operations and products, and paying workers;

❑ the development and application of job evaluation schemes based on job descriptions;

❑ the specification of plant facilities, layout, space utilisation and material and 'traffic' flows;

❑ the economic evaluation and optimisation of alternative combinations of personnel, materials and equipment;

❑ the development of procedures for the planning and control of work and material usage;

❑ the development of procedures for presenting to management information about work performance.

Method study is sometimes carried out by specialists, but in some organisations, supervisors might use method study themselves to analyse the work done in their section. It is aimed at discovering what is the best or most efficient method of getting a job done. This has the following implications:

❑ There is a 'best method' of doing a task, which is not always obvious and which isn't always used in practice. This means that many organisations will be inefficient because they don't use the best method.

❑ The 'best method' can be discovered through a *scientific* or *methodological* approach.

There are six basic scientific or methodological steps in method study.

1. Select the work or job to be studied.

2. Record the relevant facts about the job.

3. Examine the facts critically.

4. Develop the new method.

5. Install the new method.

6. Maintain the new method as standard practice.

The need for a method study may arise from a number of different circumstances, such as the introduction of new products, processes or equipment. The commonest reason for a desired change in methods is to reduce production costs. There should therefore be a constant examination of costing figures. Other indications of the need for a method study are:

❑ bottlenecks, generating a high level of work-in-progress, long delivery times or unbalanced work-flow;

❑ idle plant or workers, giving rise to under-use of resources;

❑ poor morale, indicated by petty or trivial complaints or absenteeism. This may also be the result of unnecessarily tiring work;

❑ excessive scrap;

❑ inconsistent earnings, where the earnings of employees are tied to output.

Work measurement techniques are intended to reveal the work content of a task or quite simply the means for establishing the time to carry out work.

In order to express the amount of work that can be produced by a given number of men or machines, or the work which has to be done during the process of making a certain product, some common scale of measurement is needed. Standard time provides this, but only in situations where work is of a repetitive and fairly predictable nature.

❑ *Standard time* is the total time in which a job should be completed at standard performance level by a reasonably competent individual in normal conditions.

❑ *Standard performance* is the rate of output which qualified workers will naturally achieve without over-exertion as an average over the working day or shift, provided they adhere to the specified method and provided that they are motivated to apply themselves to their work.

Standard times are used for a variety of purposes:

❑ as a basis for pay incentive schemes;

❑ for production planning, machine loading, and planning labour times and overtime/short-time working;

❑ as a means of calculating delivery dates and promises;

❑ to assist in method study;

❑ to determine standard costs;

❑ to provide data for budgetary control, estimating and planning;

❑ to provide a system of management control through comparisons of work output.

There are four common methods of measuring work which can be split into two classes:

1. *Direct observation methods*:

    ❏   stop-watch studies (time study);

    ❏   activity or work sampling.

2. *Synthetic methods*:

    ❏   using standard data;

    ❏   predetermined motion time system (PMTS).

Direct observation methods involve seeing the job going on in practice, but *synthetic methods* are used to estimate the work content of jobs without having to observe them.

There is also guesswork, of course. When work is non-routine or unpredictable, guessing the time needed to complete jobs might be the only thing work planners can do.

Direct observation methods

Time study using the stop-watch is the basic technique of work measurement and is used mainly on repetitive work where direct observation of the work is possible.

In addition to timing the elements of a task, it is also necessary to assess the speed and effectiveness of the worker performing it, since all workers vary in both of these respects.

By assessing speed and effectiveness in this way and equating them to the standard performance, times can be adjusted to cater for all types of workers, so that a fair and equitable time is issued for each task studied. This is known as rating, and is perhaps the most controversial part of work study.

The standard rating is the average rate at which qualified operators will naturally work, provided they follow the correct method and have sufficient motivation. This is also known as 'piecework' speed.

With some jobs it is either impractical or uneconomic to measure the work content by time study or other means because:

❏   there is a wide variety of work being done; or

❏   there may be a large number of people involved in doing the work.

In such cases it is more convenient to use the technique of activity sampling which consists of taking a number of observations during the work cycle, at predetermined intervals which are based on 'random number tables'. From the observations made it is possible to calculate the working and idle times: in this way activity or work can be measured with reasonable accuracy without having to stand at the work-place for long periods taking observations.

Synthetic methods

There are some occasions when observation is not a suitable method.

In these circumstances it is possible to estimate a standard time on the basis of accumulated data about previous experience from similar jobs. (Within any organisation, the same elements of work will recur, even where the actual jobs differ. Work measurement can be achieved by adding together times for the common elements). Time standards arrived at in this way are called synthetics and the technique of calculating times in this way is called 'synthesis'.

There are several advantages in the synthetic method of work measurement.

☐ It is reliable and consistent, since data from many studies is used.

☐ It eliminates standard time and money spent on making new time studies.

☐ It enables standard times to be spent on short-run work, and work of a varying nature, such as jobbing work.

☐ It enables time standards to be set before work starts.

☐ A small number of work study personnel can deal with a large volume and variety of work.

There are two methods of deriving synthetic time standards:

☐ using standard data built up from time studies of component elements of jobs;

☐ using pre-determined motion time systems (PMTS).

The scheme of synthetic times is built up by individual firms and applies to the circumstances of these firms. Similar systems have been built up for general applications by several companies. Initially these systems involve measurement of very much smaller elements or basic hand motions and these are known as 'predetermined motion times standards' (PMTS). Their most common application is in highly repetitive and complex operations involving large numbers of operators.

One of the best known and most widely used PMTS systems is called MTM (Method Time Measurement). It involves the study of hand and arm movements, recognising a number of basic motions (reach, move, turn, apply pressure, grasp ... and so on) and tables of times for these elementary movements under varying conditions are available.

The tables can be used to estimate standard times for operations by:

a) breaking down the operation into elements and identifying individual motions;

b) working out the individual motion times, with the aid of MTM data cards and tables;

c) calculating the total times; and

d) recording the proposed work-place layout and the equipment involved so that it is clear which set of circumstances the estimate is for.

Organisation and Method Study (O & M)

Work study is applied to work out of the office, in particular production work. Similar techniques are used to study office work and methods, and these are referred to as *Organisation and Method* study, or *O & M*.

The differences between O & M and work study are:

☐ O & M concentrates on office work;

☐ the aim of O & M, like the aim of work study, is to improve efficiency (productivity) and effectiveness of working, but O & M generally seeks to achieve improvements through:

1. improvements in management (e.g. better planning and control systems);

2. improvements in work organisation (e.g. changing the organisation structure and authority structure of jobs in the office);

3. improvements in methods (like work study) but with less emphasis on work measurement and establishing standard times (unlike work study). However, some office routines lend themselves to work measurement.

The approach to an O & M study is much the same as for method study in the factory.

1. Establish an area for investigation.

2. Establish terms of reference (e.g. to improve productivity by 10%; to find how the work force in a department can take on certain extra work without increasing staff numbers etc).

3. Investigate the existing methods – by observation, asking questions, studying procedure manuals and other written records, studying documents used.

4. Record the existing methods, by narrative, or using charts and diagrams (e.g. organisation charts, procedure flowcharts).

5. Analyse the existing methods, identify weaknesses and strengths, develop alternative methods and discuss these with the operations staff and management affected.

6. Develop an alternative method.

7. Install the new method, and review and improve as necessary.

New methods might involve changes in planning and control systems, a new organisation structure, changing the numbers and location of equipment, changing methods of working or documents used.

SEE ALSO

Section 2: Control, page 86; **Job analysis**, page 113; **Manpower analysis and planning**, page 133; **Organisational objectives, policies and strategies**, page 142; **Organisational structures**, page 144; **Production control**, page 156; **Quality assurance**, page 159; **Training**, page 199.

Work study

658.542 Cemach, HP, *Work study in the office*, 6th ed, Anbar, 1986.

658.542 Currie, RM, *Work study*, 4th ed, Pitman, 1977.

658.542 Evans, F, *Applications of MTM*, MTM Association, 1980.

658.542 ILO, *Introduction to work study*, 3rd ed, ILO, 1979.

Section 3

Practice and development of skills and knowledge

Introduction

This section contains a number of *reinforcement scenarios and activities* which are arranged under the same headings as the units in Section 1. These activities are similar to the scenarios and tasks you encountered in Section 1. You may find it helpful to refer back to the relevant units in Section 1, the appropriate topics in the information bank contained in Section 2 and the recommended texts.

You should not attempt these activities until you have worked through the appropriate unit in Section 1.

Unit 1: Management and supervision

Scenario: The new supervisors

Imagine that you are working for an organisation where expansion has led to an increased need for supervisors. As part of the changes you are being promoted to assistant departmental manager and your position as supervisor has become vacant.

Your old job has been advertised, both internally and externally, together with two newly created supervisory positions. Letters have been sent to suitable applicants inviting them to attend interviews. Although some of the internal candidates are likely to be familiar with certain aspects of the job already, all the candidates will be given a short talk when they arrive introducing them to the activities of the organisation and explaining what a supervisor's job entails. You have been asked to make the presentation.

Problem-solving activity

Select an organisation with which you are familiar on which to base your talk. Prepare notes and visual aids for a 15-minute presentation covering the following key points:

☐ *the objectives of your organisation and a brief description of its activities;*

☐ *the management structure of the organisation and the position of your department in the line authority;*

☐ *a description of the supervisor's role in the department;*

☐ *a description of the overlap between management and supervision in the department.*

See the information bank in *Section 2: Communications*, page 81; *Organisational objectives, policies and strategies*, page 142; *Organisational structures*, page 144.

Scenario: Pete's problems

Pete has been employed by his company for a long time. He has been responsible for several important and successful projects and as a result has been promoted to the position of project supervisor.

Each project team comprises four or five members of staff. The staff do not work exclusively on one project at a time, but can be involved with several. Part of the administration of each project is the maintenance of records for the auditors. Much of this record-keeping is done by Pete, who also takes care of the day-to-day organisation of work.

Pete is popular and is widely regarded as a hard worker. However, lately he has had to work *longer hours than usual*, starting early and working until late into the evening. Even so, it has been noticeable that *a number of jobs are still left unfinished*. Pete adopts an 'open door' style of management; anyone can consult him at any time. His subordinates make good use of this facility and as a result he is frequently interrupted by telephone calls and people dropping into his office.

The whole project group work as a team. Pete believes that they are a hard working group. Most of the group consider that they already work at full capacity and do not take kindly to any suggestion that they might be more productive.

Problem-solving activity

i)   *What do you think might be the cause of Pete's problems?*

ii) *What actions might be taken to solve Pete's problems?*

 See the information bank in **Section 2: Delegation**, page 93; *Job analysis*, page 113; *Time management*, 190.

Scenario: Queuing at the check-out

Simon is the newly appointed supervisor at the local Tescrose supermarket. Included in his responsibilities is the stocking of shelves and the manning of the check-outs. Soon after he started at Tescrose, Mr Baines, the store manager, called him into his office and gave him some friendly advice. Amongst other things he said, 'Sometimes the check-out queues are much too long and customers get impatient. I don't know why this happens, but perhaps you could sort it out please.'

Simon made a mental note to look into this problem once he had found his feet, but several times during the next two weeks, he noticed Mr Baines ordering the staff to stop restocking the shelves and move to the check-outs. Once he saw Mr Baines working at a check-out himself! However, Mr Baines did not mention the matter to Simon again.

At the end of the month at Simon's performance appraisal, Mr Baines wrote a highly critical report stating that Simon had 'shown himself to be unable to handle delegated work'.

Problem-solving activity

i)   *Who is at fault here?*

ii)   *What should Mr Baines have done?*

iii) *What should Simon have done?*

iv)   *How could this situation have been avoided?*

 See the information bank in **Section 2: Delegation**, page 93; *Performance appraisal*, page 145.

Scenario: Who's the boss?

Anne, the new supervisor, is not very popular. It's not that she has done anything wrong; all she did was apply for the job! The reason why she's not popular is because she got the job when a lot of people in the department thought that it should have been an internal appointment and been given to Pat. After all, Pat had been the acting supervisor and knew the work inside out.

Nobody is actually rude to Anne, but they tend to by-pass her whenever they can and go to Pat or Brian, the boss. Quite often when Anne has given an instruction, the staff check with Pat to see if it should be carried out. Pat hasn't countermanded any of Anne's instructions yet.

Anne has looked at the possibility of transferring Pat to another department, but there don't seem to be any suitable openings at the moment.

Problem-solving activity

i)   *Who should sort out this problem?*

ii) *What should be done?*

> **HELP ?**
>
> See the information bank in *Section 2: Authority*, page 75; *Counselling and listening*, page 88; *Discipline*, page 94; *Non-verbal communications*, page 137.

A   Activity: Basis for authority

Think of five teachers, lecturers or managers you have worked with or for and complete the table below. For example, if the first teacher/lecturer or manager you have in mind relies hardly at all on personal authority, heavily on skills-based authority, and a little on formal authority, you might have scored him or her as 10%, 65% and 25% respectively.

Teacher/ lecturer or manager	Basis for authority			
	Personal %	Skills %	Formal %	Total %
1				100
2				100
3				100
4				100
5				100

Now consider the scores you have given for personal authority and list the reasons why you have given each score. From this you should be able to describe the qualities that you consider to be important.

> **HELP ?**
>
> See the information bank in *Section 2: Authority*, page 75.

Activity: What should I do?

One of the reasons why people fail to delegate is that they have not considered in a systematic way what tasks can or cannot be delegated. *Using your own job or one with which you are familiar:*

i) *List the major tasks involved (perhaps from a job description) and then the related activities.*

ii) *Classify the tasks and activities into those which can be delegated and those which cannot. Explain why some tasks cannot be delegated.*

iii) *Consider the list of tasks and activities which can be delegated. To whom might they be delegated? Allocate each task to the most suitable person (use their job titles) and give your reasons.*

iv) *Make a note of any difficulties that might arise.*

 See the information bank in *Section 2: Delegation*; page 93; *Time management*, page 190.

 Activity: Do you do too much?

Many people who fail to delegate are not aware that they need to. They are so wrapped up in their work that they fail to see that there may be a delegation problem. *Construct a questionnaire which would make such people aware of the need to delegate and the advantages.* You might include such questions as:

1. Do you feel that you are overworked?

2. Do you often find that there are a number of tasks unfinished at the end of the day that you feel should have been completed?

 See the information bank in *Section 2: Delegation*; page 93; *Questionnaire surveys*, page 166; *Time management*, page 190.

 Activity: Individual and organisational goals

In this exercise you will be asked to identify your own short-term and long-term goals and the short-term and long-term goals of your organisation. Further, you will be asked to determine how much conflict, if any, is present among these goals. You may find it helpful to think of goals you might have in the following areas:

❏ **Professional accomplishment**

What do you want to do professionally? Start your own business perhaps? Manage a large firm? To what positions do you aspire?

☐ **Educational and personal growth**

What aspirations do you have regarding continuing education? Is the idea of personal growth important to you? What kind of things will you do to achieve this growth?

☐ **Status**

Do you want to belong to certain groups, live in certain areas or move in specific circles?

☐ **Family and personal relationships**

What kind of relationships do you want? How important do you want these relationships to be? How significant is friendship to you?

☐ **Use of free time**

What goals do you have regarding what you will do with your free time? How much leisure time do you want? How will you use it?

☐ **Lifestyle**

What kind of lifestyle appeals to you? How will you achieve it?

☐ **Social commitment**

Do you have any plans to improve our society? If so, how? Do you plan to make a definite contribution in this area?

☐ **Spiritual growth**

What objectives do you have regarding how you will relate to a larger universe? How will you achieve peace of mind? Is this important to you?

You should also do some thinking about the objectives of your organisation before starting the exercise. You may find it difficult to state specific goals of your organisation. Sometimes they appear to be vague or very general; for example, survival or providing a service. In a small organisation it may be difficult to separate the goals of the organisation from the personal goals of the owner(s).

Required:

i) *List your five main short-term personal goals in order of priority.*

ii) *List five personal long-term goals in order of priority. Consider long-term to be over one year in the future.*

iii) *List the five short-term goals of your organisation in order of priority. Focus on what kinds of goals and objectives you think it has or probably will have, rather than what objectives you would like it to have.*

iv) *List the five long-term goals of your organisation in order of priority.*

v) *Go back to your list of short-term goals. How much conflict is there between the short-term goals of your organisation and your own short-term goals? If there is conflict, how serious is it? Does everyone know about the conflict who should know about it?*

vi) *Determine whether the long-term goals are in conflict. Determine the seriousness of any conflict.*

vii) *Are your long-term and short-term goals in conflict?*

viii) *Are the organisation's short-term and long-term goals in conflict?*

ix) *If some individual goals and the goals of your organisation are seriously in conflict, work out some ways for handling the situation.*

x) *Write an action plan covering the next twelve months which states what you will try to achieve at work and which combines your organisation's and your own goal's compatibly.*

HELP ?

See the information bank in *Section 2: Management by objectives*, page 128; *Organisational objectives*, page 142.

214

Unit 2: Managing work

Scenario: Clockwise Ltd

When Albert left the Navy and joined Clockwise Ltd, he brought with him the kind of precision and orderliness that the Managing Director much admired. Albert manages four supervisors, who in turn manage nearly 40 men and women. Albert is ruthlessly efficient and once pursuing a problem can never be diverted. Both his superiors and his subordinates know that if they are involved with one of Albert's problems, it must be faced immediately.

In Albert's office there is a clock above the door and when someone enters without an appointment he has a habit of looking at the clock and saying, 'Well, you've got two minutes,' before he has even had a chance of finding out what he or she wants. After the two minutes has passed he repeatedly glances at the clock to show that the allotted time is up. The following conversation describes the effect his attitude has on other members of staff.

MARIA   I went to see him yesterday about an urgent matter and as usual he said, 'You've got two minutes,' so I began explaining the problem. Then his telephone rang and he was talking on the 'phone for a couple of minutes. As soon as he put the 'phone down he looked at the clock and said, 'That's all the time I can spare you.' So the problem is still unresolved!

ALAN   Yes, I know; you've got to time it just right. I saw him on Friday afternoon when he'd come back from lunch and we talked for about half an hour.

MARIA   Have you heard anything about that course you were hoping to go on?

ALAN   Well, I gave all the forms to Albert and eventually got them back last Tuesday and it's all been approved. The problem is that the course started on Monday, so I've missed out!

MARIA   That sounds a familiar story. I got an urgent memo passed on to me by Albert on the 20th for reply the same day. Albert had had it since the 11th!

ALAN   We've got next year's budget tied up nicely. Albert finalised the figures today: two months early!

Problem-solving activity

    i)   *How would you make Albert aware of his poor time management?*

    ii) *Albert thinks that he makes the best use of his time. How would you point out to him that this may not be so?*

See the information bank in *Section 2: Counselling and listening*, page 88; *Management by objectives*, page 128; *Time management*, page 190.

Scenario: Lectronics Ltd

Lectronics Ltd manufactures electronic communication equipment. The following information has been extracted from the minutes of recent management meetings.

CC Control Ltd

A major order has been received from CC Control Ltd for 500 DS41 units to be delivered not later than 15th of next month. As they are a major customer we need to show we can fulfil this order. Unfortunately we do not have the production capacity to deal with it. The following solutions have been proposed:

1. take on temporary workers on a night shift until the order has been completed. The labour is available, but it would be non-union labour (former employees of KO Ltd) and inevitably this would be resisted by the union. In the past the union has also refused to agree to the operation of night shifts;

2. subcontract the work to Glen Electronics. They have the capacity and, at least at the moment, are no real threat to us. The cost of subcontracting the work would be 25% higher and therefore we would make very little profit on the order, but we would keep CC Control's goodwill;

3. refuse the contract. We have not yet accepted the contract and it might be wiser not to take on the work, especially as our order book is full.

Developments

Tachi, our Japanese competitor, has now released their new PO7 system. It is already adversely affecting our sales of the QB1. It has a higher selling price than our product, but it has a number of advanced features. What seems to be clear is that we must launch our own updated PO7. Marketing has prepared a specification which Engineering says they can put into production within three months. Marketing wants to start with advance publicity and is seeking permission to go ahead.

Laser switch assembly

Laser assembly is at a standstill at the moment because of a problem with components. A complete batch of switches has been assembled using diodes of the wrong specification. This was a supplier's error and we are now left with the following choices:

1. Scrap the entire batch at a cost of £30,000.

2. Disassemble the switches so that they can go back onto the production line and be reworked. This would cost about £20,000. It is not yet clear whether we will receive any compensation from the suppliers, but if we are successful, we would still incur a loss of some £10,000.

Problem-solving activity

i)   How would you go about finding a solution to each of these problems?

ii) Select a solution and explain how you reached your decision. You need not confine yourself to the options suggested.

| HELP | ? | See the information bank in **Section 2: Decision-making and problem-solving**, page 90; **Time management**, page 190. |

Scenario: Bill's biscuits

If you had built a business up from scratch over a period of 20 years, you would be justified in feeling very upset if you thought it might all vanish overnight because of a policy change by another company. When Bill Brickle opened the post one morning, that was exactly how he felt. One of his company's major customer had written as follows:

> ... Recent research shows that our customers want a standardised product and for this reason the variable nature of your biscuits is no longer acceptable to us. However, we recognise that we have an obligation to our suppliers as well as to our customers and I am therefore writing to let you know that when your contract falls due for renewal next month, it will contain the following new clauses:
>
> 1. The shape and packet weight of the biscuits must be standardised.
>
> 2. Within 12 months you must be registered as being able to comply with BS5750 (as will all our suppliers).
>
> Failure to comply with either of these clauses will mean the end of our business relationship ...

Bill had built his company up from a small business with two employees to the present firm with a staff of over 70. The biscuit-making process itself had changed little. The ingredients are delivered in bags which are immediately poured into the top vat. The first in is always the first out, since they are drawn from a chute at the bottom. Once mixed in accordance with the recipe (or the chargehand's interpretation of it) the mixture is rolled out and the biscuit shapes cut. The shape-cutting machine operates only if the operators remember to tighten the spindle every fifteen minutes or so. Next the biscuit shapes are put into the ovens.

Sid is in charge of the ovens and has been with Bill since the business began. He can tell whether the temperature in the ovens is right just by spitting on them! Once cool, the biscuits are packed and usually the odd-shaped ones fit into the boxes so they don't have to be thrown away. Fifteen biscuits to a box is always a bit overweight, depending on how thick they are. This is determined by the operators on the rollers and the number of misshapen biscuits.

Problem-solving activity

i) *Bill doesn't know what BS5750 is or what he should do about it. Prepare a brief report giving him a summary of its requirements.*

ii) *What immediate actions should Bill take concerning his product quality?*

HELP **?** See the information bank in *Section 2: Control*, page 86; *Quality assurance*, page 159.

Scenario: The quality issues group

A quality issues group has been formed recently in the organisation where you are employed. The group reports directly to senior management and consists of a selection of employees from all grades, chaired by a supervisor. The group's brief is to look at quality issues and to carry out a SWOT analysis, listing ideas under strengths, weaknesses, opportunities and threats.

In order to carry this out, the group has invited all the working units in the organisation to put forward their views on quality. A representative from each unit is expected to make a short presentation and answer any questions raised by the review group. The quality issues group has prepared the following brief guidelines for presentations:

```
1. Standards: validity, how set, by whom

2. The work team: selection, training, performance

3. Materials: checks, samples, reports

4. Equipment: failures, maintenance reports

5. Recommendations/conclusions
```

Problem-solving activity

i) *You have been selected to make the presentation on behalf of your work unit. Prepare your notes and make the presentation (based on your own organisation or one with which you are familiar).*

ii) *Chair a meeting at which other presentations are being made.*

You should bear in mind that some of the members of the quality issues group are likely to be non-technical and may not have a full understanding of the technical terms used in the working environment.

HELP **?** See the information bank in *Section 2: Control*, page 86; *Quality assurance*, page 159.

A Activity: A question of control

In every business there are a number of control mechanisms, such as those concerning the *receipt of money, production* or *quality*. Associated with these controls there are often charts, reports or tables.

Required:

Select two such documents or mechanisms of control and prepare a set of instructions for users showing:

❏ *the control's purpose;*

❏ *the data to be collected and its source;*

❏ *what is shown;*

❏ *what actions might be taken and by whom.*

HELP ? | See the information bank in *Section 2: Control*, page 86.

A Activity: Take your time

In order to make the best use of your time, you need to look at how it is used at the moment. You also need to be able to set priorities. By following the steps below, you will be able to analyse and prioritise your time and thus improve your personal time management.

1. *Keep a detailed diary for a week. Divide each day into one-hour sections and note how you spent each hour. Write up your diary at least twice a day, say at lunchtime and at the end of the day.*

2. *Classify what you did into suitable categories such as meetings, interruptions, reports.*

3. *Analyse who makes demands on your time and why.*

4. *From the information you have gathered, isolate those tasks that should be delegated or which take up a disproportionate amount of time.*

5. *Put the categories you have devised onto the priorities axis.*

HELP ? | See the information bank in *Section 2: Time management*, page 190.

A Activity: Work study

You are presented with the following problems.

1. The operators in the press shop seem to spend more time walking between presses and material stocks than on the job itself.

2. Even though he finished his training some months ago, one of the semi-skilled workers produces 15% less than the others.

3. Your department is using 10% more overtime than is in the budget.

4. The stores never seem to have the parts needed in stock.

Required:

What instructions and help would you give a member of your work team who was going to carry out an investigation and find a solution?

See the information bank in *Section 2: Control*, page 86; *Production control*, page 156; *Work study*, page 202.

A Activity: Planning exercise

The following list of activities relates to a proposal to open a new sales office for your organisation in the city centre. *Place a number against each activity in order of priority.*

(1 = highest priority, 20 = lowest priority)

A   Find qualified personnel

B   Measure progress

C   Identify job tasks

D   Develop strategies

E   Develop alternative courses of action

F   Arrange appropriate consequences for individual performance

G   Assign responsibility and accountability

H   Set objectives

I   Train and develop personnel

J   Gather facts about current situation

K   Establish qualifications for new positions

L   Take corrective action

M   Co-ordinate activities

N   Determine allocation of resources

O   Measure performance against objectives

P   Identify negative consequences of each course

Q   Develop individual performance objectives

R   Develop relationships, responsibility, authority etc

S   Decide course of action

T   Determine measurable checkpoints

HELP **?**   See the information bank in *Section 2: Organisational objectives*, page 142.

Unit 3: Managing others

Scenario: The transport office

The boys in the transport office enjoy their work. There is always a lot of good-natured bantering, laughing and joking. Because of the nature of the work it is quiet between 8.30am and 11am and they usually do their paperwork then. Each has his own responsibilities and by 11am all the work has been cleared. Soon after 11am the telephones start ringing and they don't usually stop until 4 or 5pm.

Although they all have their own separate jobs to do, they help each other. Sometimes they have to stay late, but they don't usually claim overtime. Occasionally they also work on Saturday mornings. Dennis, the supervisor, doesn't mind if they are late for work in the morning, especially if they have worked late the night before. When things are slack he sometimes sends them home early. When a busy period comes, it's so hectic that there's no time for breaks and anyone who has a moment to spare is expected to go and get drinks from the canteen or fetch sandwiches; even Dennis.

When Nigel Morgan joined the transport office it was during a quiet spell in August. He had moved from another department where he had been a reliable and popular employee. He soon learned his new job and works very efficiently. Now it is getting busier in the office. Yesterday Nigel went for lunch at 12.30pm and returned at 1.30pm. During the afternoon he refused to get the drinks. 'I'm not the tea-boy,' he complained. At exactly 5pm he left, remarking as he said goodnight, 'I've done my work.' The others stayed on as they still had work to do.

When Dennis arrived at work today there was a note on his desk:

> Nigel Morgan doesn't pull his weight. We won't work with him any longer. If you don't do something about it, we will. The Transport Boys

Problem-solving activity

i) Who is to blame for this situation?

ii) Dennis thinks that the situation will reflect badly on him as the supervisor. What should he do now and in the longer-term?

HELP ? | See the information bank in **Section 2: Groups and teams**, page 104; **Motivation**, page 135.

Scenario: Back home

Just before lunch Barbara and Taffy had another row. This time it was about a quality problem (Taffy's responsibility). Matters were made worse when Taffy told her that he made the decisions on quality and if he ever wanted advice, he wouldn't ask her! Barbara complained to the plant manager and told him that the rest of the team had refused to work with Taffy any more; they had had enough of him.

You have been asked by the plant manager to sort out this problem before it goes any further. Your investigations reveal the following:

Both Barbara and Taffy have been in the work group for the same length of time. Barbara seems to be the one who speaks out. The rest of the group say that they don't have strong feelings about Taffy, but they are tired of him constantly saying how things were better or done differently 'back home in Wales'. They also think he works too fast. Taffy thinks that he's in a strong position as his production levels are always higher than anyone else's.

Problem-solving activity

i)   What do you think is the cause of the problem between Barbara and Taffy?

ii) What immediate and future actions should you take to resolve this problem?

iii) What action will you suggest the plant manager takes?

See the information bank in *Section 2: Groups and teams*, page 104; *Management theories*, page 132.

Scenario: Midas Ltd

Gary has worked for Midas Ltd, a large multinational company, since he left school. He is now thirty years old, married and has two children. He has just bought a house and has a large mortgage. If he stayed with Midas for the rest of his working life, although he'd never be really well off, he could expect a reasonable standard of living and a comfortable pension when he retires.

On a training course recently he was offered a job with a small new business which has a fairly uncertain future. The job is very well paid and there is a possibility that he might be offered a partnership if the firm's plans come to fruition.

Problem-solving activity

Gary turns to you for advice. What questions would you ask him in order to help him make up his mind?

See the information bank in *Section 2: Counselling and listening*, page 88.

Scenario: Nimbiville

You are to submit a plan for the layout of a new town to be called Nimbiville.

Your aim is to construct a town for the lowest feasible cost whilst catering for all sections of the projected population, both in terms of housing and employment. The maximum possible expenditure on the project is £162m, the minimum is £150m.

Accumulate points as follows:

1. *Price*   5 points for every £1m under the maximum allowable.

2. *Open spaces*   10 points for every square mile allowed.

3. *Facilities*   1 point for every 100 service units provided.

4. *Consideration* 2 points for each valid consideration concerning the siting of the buildings etc (as judged by the referee), e.g. not putting a playground close to a river.

5. *Jobs*   1 point for every 100 jobs.

Proposed site for Nimbiville (not to scale)

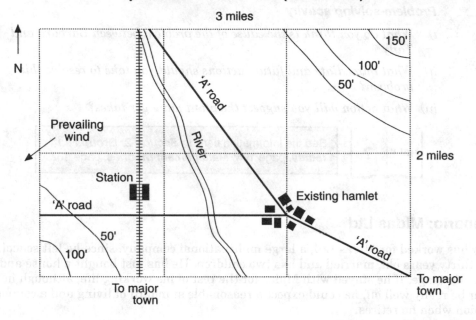

Background information

The total area to be developed is six square miles.

Population

Expected population	20,000
Families	6,000
whose income group is:	
£18,000 p.a. or more	200
£12,000 p.a. or more	1,000
£8,400 p.a. or more	3,000
£8,399 p.a. or less	1,800

Assume that the average income per annum nationally is £9,000.

Building requirements

Houses

Council:	allow 8,000 per square mile
Modern estate:	allow 4,000 per square mile
Individual dwellings:	allow 500 per square mile

Buildings (houses only) *must* take place in blocks of a quarter square mile only.

Industry

a) A chemical company has already been given permission to build a factory. This will provide 3,000 jobs and require an area of a quarter of a square mile.

b) A number of sites for manufacturing concerns should be provided. These will provide employment per unit of 1,000 and occupy one eighth of a square mile each.

Shopping facilities must be provided since the nearest big town is 20 miles away. You should allow the same area for each *service unit* (shops, banks, offices etc). Allow 500 per square mile. Shops are calculated as follows:

One comprehensive shopping centre (includes banks etc) per 15,000 people.

One centre comprises 200 units, or 1 unit of service facilities per 75 people.

Area required is one twenty-fifth of a square mile for one shopping centre.

Recreation facilities One recreation ground per 1,000 council houses, requiring one quarter of a square mile.

Costs

Housing

Houses	per unit
Council:	£18,000
Modern estate:	£24,000
Individual dwellings:	£48,000

Industry

	per square mile
All uses	£1,200,000

Service sector

	per unit
One unit	£36,000
One recreational facility (= 3 service units)	£108,000

Problem-solving activity

Produce a solution in the form of

☐ *a plan showing your siting proposals;*

☐ *your costings including a summary;*

☐ *a list showing your point scoring and total.*

See the information bank in *Section 2: Decision-making and problem-solving*, page 90.

Scenario: No singing at work

In the quality control department of a large electronics company there are seven workers testing and inspecting printed circuit boards (PCBs). In this department one of the workers Ron Wood, is having trouble with his immediate supervisor, Mike Jones, who was previously a tester in the same department. Had we been watching in this department we would have seen Ron carrying two or three PCBs at a time from the racks where they are stored to his test bench where he inspects them all. For this activity, we would have seen him log double or triple set-up time. We would have heard him occasionally singing at work and we would have seen him leaving his work bench a few minutes early to go to lunch. We would also have noticed that other employees sometimes go early with him. Had we been present on one particular occasion we would have heard Mike Jones telling him that he disapproved of these activities and that he wants Ron to stop. However, not being present to hear the actual conversation that took place let us note what each later said to the personnel officer.

In talking about his practice of logging double or triple set-up times for PCB's inspected all at once Ron said:

"This is a perfectly proper thing to do. We've been doing it for years. Mike Jones the supervisor doesn't like it though, he claims it's cheating the company. He came over to my bench a couple of days ago and said so, and boy did we have a row. It wasn't so much that he was telling me off, but more the way he did it. He treats us all like children and I'm not putting up with being spoken to like a naughty school kid. He's been like this ever since he got promoted. He used to be an easy-going, friendly bloke when he worked on the benches with the rest of us.

When he started on at me the other day I got so mad. I called in the union representative. I know what I was doing was allowed so I decided to make trouble for Mr. 'High-and-Mighty' Jones because of the way he keeps treating us. I'm trying everything I can to get transferred out of his section.

When the union questioned him about this matter of the set-up times, Mike had to back down because the rules say an employee can use any time saving method or device to speed up the process so long as the quality standards are met. I tried to tell him my method was more efficient but he wouldn't listen. He knows I do a professional job singing outside work. He hears me singing here and talking to people about my music career and he doesn't like it. He thinks I'm cocky because I have another source of income. Actually the other workers here like me singing while we work, but he thinks that I'm disturbing them. OK, sometimes I leave the job a little early to go to wash before lunch, and sometimes some of the others will go with me, so Mike Jones automatically thinks I'm the leader and I get blamed; I'm a marked man around her. He watches me like a hawk, and I don't like it. That's why I asked him for a transfer, but he won't give me one. Anyway I'm going to keep out of trouble, but if I get a chance I'll drop him right in it."

Mike said

"This trouble has been brewing for a while and I'm glad it's reached your attention. Ron Woods has been looking for a show-down with me for some time. He's been logging double and treble set-up times when he is actually inspecting one at a time and that is cheating. I've caught him at it several times and so I really gave him a dressing down this time. He's been getting away with this for too long and I'm going to put a stop to it once and for all. I really rattled him this time; a few hours later he had the union rep on my back. Well I told them both I won't tolerate this practice any more and if Wood continues it I'm going to take official action with my boss to have him fired if possible. Wood is clearly mentally deficient, talking to him is a waste of time, he just takes no notice. He seems to have some kind of grudge against me; I don't know why. I've handled him with kid gloves. It's no good though; I'm sure he is deliberately trying to provoke me and he certainly has a bad influence on the rest of the group. He thinks he's somebody just because he sings with a band and he sits there practising all day. Well that's OK with me, but when it starts interfering with the work something has got to be done, and I'm keeping a special eye on him now.

The trouble with Ron is he's got no commitment to do a real day's work. I know he can do it, I used to work with him, but lately he has slipped, his whole attitude has changed. Why, he's even encouraging the others to leave early at lunch time. I've told him about it several times but words don't seem to have a lasting impression with him. I tell you, he's mentally deficient. Well, if he keeps this up he's going to find himself out. He's asked for a transfer but I didn't give him an answer because I was so mad at the time I'd have told him to go somewhere else!"

Problem-solving activity

i) *Why did communications between Ron and Mike fail?*

ii) *Reconstruct the conversation between Ron and Mike,*

    a) *as it might have been,*

    b) *as it should have been.*

HELP ? | See the information bank in *Section 2: Communications*, page 81; *Counselling and listening*, page 88.

Activity: Are you a team builder?

To find out if you are a team builder answer the questions below by choosing a number between 1 and 7; then total your score.

1 = never, 7 = always

1. When selecting group members, I pick those
   who can meet the job requirements best, rather   1   2   3   4   5   6   7
   than considering those who will fit in.

2. I involve group members in goal-setting and   1   2   3   4   5   6   7
   problem-solving, rather than do it alone.

3. I actively encourage people to work together   1   2   3   4   5   6   7
   and to support each other.

4. I talk openly with people and encourage them   1   2   3   4   5   6   7
   to respond openly.

5. I help team members get to know one another.   1   2   3   4   5   6   7

6. I am aware and sensitive to the roles and   1   2   3   4   5   6   7
   norms of the groups I deal with.

If your total score is less than 30 you should be questioning your approach to the work team. The questions you scored lowest on are the areas needing most attention.

> **HELP ?**   See the information bank in *Section 2: Groups and teams*, page 104.

 Activity: A question of style

Consider any two managers or supervisors, teachers or lecturers of your acquaintance.

Required:

Describe their styles of leadership. Would they be more successful or less successful leaders in other situations? How much is their success or failure as leaders due to the task or their knowledge and skills?

> **HELP ?**   See the information bank in *Section 2: Leadership*, page 119.

A Activity: Body language

Examine the following sketches and write a single-sentence caption for each describing the body language, and what you think is going on in each scene.

HELP	?

See the information bank in **Section 2: Communications**, page 81; **Non-verbal communication**, page 137.

(a)

(b)

(c)

(d)

(e)

Unit 4: Individuals at work

Scenario: New ways of working

Charlene Hall has recently been appointed as general manager at Vision Electronics Ltd. She has considerable energy and enthusiasm and some very firm ideas on how to run the factory.

Last week, she called all the supervisors to attend a meeting entitled '**A new approach to management**'. At the end of her talk, she told them that she would like to discard all clock cards and put the production workers on a good weekly salary instead of an hourly wage. She also announced that she wanted to eliminate assembly lines and replace them with production unit centres. These would be made up of small numbers of workers who would work on a complete assembly rather than only doing a portion of it. In addition, the workers were to select their own teams. As a result of these changes, the supervisors' jobs would be expanded and they would be paid more. Ms Hall explained that what she proposed to do would result in increased productivity, higher standards of quality and reduced labour turnover.

Several supervisors expressed doubts about what was being proposed and said that it simply wouldn't work, especially with the type of labour on the assembly lines who would simply take advantage of not having to clock in and out. However, Ms Hall would not be deterred.

A few days later every supervisor received a memo from Ms Hall asking them to attend a second meeting where they would be expected to outline any difficulties they could foresee and how they might be overcome.

Problem-solving activity

As one of the supervisors at Vision Electronics Ltd you will be attending the meeting and will be expected to put forward your point of view. Make notes on the points you would raise.

See the information bank in **Section 2: Change management**, page 79; **Job design**, page 115; **Job evaluation**, page 117; **Quality assurance**, page 159.

Scenario: Norance Plastics Ltd

Supervisors at Norance Plastics Ltd are expected to do everything they can to meet the company's objectives, including working long hours if necessary to keep production levels up. They are paid a good weekly salary and receive a bonus based on the company's profits. Over the years the bonuses have been quite substantial, but for the last two years they have decreased owing to conditions in the industry rather than lower productivity levels. Unfortunately profits for the current year are not expected to be high.

A few weeks ago the company received an unusually large order. The workforce put in an hour a day extra and worked on Saturday mornings in an effort to meet the order, but this was not enough. The manufacturing manager informed the supervisors that the factory would have to work a seven-day week and they should tell the workforce that this would continue for a month. Employees would receive time-and-a-half for this period, and double-time for any overtime.

On the first weekend of these new working conditions five of the 20 supervisors did not turn up for work on the Sunday; nor did 10 of the key operators. This caused a serious reduction in production. The following Monday, at the weekly supervisors' meeting, the plant manager made it clear that there was no more money available and it was agreed that the problem had to be tackled quickly. A special meeting was called for the next day at which the supervisors were expected to suggest reasons why attendance was so poor and what should be done about it.

Problem-solving activity

As one of the supervisors, you will be attending the meeting. What reasons will you offer for the absenteeism and what action will you suggest you and your fellow supervisors take?

HELP **?** | See the information bank in **Section 2: Management theories**, page 132; **Motivation**, page 135.

Scenario: All change at Brooks Ltd

Brooks Ltd is a garment manufacturer. The company was established in the 1940s by Mr Leonard Brooks and is a successful family business which operates on good working practices and has an excellent labour relations record. Most of the company's employees have traditionally been women.

About five years ago the lease on the firm's city-centre premises expired and it was considered to be a good opportunity to look for more suitable premises and expand the business. A suitable unit was found on a new trading estate about 25 miles away. The move was made with little difficulty and although some of the employees moved with the company, about 60 new members of staff were recruited. Wages levels remained the same as they had been before the move. Although this was less than the norm in the new area, it was about average for the industry. This did not seem to make much difference to recruitment and labour turnover was very low.

Initially the company continued with its old methods of production. The workforce was organised into groups of four, seated at a table which held their equipment and materials. Each group decided what each individual group member should do and they made the complete garments from scratch. The supervisor gave out the tasks, trained new recruits and kept an eye on the quality. A bonus was paid according to each group's output. Different groups worked on different garments, collecting the materials and patterns from the stores and delivering the finished garments to the goods out store. Each group's daily output was displayed in the work room.

But business has been very bad recently as a result of the poor economic climate. Brooks Ltd has been forced to sell out to Matthews & Son Ltd. Les Matthews, the managing director, has agreed to retain the existing workforce. After a month Mr Matthews decided to introduce some changes as follows:

The factory will be organised into three groups of twenty. Each group member will specialise in a particular task which should take about 50 seconds. Then the piece of work will be passed on to the next person. The precise tasks and times will be worked out using work study methods. Work will flow from table to table and so a reorganisation of the factory layout will be necessary. In addition to the three large groups there will be three small groups with a membership of about four each. These will be used as reserves and for training.

The present layout of the factory, before these changes, is shown below.

Present layout

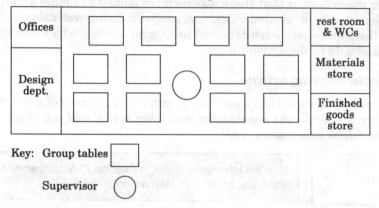

Key: Group tables □

Supervisor ○

Problem-solving activity

i) *List the advantages and disadvantages of the proposed changes.*

ii) *Design a new factory layout.*

iii) *How should the proposed changes be managed?*

iv) *What problems might arise as a result of these changes?*

See the information bank in **Section 2: Change management**, page 79; **Groups and teams**, page 104; **Job design**, page 115; **Redundancy action checklist**, page 178; **Salaries and wages**, page 180; **Stress management**, page 184.

A Are you likely to suffer from stress?

To find out if you are likely to suffer from stress, answer the following questions by choosing a number between 1 and 10, then total your score.

1 = never, 10 = always

1. I like to crowd lots of activities into each day.   1 2 3 4 5 6 7 8 9 10

2. If I make an error or mistake in my job the consequences are likely to be very serious, particularly in terms of people's safety.   1 2 3 4 5 6 7 8 9 10

3. My life is a continual fight to meet deadlines and targets within limited time.   1 2 3 4 5 6 7 8 9 10

4. I recognise that I can be quick-tempered.   1 2 3 4 5 6 7 8 9 10

5. I feel uneasy if I am just relaxing and doing nothing in particular.   1 2 3 4 5 6 7 8 9 10

6. My job demands a hostile aggressive style and approach.   1 2 3 4 5 6 7 8 9 10

7. I feel tense at work quite a lot.   1 2 3 4 5 6 7 8 9 10

8. Generally, I am more concerned with planning and preparing for the future than in taking time out to relax.   1 2 3 4 5 6 7 8 9 10

9. One of my major concerns is how I can move faster so that I can do more things in less time. 1 2 3 4 5 6 7 8 9 10

10. I make sure on most occasions that things are done my way.   1 2 3 4 5 6 7 8 9 10

HELP	?

See the information bank in *Section 2: Stress management: stress types*, page 187.

Redesigning a job

Select a job with which you are familiar (perhaps your own or one you have held in the past).

Required:

i) *Write a brief description of the job.*

ii) *Describe the main changes you would like to see made and explain how the changes might affect or be affected by other employees' attitudes, work flows, procedures, etc.*

iii) *State (a) what you and (b) what others would have to do to implement your recommendations.*

HELP **?** See the information bank in *Section 2: Change management*, page 79; *Job design*, page 115.

Why are some jobs boring?

You might think that because people have varied interests, capabilities and ambitions, what is boring for one person might not be boring for others. Or are there some jobs that people always find boring?

Required:

i) *Devise a short questionnaire to find out the common features of boring jobs.*

ii) *Conduct a survey to gather information.*

iii) *Write up your conclusions.*

HELP **?** See the information bank in *Section 2: Job design*, page 115; *Questionnaire surveys*, page 166.

Unit 5: Employee relations

Scenario: Better safe than sorry

Mike has been bored with his job for some years; routine paperwork and no prospects for promotion have made his life very dull. He has resolved to make life more interesting and with this in mind he has volunteered to be the department's health and safety representative.

Mary Cooke, the department manager, thought choosing Mike was an inspired choice 'I'll just shovel all the paperwork on safety in his direction and let him get on with it,' she thought. So she told Mike to update the company's safety policy and report anything he thinks needs the attention of the management.

Mike certainly succeeded in updating the safety policy. He turned it into a 25-page typewritten document and made everyone sign to say they'd had a copy, including Mary. Like everyone else she had neither the time nor the inclination to read it, so she filed it.

On the first Monday of the month at 8.30am sharp, Mike presented himself at Mary's office for the monthly safety review meeting. When she protested that she knew nothing about such a meeting Mike said, 'But you must; it's all in the safety policy document.'

When the meeting ended at noon, Mike had told her in detail about a whole variety of incidents which according to the safety policy demanded management action. Mary's notes on the meeting are set out below.

Mary's notes

1. Accountancy clerk trying to close a window by standing on a stool fell through it. Mike wants everyone issued with a window pole.

2. Word processor operator claims that radiation from her computer screen is giving her dizzy spells. Mike wants half-hourly breaks every two hours for computer operators.

3. Visiting sales representative slipped on the wet patch by the office door which he didn't know about. Mike suggests we put a sign up.

4. Car stolen from the staff car park was involved in a serious accident. Mike wants a security man on the car park.

5. The fumes from the cleaning fluid in the technicians room are inflammable. Mike wants 'No smoking' signs put in the corridor.

Problem-solving activity

If you were Mary, what would you do now?

HELP ?

> See the information bank in **Section 2: Employment legislation**, page 99; **Health and safety legislation**, page 109.

A question of rights

Find out the answers to the following questions:

i)   Lee Wilson, a keen football supporter, took a day's holiday without permission to watch a match in which his favourite team was playing. On his return to work his employer suspended him without pay for one day. *Could his employer do this legally?*

ii) During a busy period, Sid Stevens asks all his employees to work overtime. One employee refuses and is dismissed. *Is Sid within his rights?*

iii) Ian Jones had been given a pay rise of £25 per week. Two months later his employer, who has been faced with decreased sales, reduces his pay by £25 per week. *Can his employer do this?*

iv) An employer claims that he has the right to change the hours of work of some of his employees since they are not specified in the written contract of employment. *Does he have this right?*

v)   During the lunch-break Mr Smith, the office manager, heard strange noises in the broom cupboard. Inside he found Miss Cook, the receptionist, and Mr Robinson, one of the clerks. He dismissed Mr Robinson on the spot and gave Miss Cook a warning. *Was Mr. Smith within his rights to do this?*

 HELP ? | See the information bank in *Section 2: Employment legislation*, page 99.

 An employer's dilemma

Find out the answers to the following questions.

i)   You have a part-time female worker who has worked 12 hours per week for six years. *Is she entitled to maternity leave?*

ii)   You make a 50 year old worker redundant who has worked for you for 6 years. *What is his redundancy entitlement?*

iii) *If you do not insure against personal injury to your employees what can you be fined?*

iv)   *If you employ a 17 year old, are there any restrictions imposed on you by law because of his or her age?*

v)   You intend employing French students during the summer. *Do they need work permits?*

vi)   *Do you have to give workers Christmas Day off?*

vii) *If you do not give a written statement of particulars to an employee, how much can you be fined?*

viii) You do not want your workers to be members of trade unions. *Can you stop them?*

ix) You decide that you would like to employ married people only as you think they are more reliable than single employees. *Can you do this?*

See the information bank in **Section 2: Employment legislation**, page 99.

A Rights and wrongs

Find out the answers to the following questions:

i) *Do you have to give a trade union member of your staff time off for union duties?*

ii) You are taken to an Industrial Tribunal for unfair dismissal and lose. *Will you have to pay the employees' costs as well as compensation?*

iii) *What is the current lower rate maternity pay?*

iv) *Where is the nearest industrial tribunal to where you work or study?*

v) *Can an employee claiming unfair dismissal get legal aid?*

vi) *Over what size do firms have to employ a quota of disabled persons, and what are the details of this quota?*

vi) *Does a nurse who has committed theft in 1979 have an obligation to inform prospective employers about such a conviction?*

vii) *Is an employee entitled to paid time off for duties as a magistrate?*

viii) *Is it lawful to not employ women on the grounds that you are a small employer and have only toilet facilities for men?*

ix) *Under what circumstances would an employee be entitled to an additional award when claiming unfair dismissal?*

See the information bank in **Section 2: Employment legislation**, page 99; **Trade unions and the law**, page 192.

A A hazardous occupation

How many hazards can you identify in the picture on the following page?

See the information bank in **Section 2: Health and safety**, page 109.

(reproduced from *People at Work*, by B. Paisley and J. Parker
by kind permission of Pitman Publishing)

Unit 6: Recruitment and selection

Scenario: BCC Ltd

BCC Ltd has recently placed two advertisements in the local press, one to recruit a *chief technician* and the other for a *porter/storesperson*. A number of completed application forms have now been received by the personnel department. These, together with the following job specifications, have now been sent to the departmental managers where the vacancies exist so that they can start drawing up a shortlist.

BCC Ltd
Job specification

Post title	Chief technician	Department	Technical support
Post grage	Scale 4/5	Site	Warrington
Post number	4CO 71		

Responsible to   Head of department

Staff responsibility
　　　Technicians – 3 x Scale 2
　　　　　　　　　　6 x Scale 3
　　　　　　　　　　Labourers x 3

Duties and responsibilities *List items in descending order of importance. Percentages should be approximate and not less than 5%.*	% time
Supervision and General Organisation of 5 technicians and 3 labourers	
Supervision and General Organisation of 4 Technicians to meet the requirements of servicing 9 workshops - 1 laboratory at 5 workshops - 3 laboratories at	
Computer facilities at both	
Planning support staff depending on demand at both sites	60
Planning use of equipment where there has not been a doubling of resources on both sites	10
Monitoring expenditure of department allocation - currently £57,000	10
Installation and adaption of equipment on both sites	10
Liaison with other departments	10

BCC Ltd

Job specification

Post title	Porter/Storeperson	Department	Catering
Post grage	Scale 2	Site	Warrington
Post number	P53		

Responsible to	Catering manager

Staff responsibility

To provide a portering service to the Refectory, maintain stock to vending machines and carry out other general duties

Duties and responsibilities List Items in descending order of importance. Percentages should be approximate and not less than 5%.	% time
1. To receive and check goods inwards	20
2. To issue, maintain and order certain stock items and carry out stock control	
3. To notify Refectory Manager of stock requirements	
4. To move furniture, equipment and stores in the Refectory area	5
5. To maintain stock and clean vending machines	30
6. To empty cash from vending machines	10
7. To clean floors in refectory area including use of scrubbing machine	
8 To clean waste disposal areas and grease traps	30
9. To clean and maintain storeroom and refrigorators	5
10.To carry out such other duties as may be reasonably	

NOTES

1. The postholder must carry out all duties with regard to health and safety and be able to work under his/her own initiative. The nature of the duties require the postholder to be physically fit.

2. The postholder must be prepared to cover in all work areas and may be called in at short notice when on retainer

Problem-solving activity

What kind of person would you expect to appoint to these two positions? Draw up a job description for each vacancy giving details of the essential qualifications and experience required.

HELP **?** See the information bank in *Section 2: Recruitment, selection and induction*, page 167.

Scenario: The caretaker

Cyril, the superintendent caretaker at BCC Ltd, has recently retired after many years' service at the Nicor Training Centre. Cyril enjoyed his work despite the low pay and unsocial hours involved. His job is now being advertised, although the personnel manager recognises that it may be difficult to attract suitable applicants.

The following job description has been retrieved from the personnel files and updated.

BCC Ltd

Job specification

Post title	Superintendent caretaker	Site	Cilshire
Post grage	Scale 3/4	Section	Nicor Training Centre
Post number	UT 01		

Responsible to   Deputy Secretary

Staff responsibility

Provide day-to-day supervision of caretaking and cleaning staff at the nicor Training Centre

Duties and responsibilities List items in descending order of importance. Percentages should be approximate and not less than 5%.	% time
1. Arrangement of timetables for Caretakers' duties and Centre cleaning (including vacations).	
2. Security of buildings and equipment (including weekends and outside normal hours).	
3. Supervision of cleaning contracts	
4. Holding preliminary interviews with prospective candidates for appointment to Caretaking and Cleaning posts, prior to interview by Deputy Secretary.	
5. Preparation of rooms for special meetings and examinations.	
6. Control of Car Parking.	
7. <u>Time Sheets</u>. Checking individually prepared timesheets for non-salaried caretaking and cleaning staff for total hours worked, overtime, absences and sickness, etc.	
8. <u>Orders and Invoices</u>. Preparation of orders for cleaning materials and allied equipment, clothing and uniforms for staff. Liaise with Burser on budgeting control of cleaning materials and equipment expenditure.	

BCC Ltd

Job specification

Duties and responsibilities (cont.)	% time

9. Checking goods, received notes and signing invoices for goods received. Controlling stocks of materials and issues.

10. Making appropriate arrangements for dealing with personal property which is either 'lost' of 'found' on the premises.

11. Miscellaneous. Maintenance of inventory for cleaning equipment. Control of movement of furniture within the Centre. Minor repairs to cleaning equipment. Ensuring that all defects in buildings and surroundings are entered in the 'defects book'.

12. Such other duties which from time to time may be required by the Secretary.

Notes

This post requires shift working as the site is open 9am to 9pm 5 days a week and Saturday morning.
Current salary range is £6,000-£8,000pa with 3 weeks paid holiday.

Signature of post holder *Cyril Bear*   Date 25.4.63

Comment by section head

More emphasis should be put on the security aspects of this post.
BM
9/1/92

Signature *BMountbloggins*   Date 25/4/63

Problem-solving activity

i) *Write a job specification from the information provided.*

ii) *Devise a suitable job advertisement to be placed in the local press.*

iii) *Prepare some notes for applicants to be sent out with the application form.*

HELP ?

See the information bank in **Section 2:**
Discrimination and equality, page 98;
Employment legislation, page 99; **Recruitment, selection and induction**, page 167.

Scenario: Velop Ltd

As a manager at Velop Ltd you are expected to participate in the recruitment of staff to certain management positions. The advertisement for *one such post* is detailed below, together with *some notes from the personnel department* and the *ten candidates' completed application forms.*

Section Manager

Applicants are invited from potential managers to fill the post of evening shift section manager.

This is a new position which has arisen because of our increased production levels. The successful candidate will be expected to manage a busy section on our production line and will have responsibility for the work of 20 operators.

Applicants may have some experience of production line work and of a supervisory position, but the main qualifications are the ability to work under pressure and with commitment.

The hours of work are normally 40 hours per week 2 pm until 10 pm, Monday to Friday.

A generous salary is offered (the precise amount will depend on experience), along with substantial benefits and holidays.

Applicants should return an application form to:

K. Batty
Personnel Officer

Closing date for Applications: Tuesday 10th July.

Personnel Department notes

Job title: Section manager

Salary: Grade M 7-11

Function: Responsibility for the finishing section of the TB production line.

Duties and responsibilities:

1. To direct the work of the line operatives

2. To compile the weekly production reports

3. To advise the general manager on production and operator needs

4. To ensure that production targets are met

5. To maintain good industrial relations

6. To ensure that quality matches standards

Supervision received: Oral and written instructions from the general manager.
Supervision given: Responsible for organisation and control of up to 20 production operatives

Minimum qualifications: Ability to work and get along with people; good physical condition; leadership potential

VELOP Ltd

Application for employment as

Surname	BALL				
Forenames	ALAN				
			Title	MR	Sex MALE
			Age		
Telephone no.	—	Date of birth	15-12-57	Country of birth	ENGLAND
Address	98, SUMMER RD LEIGH PARK HAVANT HANTS	Nationality	BRITISH		
		Marital status (delete as necessary)	Married/Single/Divorced/Seperated/Widowed		
Postcode	PO9 8UE	Children's dates of birth	18-6-80 10-3-87 14-11-84		
Number of children	3	Religious denomination		Trade Union Affiliation	T.F.W.U
National Insurance no. HE 84.17 1 8.D				Current driving licence?	✓
What are your spare time interests, hobbies etc? FOOTBALL, TENPIN BOWLING, CRICKET				Notice required by current employer ONE WEEK	
Travelling arrangements if appointed BIKE					

Examinations taken		Results of examinations	
ENGLISH CSE		GRADE 3	
MATHS CSE		GRADE 3	
HISTRICY CSE		GRADE 2	
SOCIAL STUDIES GSE		GRADE 2	

Dates		Courses taken		Qualifications obtained	✓
From	To	From	To		
10 SEPT 72	22 JULY 76				

Name of last school attended	PARK (COMMUNITY)
Name of university, college or other institute	

Have you or do you suffer from any serious illness, operations or injuries? Yes/No
If yes, give details ✓

Are you a disabled person? Yes/No
If yes, give details ✓

Previous employment

Dates		Employer's name and address	Employer's business	Job title	Main duties	Salary	
From	To					Starting	Finishing
1ST SEPT '76	24 APRIL 80	LIFEGUAD ASSURANCE PETERSFIELD	ASSURANCE	POST ROOM	SORTING MAIL	£50 P.W.	£60 P.W.
8 JUNE 81	—	GILPACK LTD LIMBERLINERO HILSEA	PACKING AND SORTING	SUPERVISOR	ADMIN	£80.00 P.W	£160.00 P.W

Other relevant information in support of your application

I HAVE BEEN SUPERVISOR FOR EIGHT YEARS NOW AND HAVE FOURTEEN PEOPLE, UNDER ME.
ALSO I HAVE ~~HAVE~~ A GOOD WORKING RECORD AT MY PRESENT COMPANY, WITH THE PEOPLE I AM WORKING WITH.

VELOP Ltd

Application for employment as ....

Surname	CLEESE
Forenames	AMANDA
Title	MISS
Address	27 TEWKESBURY AVE BROCKHURST GOSPORT
Telephone no.	513 743
Date of birth	07.4.67
Age	23
Sex	F.
Postcode	PO14 6BT
Nationality	BRITISH
Country of birth	WALES
Marital status (delete as necessary)	Married/Single/Divorced/Separated/Widowed
Number of children	NONE
Children's dates of birth	/
National Insurance no.	NM 64 89 17 B
Religious denomination	CATHOLIC
Trade Union Affiliation	ASTMS
What are your spare time interests, hobbies etc?	READING, NETBALL, SCUBA DIVING, AEROBICS, SWIMMING
Travelling arrangements if appointed	
Notice required by current employer	1 MONTH
Current driving licence?	YES

Examinations taken

Dates		Examinations taken	Results of examinations
From	To		
1978	1981	O'LEVEL ENGLISH HISTORY ECONOMICS ACCOUNT ARITHMETIC FOOD+NUTRITION	FASHION + FABRIC BUSINESS STUDIES 'B' PASSES FOOD & NUTRITION ENGLISH ARITHMETIC

Name of last school attended	ST COLUMBA'S HIGH SCHOOL

Courses taken

Dates		Courses taken	Qualifications obtained
From	To		
1981	1984	ENGINEERING DEGREE	BSc

Name of university, college or other institute	NORTHERN COLLEGE

Have you or do you suffer from any serious illness, operations or injuries? Yes/No
If yes, give details

Are you a disabled person? Yes/No
If yes, give details

Previous employment

Dates		Employer's name and address	Employer's business	Job title	Main duties	Salary	
From	To					Starting	Finishing
JAN 1985	OCT 1985	TEAM SALES. THE RETREAT OLD TURNPIKE FAREHAM	SAIL MAKER	PACKER + MACHINIST	MAKING & PACKING SAILS	4,000	5,000
1985	1987	MITHS CRISPS SOUTHAMPTON	MAKING CRISPS	S.P.O.	PACKING	5,000	6,000
JAN 1988	DEC 1988	MITHS CRISPS (AS ABOVE)	MAKING CRISPS	TRAINER	TRAINING PEOPLE ON MACHINES.	6,000	6,500
JAN 1989		(AS ABOVE)	MAKING CRISPS	SUPERVISOR	SUPERVISING + ORGANISING PEOPLE	10,000	12,000

Other relevant information in support of your application

I am keen and willing to learn. I also think I am a hard worker. & adapt very well to changes.

I have done a course on supervisory skills & interviewing techniques and I am at present doing a N.G.B.S.M. course.

I have also done various courses on Health & Safety & C.O.S.S.

VELOP Ltd

Application for employment as

Surname	Forenames	Title	
COOKSON	JEANETTE	MRS	**Sex** F.

Address	201 DERSON RD	**Date of birth** 16/2/52	**Age** 38
	EASTNEY PORTSMOUTH HANTS	**Country of birth** GREAT BRITAIN	

Nationality BRITISH

Postcode

Marital status (delete as necessary)
Married/~~Single~~/~~Divorced~~/~~Separated~~/~~Widowed~~

Telephone no. /

Number of children

Children's dates of birth

National Insurance no. NS270907

Religious denomination C.of E

Trade Union Affiliation NUPE

What are your spare time interests, hobbies etc?
DRESSMAKING, DARTS, ROCK CLIMBING

Current driving licence? YES

Travelling arrangements if appointed
PUBLIC TRANSPORT

Notice required by current employer 1 WEEK

Examinations taken NONE

Name of last school attended
MEON RD SECONDARY SCHOOL

Dates	
From	To
SEP 1963	JULY 1967

Results of examinations /

Name of university, college or other institute
SOUTH DOWNS
"

Courses taken
RSA I TYPING
RSA 2 TYPING
WORDPROCESSING

Dates	
From	To
1982	1983
1983	1984
1985	

Qualifications obtained
PASS
PASS
PASS

Have you or do you suffer from any serious illness, operations or injuries? ~~Yes~~/No

If yes, give details

Are you a disabled person? ~~Yes~~/No

If yes, give details

Previous employment

Dates		Employer's name and address	Employer's business	Job title	Main duties	Salary	
From	To					Starting	Finishing
1967	1977	BABYBIRD CLOTHING FACTORY	CHILDREN'S CLOTHING MANUFACTURE	MACHINIST	SEWING		
1977	1980	H.M. DOCKYARD	MANUFACTURE OF UPHOLSTERY, FLAGS & OVERALLS	"	"		
1980		NATIONAL HEALTH SERVICE	LINEN SERVICES	SUPERVISOR	ORDERING STOCK, OVERSEEING WORK		

Other relevant information in support of your application

I have experience of working on a production line also of supervising a production line of 18 staff. I am also motivated at the thought of a challenge, so feel this job would be suited to me.

VELOP Ltd

Application for employment as: M.E.

Surname	GREEN
Forenames	M.F.
Title	MR
Sex	M
Date of birth	2.8.64
Age	26
Country of birth	ENGLAND
Telephone no.	0705 201411
Nationality	BRITISH
Marital status (delete as necessary)	Married/~~Single~~/Divorced/Separated/Widowed
Address	12 NETTLE PL. SOUTHSEA HANTS
Postcode	PO8 3NG
Number of children	NONE
Children's dates of birth	
National Insurance no.	NB 596613
Religious denomination	C of E
Trade Union Affiliation	No
Current driving licence?	YES
What are your spare time interests, hobbies etc?	MOTOR RACING, WINDSURFING, SWIMMING
Notice required by current employer	1 MONTH
Travelling arrangements if appointed	OWN CAR

Examinations taken: O'LEVEL MATHS, ENGLISH, GEOGRAPHY, TECHNICAL DRAWING
Dates From 1975 To 1980
Results of examinations: GRADE B, ", ", "

Name of last school attended: BROADWATER SEC' SCHOOL FARNHAM SURREY

Courses taken: BTEC ELECTRONICS, BTEC ELECTRONICS, NEBSM CERT
Dates From: 1987, 1988, 1989 To: 1988, 1989, 1990
Qualifications obtained: DISTINCTION, DISTINCTION, PASS

Name of university, college or other institute: HIGH COLLEGE OF TECH

Have you or do you suffer from any serious illness, operations or injuries? Yes/No
If yes, give details

Are you a disabled person? Yes/No
If yes, give details

Previous employment

| Dates | | Employer's name and address | Employer's business | Job title | Main duties | Salary | |
From	To					Starting	Finishing
1980	1983	SOUTHERN ELECTRICITY BOARD ALDERSHOT, HANTS	ELECTRICAL CONTRACTOR	ELECTRICIAN	——	4000	6000
1983	1988	BRITISH TELECOM TELEPHONE HOUSE GUILDFORD SURREY	SUPPLY & MAINTAIN THE UK TELEPHONE NETWORK	MAINTENANCE ENGINEER	REPAIR OF TECHNICAL EQUIPMENT	9500	10850
1988		AS ABOVE	—— " ——	FAULT DISTRIBUTION OFFICER	CONTROL OF FIELD STAFF	11000	14500

Other relevant information in support of your application

I AM CURRENTLY RESPONSIBLE FOR 15 STAFF AND HAVE TO ORGANISE STAFF TO MEET TIGHT OPERATIONAL TARGETS.

VELOP Ltd

Application for employment as SECTION MANAGER

Surname	BLOGGS	Forenames	JOSEPH	Title	MR

Address	Telephone no. 274 932	Date of birth 5·5·55	Age 35	Sex M
31 WAYSIDE AVE	Nationality IRISH	Country of birth SCOTLAND		
NEARDEAN				
WALTON WILTS	Marital status (delete as necessary)			
Postcode	Married/Single/Divorced/Separated/Widowed			

| Number of children 7 | Children's dates of birth | 4·5·78 5·4·79 1·7·80 9·4·51 | | |
| | | 9·5·82 10·5·83 11·7·84 | | |

National Insurance no. AN 76 54 32 18 9	Religious denomination R.C.	Trade Union Affiliation A.E.U

What are your spare time interests, hobbies etc?	Notice required by current employer 2 MONTH'S	Current driving licence? Yes/No 4E3 20 yrs
READING, SPORT, MUSIC		

Travelling arrangements if appointed CAR	Examinations taken 8 'O' LEVELS	Results of examinations 4 GRADE B / 4 GRADE C

Name of last school attended KINGS HILL COMP	Dates From 1962 / To 1970	Courses taken INDUSTRIAL MANAGEMENT	Qualifications obtained NATIONAL DIPLOMA

Name of university, college or other institute MILCE'S COLLEGE	Dates From 1972 / To 1976	Have you or do you suffer from any serious illness, operations or injuries? Yes/No CONTROLLED EPILEPSY	
		If yes, give details	
		Are you a disabled person? Yes/No	
		If yes, give details	

Previous employment

Dates		Employer's name and address	Employer's business	Job title	Main duties	Salary	
From	To					Starting	Finishing
1974	1984	RJ JONES LTD	PRODUCING INDUSTRIAL CLEANING FLUIDS	CHARGEHAND	PACKAGE AND DISTRIBUTION	5,000	8,000
1984		FORD MOTOR COMPANY	PRODUCING CARS	SECTION SUPERVISOR	PRODUCING CHASIS	10,150	15,000

Other relevant information in support of your application

I have gone as far as I can with the ford motor co unless I move 400 miles north and with 7 children at school age I have no desire to do so.
So I feel that a new challenge would be in mine and your co best interest

VELOP Ltd

Application for employment as SECTION MANAGER

Surname	RAYMOND	Forenames	JACK		Title	MR		
Address 8 ALLANS ROAD SOUTHSEA HANTS		**Telephone no.** 82-0793)		**Date of birth** 19-12-55		**Age** 35	**Sex** M	
Postcode		**Nationality** BRITISH		**Country of birth** ENGLAND				

Marital status (delete as necessary)
Married/~~Single~~/~~Divorced~~/~~Separated~~/~~Widowed~~

Number of children	ONE	Children's dates of birth	1-4-86

National Insurance no.	XY 73 61 24 D	Religious denomination	C/E	Trade Union Affiliation	T.G.W.U.

What are your spare time interests, hobbies etc? POOL, DARTS, SWIMMING

Current driving licence? YES

Travelling arrangements if appointed: CAR

Notice required by current employer: ONE WEEK

Name of last school attended	TRIPTON SEC. MOD.	Examinations taken	C.S.E. MATHS / C.S.E. ENGLISH	Dates From 1965 To 1970	Results of examinations	GRADE 2 / GRADE 1

Name of university, college or other institute	HIGHBURY INST.	Courses taken	N.E.B.S.M.	Dates From 1990 To 1991	Qualifications obtained	PASS

Have you or do you suffer from any serious illness, operations or injuries? ~~Yes~~/No — (Yes)
If yes, give details: CONTROLLED DIABETIC SINCE 1987

Are you a disabled person? ~~Yes~~/No
If yes, give details

Previous employment

Dates		Employer's name and address	Employer's business	Job title	Main duties	Salary	
From	**To**					**Starting**	**Finishing**
1970	1976	ROYAL NAVY	NAVY	A.B. MISSILE-MAN	—	1456	3640
1976	1977	FORD MOTOR COMPANY	MAKING CARS	INSPECTOR	FINDING FAULTS	3700	4105
1978	1979	MAY AND BAKERS	CHEMICALS	FORKLIFT DRIVER		6344	7320
1979	1983	NORTH THAMES GAS	—	CHARGE HAND		8330	9340
1983	—	I.B.M.	COMPUTERS	SUPERVISOR		10800	—

Other relevant information in support of your application: I HAVE A WIDE RANGE OF MAN MANAGEMENT IN ALL WALKS. I HAVE WORKED ON A PRODUCTION LINE WHEN I WORKED AT FORDS I KNOW THE PROBLEM THAT CAN ARISE ON THE LINE

VELOP Ltd

Application for employment as ....

Surname	JONES
Forenames	STEPHEN
Title	MR
Age	22
Sex	MALE
Date of birth	14-1-68
Country of birth	ENGLAND
Telephone no.	639236
Nationality	BRITISH
Marital status (delete as necessary)	Married/Single/Divorced/Separated/Widowed
Address	4 NEW RD PORTSMOUTH HANTS
Postcode	POG 7HW
Children's dates of birth	17-11-8 5-10-
Number of children	2
National Insurance no.	11 HW 667263
Religious denomination	C of E
Trade Union Affiliation	NONE
What are your spare time interests, hobbies etc?	DIM, DARTS, WATHING, FOOTBALL
Current driving licence?	YES
Travelling arrangements if appointed	SELF DRIVE
Notice required by current employer	4 WEEKS
Examinations taken	ENGLISH MATHS TECHNICAL DRAWING BIOLOGY PHYSICS
Results of examinations	ALL PASSES CSE GRADE 2 3M - 2 - 1 ... II
Name of last school attended	BISHOPFIELD SEC. MOD.
Dates From 1964 To 1970	
Name of university, college or other institute	NONE
Courses taken	
Dates From To	
Qualifications obtained	
Have you or do you suffer from any serious illness, operations or injuries? Yes/No. If yes, give details	
Are you a disabled person? Yes/No. If yes, give details	

Previous employment

Dates		Employer's name and address	Employer's business	Job title	Main duties	Salary	
From	To					Starting	Finishing
1782	1986	DAVIS WORLD TRAVEL	TRAVEL AGENT	TRAVEL CLERK	BOOKING & TICKETING OF TRAVEL	£4,800	£6,300
1986	1987	SHOGG ROBINSON	— " —	ASST. MANAGER	— " —	£6,300	£7,500
1987	PRESENT	HEALTH AUTHORITY	DISTRICT LINEN SERVICE	ASST. LINEN SERVICES MANAGER	RUN PRODUCTION IN AN INDUSTRIAL LAUNDRIES	£6,500	£8,500

Other relevant information in support of your application

OVER THE LAST THREE YEARS I HAVE SERVED AS A PRODUCTION MANAGER AND HAVE BEEN PROMOTED THROUGH THE RANK TWICE. I ENJOY THIS TYPE OF WORK AND HAVE VERY GOOD ATTENDANCE AND SICKNESS RECORDS.

VELOP Ltd

Application for employment as **SECTION MANAGER**

Surname	VOROEVERS
Forenames	Deborah
Title	MISS
Address	7 ANSHILL STREET, GOSPORT, HANTS
Telephone no.	G 567347
Date of birth	12/3/164
Country of birth	ENGLAND
Age	26
Sex	F
Postcode	PO12 6B
Nationality	BRITISH
Marital status (delete as necessary)	Married/Single/Divorced/Separated/Widowed
Number of children	NINE
Children's dates of birth	
National Insurance no.	NB 96 234G D
Religious denomination	C.E.
Trade Union Affiliation	EETPU
What are your spare time interests, hobbies etc?	SWIMMING, D.I.Y., AMATEUR DRAMATICS
Current driving licence?	YES
Travelling arrangements if appointed	DRIVE OWN CAR
Notice required by current employer	1 MONTH
Name of last school attended	HENRY CORT COMP
Examinations taken	C.S.E. MATHS, O'LEVEL ENGLISH, " DRAMA, " ART, " TEXTILES, C.S.E. SOCIAL SCIENCE + SCIENCE
Dates From 1975 To 1980	
Results of examinations	PASSES
Name of university, college or other institute	WINCHESTER INST. OF DRAMA
Courses taken	DRAMA
Dates From 1980 To 1982	
Qualifications obtained	R.S.D.A.
Have you or do you suffer from any serious illness, operations or injuries?	Yes/No
If yes, give details	
Are you a disabled person?	Yes/No
If yes, give details	

Previous employment

Dates From	Dates To	Employer's name and address	Employer's business	Job title	Main duties	Salary Starting	Salary Finishing
1982	1983	MORRIS FILTEC INDUSTRIAL SITE	PHOTOGRAPHIC FILTERS	PHOTOGRAPHIC TECHNICIAN AND LAB TECHNICIAN	WORK IN DARK ROOM AND CONVERSE WITH CLIENTS	6.000	9.000
1983		Feiguson Ltd	MAKE TV's + SATALITE	LINE FEED + FLOAT	ORDER materials and look after line running Also stand in for manager when absent	7.000	- 9.500

Other relevant information in support of your application

Have attended a one year NEBSM course at Exbury college.
Also attended night ~~school~~ school on a typing course.

VELOP Ltd

Application for employment as ....

Surname	MILL
Forenames	DAVID GEORGE
Title	MR
Age	48
Sex	MALE
Address	14 NEWTOWN, PORCHESTER, HANTS
Telephone no.	—
Date of birth	05 02 42
Country of birth	ENGLAND
Postcode	PO16 8B
Nationality	BRITISH
Marital status (delete as necessary)	Married/Single/Divorced/Separated/Widowed
Number of children	2
Children's dates of birth	140372 / 231273
National Insurance no.	YD 63 18 24 D
Religious denomination	CHURCH OF ENGLAND
Trade Union Affiliation	—
What are your spare time interests, hobbies etc?	DARTS, COMPUTERS, FOOTBALL,
Current driving licence?	—
Travelling arrangements if appointed	PUBLIC TRANSPORT
Notice required by current employer	1 MONTH
Name of last school attended	ANTHONY GELL COMPREHENSIVE DERBYSHIRE
Examinations taken	CSE's
Results of examinations	METALWORK 2, WOODWORK 3, GEOGRAPHY 2, ART 2, ENGLISH 2, MATHS 2

Dates: From 1964 To 1968

Name of university, college or other institute	NONE
Courses taken	—
Qualifications obtained	—

Dates: From — To —

Have you or do you suffer from any serious illness, operations or injuries? Yes/No	APENDIX REMOVED 1979
Are you a disabled person? Yes/No	

Previous employment

| Dates | | Employer's name and address | Employer's business | Job title | Main duties | Salary | |
From	To					Starting	Finishing
1785	1991	PACK SYSTEMS LTD, HEDGE END	PORTION PACKING	SHIFT SUPERVISOR	SUPERVISING PRODUCTION STAFF	£7,500	£11,520
1960	1985	ROYAL NAVY	—	L.M.E.M. (M)	ENGINEER	£2 per week	£10,000

Other relevant information in support of your application

I HAVE BEEN IN A SUPERVISORY POSITION FOR THE LAST 2½ YEARS IN A PRODUCTION LINE ENVIROMENT, IN CHARGE OF UP TO SIXTY STAFF. IN THIS JOB YOU HAVE TO SET TARGETS AND GET THE STAFF TO REACH THESE TARGETS. YOU HAVE TO BE ABLE TO CONTROL WASTE TO A LOW STANDARD. YOU HAVE TO BE ABLE TO COMMUNICATE WITH OTHER SUPERVISORS HAS WELL HAS QUALITY CONTROL INSPECTORS, ENGINEERS STORES DEPARTMENT AND SENIOR MANAGEMENT. IN THE ABSENCE OF THE PRODUCTION MANAGER DUE TO SICKNESS OR HOLIDAYS I HAVE BEEN HIS STAND IN.

I HAVE ALSO SUCCESSFULLY COMPLETED A N.E.E.B.S. COURSE.

VELOP Ltd

Application for employment as ... EVENING SHIFT SECTION MANAGER

Surname	COLLINS
Forenames	DAVID JAMES
Title	MR
Age	40
Sex	MALE
Address	17, MURRAY AVE., COPNOR, PORTSMOUTH, HANTS.
Postcode	PO2 16XT
Telephone no.	0705 244450
Date of birth	11.5.50
Nationality	BRIT/ENG.
Country of birth	ENGLAND
Marital status (delete as necessary)	Married/Single/Divorced/Separated/Widowed
Number of children	TWO
Children's dates of birth	23 01 73 01 02 76
National Insurance no.	ADL12326
Religious denomination	C of E
Trade Union Affiliation	20
What are your spare time interests, hobbies etc?	SQUASH, STOCK CAR RACING, SEMI-PROFESSIONAL GOLFER.
Current driving licence?	FULL
Travelling arrangements if appointed	CAR
Notice required by current employer	TWO MONTHS

Name of last school attended: RYE SECONDARY MODERN
Dates: From SEPT 1951 To FEB 1966

Examinations taken: C.S.E. MATHS ENGLISH TECH DRAWING WOODWORK

Results of examinations: B. PASS IN 2 ALL BUT WOODWORK A PASS.

Name of university, college or other institute: EXBURY TSCH
Dates: From SEPT 1989 To JUNE 1990

Courses taken: NEBSM SUPERVISORY MANAGEMENT

Qualifications obtained: PASS

Have you or do you suffer from any serious illness, operations or injuries? Yes/No
If yes, give details

Are you a disabled person? Yes/No
If yes, give details

Previous employment

Dates		Employer's name and address	Employer's business	Job title	Main duties	Salary	
From	To					Starting	Finishing
APRIL 1966	MARCH	HM FORCES (ARMY)	DEFENCE	STORES MANAGER	DEMAND, RECEIPT, STOCK CONTROL, ISSUE CONTROL	£10,000	£16,500

Other relevant information in support of your application

Between 1977 and 1988 workshop supervisor of a welding & filter shop manufacturing and repairing bridge sections for mobile bridges used by the forces. Controlling 27 staff and doing time sheets, job allocations, arranging Quality control.

Problem-solving activities

i)   *Draw up a shortlist of four candidates you would wish to interview.*

ii) *Prepare your interview questions.*

iii) *Devise a decision sheet to use in conjunction with your interview questions to help you select the most suitable applicant.*

| HELP ? | See the information bank in *Section 2: Employment legislation*, page 99; *Recruitment, selection and induction*, page 167. |

Scenario: The chosen few

Guson Ltd has two factories: one in Appleton and the other in Lymm. Over the last twelve months demand for the company's products has fallen drastically as a result of the economic recession and management has decided to close the Lymm factory. Some of the redundant employees at Lymm will be offered jobs at the Appleton factory, but only a few vacancies exist. It has been decided that the chosen few will be selected on the basis of last year's job appraisals.

One of the jobs available at Appleton is that of *technician supervisor*. This job has fallen vacant because the previous holder has emigrated to Australia. The personnel department has drawn up a shortlist of four candidates and their appraisal forms are shown below.

EMPLOYEE APPRAISAL FORMS

Employee's name   *Keith Harrington*

Occupation   *Technician*

The following general definitions apply to each factor rated below.

Satisfactory   The employee's performance with respect to a factor meets the full job requirements as the job is defined at the time of rating. A satisfactory rating means good performance. *This is the basic standard for rating any factor below.*

Fair   The employee's performance with respect to a factor is below the requirements for the job and must improve to be satisfactory.

Very good   The employee's performance with respect to a factor is beyond the requirements for satisfactory performance for the job.

Unsatisfactory   The employee's performance with respect to a factor is deficient enough to justify release from present job unless improvement is made.

Exceptional   The employee's performance with respect to a factor is extraordinary, approaching the best possible for the job.

Rate on factors below

Unsatisfactory	*Fair*	*Satisfactory*	*Very good*	*Exceptional*

Effectiveness in dealing with people: extent to which employee cooperates with, and effectively influences those with whom he comes in contact.

Relations too ineffect- ive to retain in job without improvement	Somewhat less effective than required by the job	Maintains effective working relations with others	☒ Ability superior to normal job require- ments	Extraordinary. Beyond that which present job can utilise

Personal efficiency: speed and effectiveness in performing dutires not delegated to subordinates.

Efficiency too poor to retain in job without improvement	Efficiency below job requirements in some respects	Personal efficiency fully satisfies the job requirements	Superior efficiency	☒ Extraordinary degree of personal efficiency

Job knowlege: extent of job information and understanding possessed by employee.

Knowledge inade- quate to retain in job without improvement	Lacks some knowledge required	☒ Knowledge fully satisfies the job requirements	Very well informed on all phases of work	Extraordinary. Beyond scope which present job can fully utilise

Judgement: Extent to which decisions and actions are based on sound reasoning and weighing of outcome.

Extent to which deci- sions and actions are based on sound reasoning and weigh- ing of outcome	Decisions not entire- ly adequate to meet demands of job	☒ Makes good deci- sions in various situa- tions arising in the job	Superior in deter- mining correct decisions and actions	Extraordinary. Beyond that which present job can fully utilise

Initiative: extent to which employee is a 'self-starter' in attaining objectives of job.

Lacks sufficient ini- tiative to retain in job without improvement	Lacks initiative in some respects	☒ Exercises full amount of initiative required by the job	Exercises initiative beyond job requiremens	Extraordinary. Beyond that which present job can fully utilise

Job attitude: amount of interest and enthusiasm shown in work.

Attitude too poor to retain in job without improvement	Attitude needs improvement to be satisfactory	Favourable attitude	☒ High degree of enthusiasm and interest	Extraordinary degree of enthusiasm and interest

Dependability: extent to which employee can be counted on to carry out instructions, be on the job, and fulfil responsibilities.

Too unreliable to retain in job without improvement	Dependability not fully satisfactory	Fully satisfies dependability demands of job	☒ Superior to normal demands	Extraordinary dependability in all respects

Overall evaluation of employee performance:

Performance inadequate to retain present job	Does not fully meet requirements of the job	☒ Good performance. Fully competent	Superior. Beyond sat- isfactory fulfilments of job requirements	Extraordinary. Perfor- mance approaching the best possible for the job

Use this item only if the employee is still in the learning stage of the job.

Unsatisfactory	Fair	Satisfactory	Very good	Exceptional
☐ Progress too slow to retain job	☐ Progressing but not as rapidly as required	☐ Making good progress	☐ Progressing very rapidly	☐ Doing exceptionally well. Outstanding rate of development

1. Outstanding abilities and accomplishments.

Reliability, once set a job he always sees it through usually without supervision

2. Weaknesses.

Sometimes he tries to get the job done at any cost

Recommendations for improvement.

Try to consider the "bigger" picture

3. General remarks concerning employee's performance.

Valued employee who does a very good job

4. Specific suggestions for further development.

Some training on new equipment would be of value

Rated by: *P Kay*	Date *29/1/92*	Reviewed by: *M Cooke*	Date *29/1/92*

To rater: Initial and date this space when you have discussed this rating with the employee.

BL

Supervisor

Signature of employee* *K Harrington* ---

* This signature merely verifies that this evaluation has been discussed with the employee, and it does not express approval or disapproval of the above.

EMPLOYEE APPRAISAL FORMS

Employee's name *Dennis Fowler*

Occupation *Technician*

The following general definitions apply to each factor rated below.

Satisfactory The employee's performance with respect to a factor meets the full job requirements as the job is defined at the time of rating. A satisfactory rating means good performance. *This is the basic standard for rating any factor below.*

Fair The employee's performance with respect to a factor is below the requirements for the job and must improve to be satisfactory.

Very good The employee's performance with respect to a factor is beyond the requirements for satisfactory performance for the job.

Unsatisfactory The employee's performance with respect to a factor is deficient enough to justify release from present job unless improvement is made.

Exceptional The employee's performance with respect to a factor is extraordinary, approaching the best possible for the job.

Rate on factors below

Unsatisfactory	Fair	Satisfactory	Very good	Exceptional

Effectiveness in dealing with people: extent to which employee cooperates with, and effectively influences those with whom he comes in contact.

Unsatisfactory	Fair	Satisfactory	Very good	Exceptional
☐ Relations too ineffect-ive to retain in job without improvement	☐ Somewhat less effective than required by the job	☒ Maintains effective working relations with others	☐ Ability superior to normal job require-ments	☐ Extraordinary. Beyond that which present job can utilise

Personal efficiency: speed and effectiveness in performing dutires not delegated to subordinates.

Unsatisfactory	Fair	Satisfactory	Very good	Exceptional
☐ Efficiency too poor to retain in job without improvement	☐ Efficiency below job requirements in some respects	☐ Personal efficiency fully satisfies the job requirements	☒ Superior efficiency	☐ Extraordinary degree of personal efficiency

Job knowlege: extent of job information and understanding possessed by employee.

Unsatisfactory	Fair	Satisfactory	Very good	Exceptional
☐ Knowledge inade-quate to retain in job without improvement	☐ Lacks some knowledge required	☐ Knowledge fully satisfies the job requirements	☒ Very well informed on all phases of work	☐ Extraordinary. Beyond scope which present job can fully utilise

Judgement: Extent to which decisions and actions are based on sound reasoning and weighing of outcome.

Unsatisfactory	Fair	Satisfactory	Very good	Exceptional
☐ Extent to which deci-sions and actions are based on sound reasoning and weigh-ing of outcome	☐ Decisions not entire-ly adequate to meet demands of job	☐ Makes good deci-sions in various situa-tions arising in the job	☒ Superior in deter-mining correct decisions and actions	☐ Extraordinary. Beyond that which present job can fully utilise

Initiative: extent to which employee is a 'self-starter' in attaining objectives of job.

Unsatisfactory	Fair	Satisfactory	Very good	Exceptional
☐ Lacks sufficient ini-tiative to retain in job without improvement	☐ Lacks initiative in some respects	☐ Exercises full amount of initiative required by the job	☒ Exercises initiative beyond job requiremens	☐ Extraordinary. Beyond that which present job can fully utilise

Job attitude: amount of interest and enthusiasm shown in work.

Unsatisfactory	Fair	Satisfactory	Very good	Exceptional
☐ Attitude too poor to retain in job without improvement	☐ Attitude needs improvement to be satisfactory	☒ Favourable attitude	☐ High degree of enthusiasm and interest	☐ Extraordinary degree of enthusiasm and interest

Dependability: extent to which employee can be counted on to carry out instructions, be on the job, and fulfil responsibilities.

Unsatisfactory	Fair	Satisfactory	Very good	Exceptional
☐ Too unreliable to retain in job without improvement	☒ Dependability not fully satisfactory	☐ Fully satisfies dependability demands of job	☐ Superior to normal demands	☐ Extraordinary dependability in all respects

Overall evaluation of employee performance:

Unsatisfactory	Fair	Satisfactory	Very good	Exceptional
☐ Performance inadequate to retain present job	☐ Does not fully meet requirements of the job	☒ Good performance. Fully competent	☐ Superior. Beyond sat-isfactory fulfilments of job requirements	☐ Extraordinary. Perfor-mance approaching the best possible for the job

Use this item only if the employee is still in the learning stage of the job.				
Unsatisfactory	*Fair*	*Satisfactory*	*Very good*	*Exceptional*
☐ Progress too slow to retain job	☐ Progressing but not as rapidly as required	☐ Making good progress	☐ Progressing very rapidly	☐ Doing exceptionally well. Outstanding rate of development

1. Outstanding abilities and accomplishments.

Technically very sound, though seems a little less able on some of the very latest equipment

2. Weaknesses.

Has some well intentioned but irritating ways of dealing with other staff, especially female staff

Recommendations for improvement.

3. General remarks concerning employee's performance.

Able and valued employee but he has a tendancy to assume authority greater than that given

4. Specific suggestions for further development.

Training on technical and interpersonal skills would be of value

Rated by: *PKay*	Date *29/1/92*	Reviewed by: *M Cooke*	Date *29/1/92*

To rater: Initial and date this space when you have discussed this rating with the employee.

BL

Supervisor

Signature of employee* *D Fowler*
----

* This signature merely verifies that this evaluation has been discussed with the employee, and it does not express approval or disapproval of the above.

EMPLOYEE APPRAISAL FORMS

Employee's name *Mark Harris*

Occupation *Technician*

The following general definitions apply to each factor rated below.

Satisfactory The employee's performance with respect to a factor meets the full job requirements as the job is defined at the time of rating. A satisfactory rating means good performance. *This is the basic standard for rating any factor below.*

Fair The employee's performance with respect to a factor is below the requirements for the job and must improve to be satisfactory.

Very good The employee's performance with respect to a factor is beyond the requirements for satisfactory performance for the job.

Unsatisfactory The employee's performance with respect to a factor is deficient enough to justify release from present job unless improvement is made.

Exceptional The employee's performance with respect to a factor is extraordinary, approaching the best possible for the job.

Rate on factors below

Unsatisfactory	Fair	Satisfactory	Very good	Exceptional

Effectiveness in dealing with people: extent to which employee cooperates with, and effectively influences those with whom he comes in contact.

Unsatisfactory	Fair	Satisfactory	Very good	Exceptional
Relations too ineffective to retain in job without improvement	Somewhat less effective than required by the job	Maintains effective working relations with others	Ability superior to normal job requirements	☒ Extraordinary. Beyond that which present job can utilise

Personal efficiency: speed and effectiveness in performing duties not delegated to subordinates.

Unsatisfactory	Fair	Satisfactory	Very good	Exceptional
Efficiency too poor to retain in job without improvement	☒ Efficiency below job requirements in some respects	Personal efficiency fully satisfies the job requirements	Superior efficiency	Extraordinary degree of personal efficiency

Job knowlege: extent of job information and understanding possessed by employee.

Unsatisfactory	Fair	Satisfactory	Very good	Exceptional
Knowledge inadequate to retain in job without improvement	Lacks some knowledge required	☒ Knowledge fully satisfies the job requirements	Very well informed on all phases of work	Extraordinary. Beyond scope which present job can fully utilise

Judgement: Extent to which decisions and actions are based on sound reasoning and weighing of outcome.

Unsatisfactory	Fair	Satisfactory	Very good	Exceptional
Extent to which decisions and actions are based on sound reasoning and weighing of outcome	Decisions not entirely adequate to meet demands of job	☒ Makes good decisions in various situations arising in the job	Superior in determining correct decisions and actions	Extraordinary. Beyond that which present job can fully utilise

Initiative: extent to which employee is a 'self-starter' in attaining objectives of job.

Unsatisfactory	Fair	Satisfactory	Very good	Exceptional
Lacks sufficient initiative to retain in job without improvement	Lacks initiative in some respects	☒ Exercises full amount of initiative required by the job	Exercises initiative beyond job requiremens	Extraordinary. Beyond that which present job can fully utilise

Job attitude: amount of interest and enthusiasm shown in work.

Unsatisfactory	Fair	Satisfactory	Very good	Exceptional
Attitude too poor to retain in job without improvement	Attitude needs improvement to be satisfactory	☒ Favourable attitude	High degree of enthusiasm and interest	Extraordinary degree of enthusiasm and interest

Dependability: extent to which employee can be counted on to carry out instructions, be on the job, and fulfil responsibilities.

Unsatisfactory	Fair	Satisfactory	Very good	Exceptional
Too unreliable to retain in job without improvement	☒ Dependability not fully satisfactory	Fully satisfies dependability demands of job	Superior to normal demands	Extraordinary dependability in all respects

Overall evaluation of employee performance:

Unsatisfactory	Fair	Satisfactory	Very good	Exceptional
Performance inadequate to retain present job	Does not fully meet requirements of the job	☒ Good performance. Fully competent	Superior. Beyond satisfactory fulfilments of job requirements	Extraordinary. Performance approaching the best possible for the job

Use this item only if the employee is still in the learning stage of the job.

Unsatisfactory	Fair	Satisfactory	Very good	Exceptional
☐ Progress too slow to retain job	☐ Progressing but not as rapidly as required	☐ Making good progress	☐ Progressing very rapidly	☐ Doing exceptionally well. Outstanding rate of development

1. Outstanding abilities and accomplishments.

Easy going and cheerful manner
Technically sound.
Well liked by the other staff

2. Weaknesses.

Over reliance on interpersonal skills to "sell" his ideas.

Recommendations for improvement.

Concentrate more on technical aspects especially new developments

3. General remarks concerning employee's performance.

Good performance in general, he is a particular asset where careful handling of people is needed

4. Specific suggestions for further development.

Needs to further develop in technical abilities

Rated by: *P Kay*	Date 29/1/92	Reviewed by: *M Cooke*	Date 29/1/92

To rater: Initial and date this space when you have discussed this rating with the employee.

BL

Supervisor

Signature of employee* *M Harris* ---

* This signature merely verifies that this evaluation has been discussed with the employee, and it does not express approval or disapproval of the above.

EMPLOYEE APPRAISAL FORMS

Employee's name ___*David Knight*___

Occupation ___*Technician*___

The following general definitions apply to each factor rated below.

Satisfactory The employee's performance with respect to a factor meets the full job requirements as the job is defined at the time of rating. A satisfactory rating means good performance. *This is the basic standard for rating any factor below.*

Fair The employee's performance with respect to a factor is below the requirements for the job and must improve to be satisfactory.

Very good The employee's performance with respect to a factor is beyond the requirements for satisfactory performance for the job.

Unsatisfactory The employee's performance with respect to a factor is deficient enough to justify release from present job unless improvement is made.

Exceptional The employee's performance with respect to a factor is extraordinary, approaching the best possible for the job.

Rate on factors below

Unsatisfactory	Fair	Satisfactory	Very good	Exceptional

Effectiveness in dealing with people: extent to which employee cooperates with, and effectively influences those with whom he comes in contact.

Relations too ineffective to retain in job without improvement	☒ Somewhat less effective than required by the job	Maintains effective working relations with others	Ability superior to normal job requirements	Extraordinary. Beyond that which present job can utilise

Personal efficiency: speed and effectiveness in performing dutires not delegated to subordinates.

Efficiency too poor to retain in job without improvement	☒ Efficiency below job requirements in some respects	Personal efficiency fully satisfies the job requirements	Superior efficiency	Extraordinary degree of personal efficiency

Job knowlege: extent of job information and understanding possessed by employee.

Knowledge inadequate to retain in job without improvement	Lacks some knowledge required	Knowledge fully satisfies the job requirements	Very well informed on all phases of work	☒ Extraordinary. Beyond scope which present job can fully utilise

Judgement: Extent to which decisions and actions are based on sound reasoning and weighing of outcome.

Extent to which decisions and actions are based on sound reasoning and weighing of outcome	☒ Decisions not entirely adequate to meet demands of job	Makes good decisions in various situations arising in the job	Superior in determining correct decisions and actions	Extraordinary. Beyond that which present job can fully utilise

Initiative: extent to which employee is a 'self-starter' in attaining objectives of job.

Lacks sufficient initiative to retain in job without improvement	Lacks initiative in some respects	Exercises full amount of initiative required by the job	Exercises initiative beyond job requiremens	☒ Extraordinary. Beyond that which present job can fully utilise

Job attitude: amount of interest and enthusiasm shown in work.

Attitude too poor to retain in job without improvement	Attitude needs improvement to be satisfactory	Favourable attitude	☒ High degree of enthusiasm and interest	Extraordinary degree of enthusiasm and interest

Dependability: extent to which employee can be counted on to carry out instructions, be on the job, and fulfil responsibilities.

Too unreliable to retain in job without improvement	Dependability not fully satisfactory	Fully satisfies dependability demands of job	☒ Superior to normal demands	Extraordinary dependability in all respects

Overall evaluation of employee performance:

Performance inadequate to retain present job	Does not fully meet requirements of the job	☒ Good performance. Fully competent	Superior. Beyond satisfactory fulfilments of job requirements	Extraordinary. Performance approaching the best possible for the job

Use this item only if the employee is still in the learning stage of the job.

Unsatisfactory	Fair	Satisfactory	Very good	Exceptional
☐ Progress too slow to retain job	☐ Progressing but not as rapidly as required	☐ Making good progress	☐ Progressing very rapidly	☐ Doing exceptionally well. Outstanding rate of development

1. Outstanding abilities and accomplishments.

Technically brilliant and highly motivated to solve the problem presented. Often puts in hours outside the job requirements

2. Weaknesses.

Interpersonal relations

Recommendations for improvement.

3. General remarks concerning employee's performance.

He is effective on the technical side, but forgets the human aspects when making decisions

4. Specific suggestions for further development.

Interpersonal skills/communication training

Rated by: *PKay*	Date *29/1/92*	Reviewed by: *M Cooke*	Date *29/1/92*

To rater: Initial and date this space when you have discussed this rating with the employee.

BL

Supervisor

Signature of employee* ___*DKnight*_____

* This signature merely verifies that this evaluation has been discussed with the employee, and it does not express approval or disapproval of the above.

Problem-solving activity

i) *Select the most appropriate candidate and give your reasons.*

ii) *What other information should have been available?*

iii) *Is it reasonable to promote employees on the basis of appraisal forms alone?*

iv) *How should the unsuccessful employees be told?*

HELP ?	See the information bank in **Section 2: Counselling and listening**, page 88; **Performance appraisal**, page 145; **Recruitment, selection and induction**, page 167.

Induction procedures

State whether in your opinion the following statements are true or false. If possible relate your opinions to your own place of work.

	True	False
1. Induction programmes are crucial to the retention and motivation of staff.	☐	☐
2. Induction programmes should be carried out at intervals over an employees' first six months.	☐	☐
3. Induction can be carried out by means of booklets.	☐	☐

Now list ten items you would put on a list of matters to be included in an induction programme and rank them in order of importance.

 | **HELP** | **?** | See the information bank in *Section 2: Recruitment, selection and induction*, page 167.

 Personnel policies

Identify five major employers in your locality, if possible one from each of the following sectors:

retailing   industrial   banking   insurance   chemical

Required

Answer the following questions by carrying out a survey of job advertisements in the local and/or national press and write a brief statement about the personnel policy of each organisation.

1. *Do they pay well?*
2. *Do they provide training?*
3. *Do they put a high value on training?*
4. *Are they a prestigious employers?*
5. *What do their job advertisements stress?*
6. *What fringe benefits are offered?*
7. *Is there a particular type of person they wish to recruit?*
8. *Is there any evidence of trade union presence?*

 | **HELP** | **?** | See the information bank in *Section 2: Organisational objectives, policies and strategies*, page 142; *Personnel management*, page 154.

Unit 7: Development and retention

Scenario: Restructuring at Hardings

Harding Ltd is a specialist chemical engineering company. The business has grown steadily over the last 25 years and by the start of last year employed nearly 300 specialist engineers. Staff promotion at Hardings was based largely on technical expertise, consequently all the department managers had good technical skills but no other training.

A fall in demand persuaded Hardings that they needed to restructure in order to save money and although they hoped to do this through early retirement and voluntary redundancy, compulsory redundancy was not ruled out. An announcement to this effect was made last August by the managing director, Walter Derbyshire.

Several new organisational structures were published and then withdrawn (without explanation) but in December the final version was announced. This final structure was a result of 'trading' between the eight department heads. In addition, it was stated that job descriptions would be available soon, and that a policy of 'slotting in' would take place, that is people would be ear-marked for jobs in the new structure and put into them. There would be an appeals procedure, but it was clear that those who didn't like the new structure had a choice: to stay or to leave. At no time were any but the top eight people in the organisation consulted on the changes and the implementations.

When the job descriptions were finally published just as the company closed for Christmas, many fairly senior employees as well as the most junior, were at first confused and then outraged at the new situation. The redistribution of duties combined with the early retirement for older staff effectively stopped any prospects of promotion for the foreseeable future. In addition, staff who already considered themselves hard pressed found their job descriptions increased and anomalies in the system meant supervisors were paid less than the people they managed.

In July, Walter Derbyshire left to take up a job with another company and his replacement, Ian Cooke, reviewed the situation.

Demand in the industry has now picked up again, but labour turnover, which had always been low, was now increasing and giving cause for concern. An attitude survey revealed low morale and commitment, and many staff refused to consider tasks not specifically within their job descriptions.

Problem-solving activities

i) What went wrong at Hardings and why did it happen?

ii) Ian Cooke has called a meeting of all the management. If you were attending that meeting, what suggestions would you put forward as solutions to the problem?

See the information bank in **Section 2: Change management**, page 79; **Job evaluation**, page 117; **Motivation**, page 135, **Training**, page 199.

Scenario: Computers and appraisals

Mosham City Council installed a computer network over five years ago, but as far as most people were concerned the impact was quite small. Peter Robinson, the union representative, has assumed, just like everyone else, that it was being used for word processing and electronic mail and a few technical matters.

The last pay award made to the members of Robinson's union, contained a clause stating that 'a system of appraisal will be implemented for all clerical staff within 12 months'.

The management style of the senior staff in the council is very autocratic and one senior manager has been quoted as saying, 'There's nothing to this appraisal business; you just tell them what you think of them. There's no point in pussy-footing around'. He's also quoted as saying, "We'll put all the appraisals on the computer system so that the right people can have access to them".

Peter Robinson is going to a meeting to discuss implementing the appraisal system in a week's time. At a recent union meeting, several of the union members had expressed concern about the method of appraisals to be used and the use of the computer to store the information.

Problem-solving activities

i)   *Can the Council keep employees' records on the computer and do the employees have any rights concerning the computer records?*

ii) *Formulate a policy for the union concerning the appraisals for use at the forthcoming meeting.*

> See the information bank in *Section 2: Data protection legislation*, page 89; *Performance appraisal*, page 145.

A   The learning style inventory

This inventory is designed to assess your method of learning. As you take the inventory, give a high rank to those words which best characterise the way you learn and a low rank to the words which are least characteristic of your learning style.

You may find it hard to choose the words that best describe your learning style because there are no right or wrong answers. Different characteristics described in the inventory are equally good. The aim of the inventory is to describe how you learn, not to evaluate your learning ability.

Required:

There are nine sets of four words listed below. Rank order each set of four words assigning a 4 to the word which best characterises your learning style, and 3 to the word which next best characterises your learning style, a 2 to the next most characteristic word, and a 1 to the word which is least characteristic of you as a learner.

Be sure to assign a different rank number to each of the four words in each set. Do not make ties.

	A	**B**	**C**	**D**
1.	discriminating	tentative	involved	practical
2.	receptive	relevant	analytical	impartial
3	feeling	watching	thinking	doing
4.	accepting	risk-taker	evaluative	aware
5.	intuitive	productive	logical	questioning
6.	abstract	observing	concrete	active
7.	present-oriented	reflecting	future-oriented	pragmatic
8.	experience	observation	conceptualisation	experimentation
9.	intense	reserved	rational	responsible

Scoring:

A [   ]   B [   ]   C [   ]   D [   ]
(234578)   (136789)   (234589)   (136789)

Add the columns using only the scores for the row numbers shown in brackets then plot the scores for A B C & D on the learning style axis.

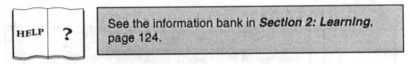

HELP ? See the information bank in **Section 2: Learning**, page 124.

A Discovering your own learning style

Think of a skill you have taught yourself to do recently. Perhaps it was how to operate a video recorder, mend a window, drive a car, use a computer, learn a language, patch your jeans, play a musical instrument or fill in a tax return! Now consider how you set about learning the skill. What method did you use? Make a few notes on this or draw a diagram.

You may find it helpful to compare notes with others in your group about the learning methods you used for different skills.

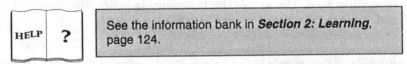

HELP ? See the information bank in **Section 2: Learning**, page 124.

Index

Page numbers in bold indicate the main reference

ACAS (Advisory, Conciliation
  and Arbitration Service)   193
acceptance theory
Adair, Professor John   120
appraisal interviews
  see performance appraisal
attitude   **73**
  survey   73
audio-visual aids   82
authority   **75**
  acceptance theory   75
  institutional theory   75
  McGregor, Douglas   75
  Theory X and Theory Y   75

batch production *see* production systems
behaviour   105
  ,classifying leadership   123
  group norms   106
  Hawthorne experiments   105
Blake, Robert   122
body language   137
bonus schemes   181
brainstorming   90
British Standard 5750   160
budgetary control   **77**

cascade networks   81
cause and effect analysis   90
change   79
  ,barriers to   80
  management   **79**
closed shop   193
codes of practice   193
communication   **81**
  ,guidelines for improving   83
  information points   82
  in-house journals/newsletters   82
  listening   88
  non-verbal communications   **137**
  ,poor   81
  ,written   82
conferences   82
contingency theories
  see leadership theories
control   **86**
COSHH (Care of Substances
  Hazardous to Health)   111
counselling   **88**

Data Protection   **89**
  Act 1984   89, 99
  Register   89
decision making   **90**
delegation   **93**
  checklist for effective   93
Disabled Persons (Employment) Acts   99
discipline   **94**
  checklist for handling
    disciplinary situations   94

disciplinary interview   95
discrimination   **98**
dismissal, unfair   193

employee
  benefits   183
  ,duties of   100
  handbooks   82
  reports   82
  rights to time off work   103
employer, duties of   99
employment legislation   **99**
Employment Act
  1980   192
  1982   194
Employment Protection
  (Consolidation) Act 1978   99
equal opportunities   98
  Equal Pay Act 1970   100
  equality of opportunity in selection   177
exit interview   88

Fayol, Henri *see* management theories

Gantt chart   157
groups and teams   **104**
  ,developing   106
  ,differences between   105
  ,informal   106

Handy, Charles *see* management theories
Health and Safety at Work Act 1974   101
Health and Safety Executive   112
health and safety legislation   **109**
Herzberg, Frederick *see* motivation
hygiene factors *see* motivation

institutional theory *see* authority
interviews   169
  assessment form   170
  guide   174
  ,performance appraisal   147
job
  analysis   **113**
  design   **115**
  enlargement   **115**
  pressures   186
  specification   167
job production *see* production systems

leadership behaviours
  ,classifying   123
leadership   **119**
  contingency theories   120
  management grid   121
  Michigan studies   121
  theories   119
learning   **124**
  styles   125
listening   88

management by objectives **128**
management grid *see* leadership theories
management theories **132**
   Drucker, Peter 132
   Fayol, Henri 132
   Handy, Charles 132
managerial responsibilities 179
manpower
   analysis and planning **133**
   utilisation 134
Maslow, Abraham *see* motivation
maternity leave 193
Mayo, Elton 104
McGregor, Douglas *see* authority
measured day work *see* pay structures
meetings 81
Michigan studies *see* leadership theories
Mouton, Jane 122
motivation **135**
   Herzberg, Frederick 136
   hygiene factors 136
   Maslow, Abraham 135
   Vroom, VH 136

NIIP Seven-point plan 170
network analysis 158
   PERT 158
non-verbal communications **137**
'norms' *see* behaviour

organisational objectives **142**
organisational structures **144**

pay structures
   bonus schemes 181
   group incentive schemes 181
   ,main types 180
   measured day work 181
   profit sharing 181
   salary levels 182
performance appraisal **145**
   interviews 146
performance, measuring 86
personnel management **154**
   policy 158
PERT (programme evaluation and review
   technique) *see* network analysis
picketing 194
positive reinforcement 130
presentations 85
problem solving **90**
profit sharing *see* pay structures
production control **156**
production systems
   ,batch 156
   ,job 156
   ,mass 156
promotion 146
   policy 146

quality
   assurance **159**
   BS 5750 160
   circles 159
   control 159
   standards 159
questionnaires **166**

racial discrimination 98
Racial Equality, Commission for 98
recruitment, selection and induction **167**
   school and college leavers 175
   tests 175
redundancy action checklist **178**
report writing 84
responsibility **179**
RIDDO (Reporting of Injuries,
   Diseases and Dangerous Occurrences)
   Regulations 1985 110

salary levels *see* pay structures
secret ballots 192
selection *see* recruitment
seminars 82
sex discrimination 98
   Sex Discrimination Act 1975 102
standards *see* quality
stock control 161
stress
   ,causes of 184
   management **190**
   ,types of 187
structure tree 91
style theories of leadership *see* leadership
   theories
supervisory responsibilities 179

targets 142
teams and groups
   ,developing 106
   ,differences between 105
   , effective and ineffective work 107
   teamwork 108
tests *see* recruitment, selection and
   induction
Theory X or Theory Y *see* Authority
time management **190**
trade unions
   and the law **192**
   recognition 193
   unfair dismissal 193
training **199**
   'off the job' 124
   'on the job' 124

Vroom, V H *see* motivation

wages *see* pay structures
work study **202**

Finance for Non-financial Managers

An Active-Learning Approach

AH Millichamp

ISBN: **1 873981 06 6** • Date: **June 1992** • Edition: **1st**
Extent: **400 pp (approx)** • Size: **275 x 215 mm**
Lecturers' Supplement ISBN: **1 873981 77 5**

Courses on which this book is expected to be used
BTEC Higher National, professional courses (eg ACCA Certified Diploma in Accounting and Finance), and all courses (eg engineering, personnel, sales, purchasing, catering, tourism, etc) on which students need an understanding of accountancy in order to communicate with accountants and implement necessary financial controls and plans as part of their management role.

This book provides a complete course of study in the areas of accounting and finance that students on many professional, vocational and degree courses are required to cover. It is structured in such a way that the student is led through the various finance-related problems of the non-financial manager via a single, realistic scenario of a non-accountant setting up a small business, which rapidly expands (Section 1). The problems and situations that the scenario introduces enable the student to gain a practical knowledge of accounting in an integrated way. To solve particular problems students may need to apply techniques from the areas of financial accounting, management accounting and financial management (Section 2).

This approach ensures that the student sees the practical applications of the techniques that he/she has to acquire. Case exercises (with and without answers) develop knowledge and skills (Section 3).

Contents:

Section 1 – Scenarios and Related Tasks

Section 2 – Student Information Bank
Financial Accounting: The Profit and Loss Account • The Balance Sheet • Depreciation • Stocks • Manufacturing Accounts • Company Accounts • Accounting Conventions • Ratio Analysis • Cash Flow Statements • Current Topics (Accounting Regulation • Accounting for Changing Price Levels)
Management Accounting: Total Absorption Costing • Cost Behaviour and Marginal Costing • Uses of Marginal Costing • Budgeting • Standard Costing
Finance: Cash Flow Forecasting • Investment Appraisal • Sources of Finance • Working Capital • The Stock Exchange.

Section 3 – Developing Knowledge and Skills

Free
Lecturers' Supplement

A First Course in
Cost and Management Accounting
T Lucey

ISBN: **1 870941 54 3** · Date: **1990** · Edition: **1st**
Extent: **272 pp** · Size: **245 x 190 mm**
Lecturers' Supplement ISBN: **1 873981 51 1**

Courses on which this book is known to be used
BTEC National Business and Finance; DMS; RSA; LCCI; AAT; Management and Supervisory
Studies; Business Studies and Marketing courses; Access courses; Purchasing and Supply and
other courses requiring a broad, non-specialist treatment of cost and management accounting.

This book provides a broad introduction to cost and management accounting for those who have not
studied the subject before. It is written in a clear, straightforward fashion without technical jargon or
unnecessary detail. The text includes many practical examples, diagrams, exercises and examination
questions. Features include several objective tests for self-assessment and assignments for activity-
based learning.

Contents:
Cost Analysis and Cost Ascertainment • What is Product Costing and Cost Accounting? • Elements of
Cost • Labour, Materials and Overheads • Calculating Product Costs • Job, Batch and Contract
Costing • Service, Process and Joint Product Costing • Information for Planning and Control • What is
Planning and Control? • Cost Behaviour • Budgetary Planning • Budgetary Control • Cash Budgeting •
Standard Costing • Variance Analysis • Information for Decision Making and Performance Appraisal •
What is Decision Making? • Marginal Costing • Break-even Analysis • Pricing Decisions • Investment
Appraisal • Performance Appraisal of Departments and Divisions.

Management Theory and Practice

GA Cole

ISBN: **1 870941 60 8** • Date: **1990** • Edition: **3rd**
Extent: **608 pp** • Size: **215 x 135 mm**
Lecturers' Supplement ISBN: **1 873981 60 0**

Courses on which this book is known to be used
CIMA; ACCA; AAT; IComA; BTEC HNC/D; IIM; BA Business Studies; BA Accounting; MSc
Information Technology; BSc Software Engineering; Hotel and Catering Management courses;
CIB; CIM; IAM; DMS; CIPFA; IPS; CBA; ICM; DMS; CBSI; ABE; IOM; NEBSM; DBA; MIOM; Dip.
HSM; BTEC ND; Dip. in Administrative Management; BSc (Hons) Software Engineering; MSc
Computing; HND IT.

**On reading lists of CIMA , ACCA, ACCA Cert Dip, LCCI, IComA, ABE, AAT, IAM, ICSA and
ICM**

This book aims to provide, in one concise volume, the principal ideas and developments in the theory
and practice of management as required by business and accountancy students. This edition was
revised and updated in such areas as employment law and employee relations and has a number of
new chapters, including *Japanese Approaches to Management*.

Contents:

Glossary of Management Terms • Introduction to Management Theory • Classical Theories • Human
Relations Theories • Systems Approaches to Management Theory • Management in Practice •
Planning • Organising – Leadership and Groups • Control in Management • Marketing Management •
Production Management • Personnel Management • Appendices: Guide to Further Reading –
Examination Technique – Outline Answers to Examination Questions at Section Ends – Further
Examination Questions.

Review Comments:

*'I have used this text for the past four to five years. Content, price, conciseness, style will take a lot of
beating [ACIS,CIMA,CIOB].' 'Excellent textbook for any management student.' 'One of the clearest
presentations available.' 'Very clear – excellent chapter design.' 'The right mix of diagrams, charts
and reading text ...' 'Our students find your approach to topics and logical progression beneficial and
easy to understand.' – Lecturers*

'This book provides a thorough introduction for students of management'

"Journal of Managerial Psychology"

Personnel Management

GA Cole

ISBN: **1 870941 16 0** • Date: **1988** • Edition: **2nd**
Extent: **512 pp** • Size: **215 x 135 mm**
Lecturers' Supplement ISBN: **1 873981 63 5**

Promoting Active Learning

Courses on which this book is known to be used
IPM; ICSA; Association of Business Executives; HNC/D Business and Finance; CNAA Diploma in Personnel Management; CNAA Degrees in Business Studies (Personnel Management Options); CIB; Institute of Training and Development; A Level Business Studies; CPP; HNC/D Human Resource Management; DMS; MIOM; IMS; BA Business Studies; IOH.

On reading list of ICSA

This book is intended to meet the need of students and lecturers for an introductory textbook that can offer a variety of learning opportunities in the form of discussion questions, case studies, examination questions and suggested answers.

Contents:

The Scope of Personnel Management • The Personnel Function in Organisations • Personnel Policies and Strategies • **The Organisational Context** • Organisations – Key Issues • Organisation Structures • Leadership • Groups at Work • Motivation Theory • **Planning the Organisation's Manpower** • Manpower Planning • Job Analysis • Job Evaluation • Recruitment • Selection • Job Design • Organisation Development • Retirements, Redundancies and Redeployments • Personnel Records and Administration • **Conditions of Employment** • The Employment Contract • Hours of Work • Payments Systems – Key Issues • Wage Payments Systems • Salary Systems and Employee Benefits • Health, Safety and Welfare • **Employee Development** • Performance Appraisal • Key Theories of Learning • Systematic Training • Training Needs and Training Plans • Designing Training Programmes • Evaluation of Training • Management Development • **Employee Relations** • Introduction to Employee Relations • Formal Communication in Organisations • Collective Bargaining • Disputes and Strikes • Grievances, Discipline and Employee Participation • Employment Law and Personnel Management.

Review Comments:

'Best value for students taking Personnel Management or Employment Relations options [BTEC Higher].' 'Excellent for this course [IPM Cert. in Personnel Practice].' 'Good case studies.' 'Short, sharp, punchy, easy to follow, good layout.' 'Quality product at an affordable price.' 'Clear, comprehensive and helpful.' 'Syllabus well covered, set out clearly, competitive price.' 'Covers all elements of course [HND], competitively priced.' – **Lecturers**

Free Lecturers' Supplement

Management Information Systems

T Lucey

ISBN: **1 870941 80 2** • Date: **1991** • Edition: **6th**
Extent: **336 pp** • Size: **215 x 135 mm**
Lecturers' Supplement ISBN: **1 873981 59 7**

Courses on which this book is known to be used
ACCA; HND Yr 1; HNC BIS; Info. Systems Fundamentals; DAS; MSD; DBA; HNC Industrial
Studies; NEBSM; CMS; IPM (PMFP); Dip. in Int. Audit; Nat. Cert. in Computer Studies; CIPFA;
AAT; HND BIT; HND Computing; BSc Computing; IAM; BSc (Bus. Studies); DMS; BEd Bus.
Studies; CIMA; CIML Software Eng. Man.; MSc Computing; ICSA; MBA; IMS.

On reading lists of ACCA, AAT, IComA, ABE, ICM, IAM and BCS

The book deals with the design and application of management information systems in private and
public sector organisations.

For the new edition the text has been substantially updated and revised including assignments, case
studies and more detail on information technology.

Contents:

Management Information Systems – An Overview • Information, Data and Communications •
Systems Concepts – Structure and Elements • Systems concepts – Objectives and Types •
Organisations – Principles and Structure • Organisations – Adaptability and Behaviour •
Organisations – Configuration, Culture and Information Management Levels and Functions •
Motivation and Leadership • Organising and Co–ordinating • Planning • Decision Making • Control –
Concepts, Loops and Information • Control in Organisations • Information Technology and MIS •
Influences on MIS Design • Answers to End of Chapter Questions.

Review Comments:

*'...an excellent work on general management with the emphasis on MIS. I have chosen it in
preference to the many management books I have recently reviewed.' 'Good coverage at an excellent
price.' 'Still the best book for an introductory organisation and information systems course.' 'Easy to
read and understand.' 'Excellent value as a first text on MIS.' 'Much improved edition [6th[for this
syllabus [ICSA].' 'I like it for its broad management approach.' – Lecturers*

*'The book is highly recommended to students, to accountants and to business managers who want a
simple guide to modern systems theory.'*

"Management Accounting"

Small Business Management
An Active-Learning Approach

D Stokes

ISBN: **1 873981 12 0** • Date: **June 1992** • Edition: **1st**
Extent: **300 pp (approx)** • Size: **275 x 215 mm**
Lecturers' Supplement ISBN: **1 873981 88 0**

Courses on which this book is expected to be used
Any course with a Small Business Management or New Venture Management option. All courses where students are required to present a **business plan** or **feasibility study** as part of a business management module, eg BTEC Higher National, DMS, CIM and the many part-time courses in small business management.

This book provides all the teaching material for a course on Small Business Management. The two-section structure of the text ensures that students first identify problems in a realistic context (Section 1) and are then directed to the appropriate information on principles and practice (Section 2) to solve them. Section 1 has scenarios, covering all the main business situations a small business manager is likely to encounter, together with related issues and problems as tasks. An ongoing assignment centres around a business idea chosen by the student.

Section 2 is an information bank covering the theory and practice of small business management. It provides an invaluable summary, bridging the gap between more theoretical research papers which describe aspects of the small business environment, and practical guides which prescribe methods of small business management.

Contents:
Section 1 – Scenarios and Related Tasks (including ongoing assignment).

Section 2 – The Information Bank Small Businesses and the National Economy • The Small Business Environment • Government Policy • The Entrepreneur • The Customer and Competition • Research for the Small Business • The Small Business Startup • Franchising • Buying an Existing Business • Legal Types of Business (Sole Trader, Partnership, Limited Company, Co-operative) • The Business Plan • Successful Small Business Strategies • Management of Resources (especially people) • Marketing, Strategy and Methods • Money: Raising Finance and Using It.

Free Lecturers' Supplement